"E" is for English

Mainstream America Issues a Challenge to Barack Obama

Jeff Willis

CONTENTS

Dedication

To my beloved Olga, my wife,
friend,companion and partner.

Я не имею жизни без тебя...

6

Acknowledgements

I wish to acknowledge :

My father, Henry Clinton Willis, Jr., a veteran of WWII's Europeon Theatre that included action at Omaha Beach and The Ardennes, who later aided underprivileged boys as a Public School Teacher.

Katherine (AKA Katya) Willis, my youngest daughter who has truly proven to be the sunshine of my life with her quick wit, intelligence and sensitivity.

My son, Clint Willis, currently serving his country in the Air Force who redefined courage and character in my eyes.

My daughter Stephanie Willis who shared with me an "underestimated frequency."

Samuel and Rosemary Freas, two of the finest people that I have met.

Warren Huff, who allowed me to gain insight into "the great land" and the plight of Alaska natives.

Russell Harrington, a college friend who introduced me to the pleasures of Acadian Louisiana living.

Pat and Nancy McKay, whom I consider true reflections of Reagan Democrats.

Armando Diaz and Anna (Yosi) Tavaras, two gritty Cubanos who reflect the class and entrepreneurship of Cuban Americans, further exemplifying the foolishness and shortsightedness of the Teller Amendment.

Marco Rubio who possesses the intelligence, enthusiasm and insight to be a future U.S. President.

Elizabeth Patricia Sonnen, a native of Scotland, who immediately embraced and fertilized America upon arrival.

Teddy Roosevelt Speaks

Ideas on Immigrants and being an AMERICAN in 1907

"In the first place, we should insist that if the immigrant who comes here in good faith becomes an American and assimilates himself to us, he shall be treated on an exact equality with everyone else, for it is an outrage to discriminate against any such man because of creed, or birthplace, or origin. But this is predicated upon the person's becoming in every facet an American, and nothing but an American... There can be no divided allegiance here. Any man who says he is an American, but something else also, isn't an American at all. We have room for but one flag, the American flag... We have room for but one language here, and that is the English language... And we have room for but one sole loyalty and that is a loyalty to the American people."

— President Theodore Roosevelt

Author's Introduction

A literacy test as a prerequisite for a voter identification card? *"E" is for English* redefines political incorrectness in outlining the step-by-step process for making English the official language in the United States of America via the Twenty-eighth Amendment to the Constitution.

Along the way, obstacles ranging from outdated legislation to a powerful teachers union, boldly declared part of the problem, are identified. En route to the solution, a totally unexpected direction and methodology emerge.

John Fund's account in *Stealing Elections*, painstakingly unearthed fraud in the election process and discussed preventive measures. *"E" is for English* goes one step further, tying the solution to a plan to make America smarter, while curbing identity theft and better controlling immigration.

While Dick Morris's bestseller, *Fleeced*, exposed the hypocrisy of the National Education Association, *"E" is for English* proposes an alternative union, more closely aligned with American values.

"E" is for English begins at the southernmost tip of the continental United States, before abruptly turning northeast for a journey that spans sixteen time zones. In this quest, Cuban Americans are reintroduced, the inner face of the Latin American community is unearthed, and profound parallels with Russia are revealed. The English language itself is seen from opposite ends of the spectrum – from something that can be legally avoided to the future.

The immigration issue is discussed from a different direction. With it comes a new, tough question: are we ready to rearrange our immigration priorities and should education and English proficiency be ranked ahead of family ties?

From Russia, *"E" is for English* returns to the heartland to examine something that has developed seemingly overnight – the universal use of the internet. It is here that the *Eagles for America,* a national blogging movement is introduced. Utilizing the internet, namely YouTube and other social networking sites, this grass roots movement will ultimately be made up of thousands of committed bloggers. *Eagles,* as they will be referred to, will make it their lifelong aim to spearhead a litmus test for every politician, blackballing all opposed to the "E" Amendment in its purest form.

"E" is for English graphically describes the Eagles' tireless assault on the current power structure, labeling any opponent as "un-American, un-patriotic and unfit for leadership in the United States of America." To committed Eagles, there can be no outcome save victory.

En route to its startling conclusion, *"E" is for English* proposes a basic English proficiency test, for voting, naturalization, and permanent status to a more advanced test for civil service and certain professional licenses and designations. A sophisticated voter identification card featuring photo, thumb print and retinal scan are proposed; along with a method of paying for it! The motive is very simple – the need for a smarter, more literate America outweighs corruption and inertia that have become watchwords in America's gradual decline. This is the ultimate question and challenge issued to Barack Obama. Are you simply another opportunistic, self-serving politician? Or do you truly want to make a difference?

1 Politically Incorrect

The objective of this writing is simple and easily defined – to instigate a Constitutional Amendment that will make English the Official Language of the United States of America.

The amendment will have seven points.

(a)   *English will be the one and only official language*

(b)   *Passage of an English proficiency test will be required for citizenship*

(c)   *Passage of an English proficiency test will be required for voter registration*

(d)   *Passage of an intermediate English proficiency test will be required for government employment, certain professions and permits*

(e)   *Passage of an intermediate English proficiency test will be required for all children of illegal aliens, superseding presumed Fourteenth Amendment inclusion*

(f)   *Only legal citizens will be included in any and all census counts*

(g)   *The amendment will be immune to any legal challenge in the courts*

Wow! Ouch! No way! No how! Impossible! It will never happen! It can never happen! They won't let it happen!

True, the odds will be long. But this is America. Anything is possible. Ask Barack Obama!

When introducing any idea, the first rule is to identify your opposition. The second rule is to never underestimate them.

Before we do that, however, let us take a look at the Americans who will support such an amendment. They are surprisingly large in number.

Numerous studies confirm that more than 80% of America favors making English the official language. To what degree this 80 plus percent will want this written into law is unknown. What does look promising is that the ratification process gives each state an equal vote. Americans from every corner of the country will have a voice.

Who specifically will oppose such an amendment? Let us go down the list.

Trial Lawyers –

Can you imagine the howl that you will hear from the ACLU? It will not be pretty. They will call proponents everything from racists to bigots to fascists to Nazis to bullies to elitists to segregationists to the devil incarnate. Why? Because their livelihoods will be threatened! And their very existence questioned.

Facts are facts. Americans like lawsuits. We are the most litigious peoples in the world. In one sense, this is sickening; in another, it's humorous. Adopting a Constitutional Amendment eliminating the chance of a court challenge will be considered *dangerous*, they will say. It is dangerous all right – to their pocketbooks!

In reality, without this immunity from litigation, the courts would be flooded with fights over disfranchisement.

This English proficiency test will not be modeled after the old *Jim Crow* tests of the mid-twentieth century. Nor, will they be ambiguous and inconsistent as those detailed in Robert Caro's *Lyndon Johnson, Master of the Senate.*

The test will be created by a non-partisan commission. Passing the test will require the taker be able to read English at a fourth grade level. This is not radical. In fact, it is logical.

But won't this amendment be in direct conflict with the *Civil Rights Act of 1968* and the *Voting Rights Act* adopted in 1965 and later amended in 1970, 1975, 1982 and finally again in 2006? There's the question. That's why, for the sake of keeping opportunistic lawyers from clogging up the court system, it will be better to nip the whole argument in the bud. The "E" Amendment will repeal the *Voting Rights Act*. End of story. Tough reality? Yes. But practical.

Then, there is the question of voter fraud.

In John Fund's recent book, *Stealing Elections*, the problem with voter fraud, a very real threat to our process, is underlined.

A voter registration card with photo, thumb print, and retinal scan will likewise be used as a back-up in the event a cheater manages to slip past the initial stopgaps.

I can hear the Libertarians screaming shades of big brother.

Yes, it will be like a second driver's license. But 9/11 permanently changed America. We are not living in the same country as we were twenty years ago. A lot can be ascribed to the Bush Administration. There were a lot of mistakes and misjudgments. That's a fact. But, we have not had a terror attack since, although we have thwarted several would-be terror attacks. That's also a fact.

Voter registration cards, as described, will ultimately kill two birds with one stone. But more significantly, the "E" Amendment will stipulate that "if a person cannot present a card when voting, it will be assumed that he or she was incapable of passing the proficiency test. It will also be presumed that the person is in the country illegally."

Last, but not least, is the issue of identify theft.

This is the fastest growing crime in America. A voter ID, used in conjunction with a credit card payment, might be cumbersome. While it will not totally eliminate identity theft, it will curb a large part of it.

To be sure, it will take more than voter ID cards to completely stop identity theft. Some possible ideas will be proffered later in the writing. But, make no mistake, the voter identification cards will have an impact. Just as surely as they will drastically curtail, if not completely eliminate, voter fraud.

Won't this be an expensive endeavor for a country already printing money with no end?

Yes, but the Twenty-fourth Amendment makes any attempt at charging citizens even a token fee impossible, as it should be. No American should ever be required to pay for the right to vote. By the same token, requiring voters to be able to read English at a fourth grade level is not unreasonable. It is the ultimate argument that should be decided by the states. If, three-fourths of the states say *yes*, then it should be adopted in the form of the Twenty-eighth Amendment to the Constitution.

Creating a foolproof system to eliminate voter fraud and deter identity theft is something that most political leaders will support, at least in principle. To do this would require more than a photo ID. The combination of photo, thumbprint and retinal scan, will be virtually foolproof and extremely expensive.

So how will we fund such a method to eliminate voter fraud and curtail identity theft? Most Americans will oppose a tax to fund it! In a later chapter, a comprehensive plan to totally fund both the testing and the voter identification cards will be introduced.

Who else will oppose the "E" Amendment?

Politicians dependent on the illiterate masses for election –

There is no question that passage of this legislation will change the political landscape in America. The true middle class will have much more influence than currently enjoyed. In many cases, politicians are able to use the masses to assist themselves and a few well-connected, well-funded allies into office. Lobbyists cater to these leaders.

Potentially eliminating some of their constituents will not be an attractive thought. It will likewise somewhat alter representation. Currently some states, such as California, are receiving inflated representation because illegal aliens are included in the census. Under the "E" Amendment, proof of citizenship will be a prerequisite for inclusion in the census count. Louisiana Senator David Vitter has already proposed this measure.

Without question, opponents of the proposed amendment will be vocal. They will talk about disfranchisement and discrimination. They will call the proponents of the "E" Amendment, racists, bigots, and anti-immigrant. They will refer to voter ID cards as a strategy designed to intimidate voters.

The Fourteenth Amendment was created to provide citizenship for freed slaves. The founders could never have imagined it being used to manipulate contemporary immigration law, but that has happened. The Fourteenth Amendment states that anyone born in the United States has automatic citizenship. What if the parents of that child entered the country illegally? This is a loophole in the immigration process and those attempting to break in line have found it!

Today, becoming a permanent resident appears to be as easy as coming into to the country and having a baby. This baby, born in the U.S. becomes an anchor. Then, through the anchor baby, entire extended families are allowed to stay in the country. The "E" Amendment will allow these anchor babies to stay legally and permanently; only *if* they pass a high school proficiency test. If they do not, they return with their parents to their native country and follow the process through normal channels.

After all anything short of this would be encouraging people outside of the United States to break the law!

In *Phyler v. Doe*, the 5-4 Supreme Court decision handed down in 1982 did that. In a close vote, the court chose to legislate from the bench as opposed to deferring the matter to Congress. William Rehnquist wrote the dissenting opinion. The "E" Amendment could potentially supersede this ruling.

Can we name another entity who will oppose the amendment?

Those Opposed to the Need for a Voter Registration Card –

Libertarians love this country. Their argument against this precise of an identification system has merit and I deeply respect their position. The thought of the need of a second ID is distressing. But these are dangerous times. We must make our nation more secure. In addition to fighting voter fraud, we must fight terrorism and identity theft. This is a way to do it.

A special provision of the "E" Amendment would include prohibition of any form of outsourcing where an American's social security number was required. This measure, coupled with voter identification cards would strike a blow at identity theft. Even the most private citizens would see the merit and ultimately conclude that it was an advantageous trade-off. Without question, we must gain the support of these opponents. Their fear of "big brother" is understandable. Still, the thought of illiterate people voting multiple times is an even scarier prospect. Not to mention the specter of unregulated, off shore, service sector workers having easy access to the most personal information of our people!

Who else can we expect to oppose the "E" Amendment?

Mainstream Media –

In an upcoming chapter we will discuss some of the problems and some possible solutions to address this critical issue. True, some will find it novel, but the hierarchy will oppose it. While the First Amendment must always prevail, there must be responsibility exercised by those entrusted with the stewardship of television and radio stations.

The network television and radio stations are federally licensed. In theory, they are supposed to occupy a position above partisanship. Unfortunately this doesn't always happen. Many of today's media moguls may have become bigger than the amendment itself. This places the amendment in jeopardy. It cannot be overlooked.

In short, the opponents of our proposed "E" Amendment are much fewer in number than those who will be in favor of it. But make no mistake, the opponents have money. They have lobbyists. They have allies in all levels of government. They are supported by a powerful partisan broadcast media. They are also aided by perhaps the most beguiling affliction that America has experienced since her founding, the doctrine of *political correctness,* the preamble to voluntary sedition.

In his 2000 essay, "The Origins of Political Correctness," Bill Lind wrote: "We call it *Political Correctness.* The name originated as something of a joke, literally in a comic strip, and we tend to think of it as only half-serious. In fact, it's deadly serious. It is the great disease of our century, the disease that has left tens of millions of people dead in Europe, in Russia, in China, indeed around the world. It is the disease of ideology. PC is not funny. PC is deadly serious.

"If we look at it analytically, if we look at it historically, we quickly find out exactly which it is. Political Correctness is cultural Marxism. It is Marxism translated from economic into cultural terms. It is an effort that goes back not to the 1960s and the hippies and the peace movement, but back to World War I. If we compare the basic tenets of Political Correctness with classical Marxism the parallels are very obvious."

This book redefines political incorrectness.

In Nicholas Wreden's *Unmaking of a Russian*, it is graphically explained how the Bolsheviks, with only 60,000 or so members, completely took over a huge country. Why was it able to happen? Confusion. A desire for change, any change, by a people who had spent centuries in an imperial system that had been slowly rotting. Added to this was the total lack of passion on the part of the Russian people. Before anyone truly knew what had happened, the Bolsheviks had imposed their totalitarian system on millions.

Could such happen in America?

It already is happening.

Were we to actually count the prople running the country, we would be astounded by how small their numbers truly are. Yet, they have the power, the organization, and the money to do it. It begins with political control. An ever so small change in the electorate could have monumental impact.

No doubt, any of those chosen few who take the time to read this text will ridicule and chastise me. If I have any dirt in my background, it is sure to be revealed, anything to discredit me. Anyone who might challenge the current status quo will be met with a similar fate. Ask Joe the Plumber.

Conventional wisdom suggests that it is better to not rock the boat! If you get out of line, make no mistake, you can get hurt and even ruined. It's generally considered better to go with the flow, and certainly safer!

As Wreden explained twenty years after the Bolshevik revolution, "if some one should come to me today, and tell me that twenty years from now I would be an American no longer, that every city and town in the country would know famine and war, that all my friends would be torn from their anchorages and most of them would suffer violent death, and that I would be tucked away in some distant part of the world, separated forever from my family – if some one should tell me all of this, I would think the man was insane, and dismiss the whole gloomy picture from my mind. But later, perhaps when I found myself alone, I would give free rein to my imagination, and a gnawing disquiet would take hold of me. I would remember that not so long ago I should have thought the same prediction just as ridiculous, just as absurd, and yet every word of it has actually come true."

Political correctness has become the tool of control for those limited few who constitute America's ruling class. With the aid of the media, it has become uncool to deviate from this accepted standard. Our country has reached a point where political correctness is now more important than honesty and sincerity. People would rather lie and be politically correct than tell the truth, and for good reason. Anyone deviating from this accepted norm can expect to be ridiculed and chastised, unmercifully.

The sad thing is, the need to be politically correct often distorts the actual analysis of a given person or situation. Even though a problem may be uncovered, it has become accepted to sweep it under the rug, rather than to confront it.

Let us talk about another organization certain to be opposed to the "E" Amendment.

The National Education Association –

When people think of an English proficiency test, they immediately picture frightened, bronze-skinned foreigners lining up to face the inevitable. But these actually represent a minority.

The public school system has struggled to find its way for years. When I was in school, it was a joint effort by parents and teachers. Today the Parent Teacher Association (PTA) has been pushed aside by a powerful union, which has made bullying and brainwashing their unspoken, unwritten standard operating procedure.

The NEA has scoffed at the idea of merit pay for teachers, advocating tenure as the primary barometer. In Dick Morris' recent bestseller, *Fleeced*, the NEA is identified as a muscular organization wielding an inordinate amount of influence. In a manner of speaking, they may be considered part of the problem, as opposed to part of the solution. Their habit of *floating*, as opposed to failing, underachieving students has left us with many high school graduates who are functionally illiterate.

In 1969, a public school system in a small town in South Arkansas fully integrated. A highly educated industrial arts teacher welcomed large numbers of African American students into his classroom. Then, he learned why separate but equal was partially mythical. At least one-third of these new students were functionally illiterate.

As one teacher wryly put it, "keeping them from slipping out the back window when nobody was looking was your primary duty."

In frustration, the teacher complained to the school board saying, "I can't even give a simple math test because many of these new students can't read the questions."

After an uncomfortable deliberation, the teacher received his answer. "Work with them as much as possible and help them learn the material. And, if they are unable to learn it, find a way to help them pass the class." In other words, "pass on the problem to the next level because we don't know what else to tell you."

And so it went! The term for this practice is "floating."

A proficiency test that requires a high school graduate to pass a fourth grade reading level exam will be a major embarrassment, if the exam is not passed. It will vividly reveal one of America's dirty little secrets.

Even though the NEA squawked at *No Child Left Behind*, it was at least an effort to be somewhat proactive. A standardized test probably isn't the answer. There are numerous theories relating to a better way. Perhaps the act of merely paying teachers specialized in English a premium might be the easiest and best solution.

There is a saying that absolute power corrupts absolutely. Perhaps what is needed to get the National Education Association on track is some healthy competition, as in a rival union. For the sake of clarity, we will call this proposed rival, the American Education Association.

AEA would have different points on many of these issues.

(a)   *They will support the "E" Amendment*

(b)   *They will support starting English teachers at a rate of 20% more than teachers of all other disciplines*

(c)   *They will support merit pay for all teachers*

(d)   *They will support a requirement for taking a foreign language for graduation*

Up until now, we have talked about English and only English. Why are we now talking about requiring a foreign language for high school graduation? Easy. When a foreign language is learned, the student gets a better handle on English.

Organizing a new union can, and likely will, result in a huge exodus from NEA ranks. Many teachers would love to see a change. As Morris recounted, all too many are leaving the profession. Some are the teachers who are leaving are the best ones.

Could all schools fund such a standard? I think so. These courses don't require computers or special equipment. Homework and study will do the trick. But even that is easier said than done.

As a sophomore in high school, I was lucky enough to draw a youthful English teacher by the name of Cheryl Gregory. An Ole Miss graduate, she boldly professed that, "like it or not, we were going to learn something in her classes."

The first semester went by in uneventful fashion. We spent the first two nine-week periods studying literature. The third quarter, we were introduced to transformational grammar!

When the initial comparisons between traditional grammar and transformational grammar were explained, nobody really had a clue what she was talking about. It literally transcended anything that we had previously been exposed to. We were learning the actual rules of grammar, drawing diagrams, known as trees, showing their application.

Transformational grammar is the taking of sentences from surface structure to deep structure. There were twenty-four students in the class. Ten failed. I made an A. Not that I was a great student – I had made a C the first two quarters. She had been teaching the required stuff during the first part of the year. How the school decided to allow transformational grammar to be taught is still a mystery. But, Cheryl taught it.

Afterward, she caught it from angry parents and timorous school administrators. She did not return the following year.

That one class completely changed my impression of English. I learned it and saw it for what it was – a language that had incurred three distinct changes in its evolution to its modern state. Or, as Rex Reed stated, "German with French spread over it."

In Cheryl's case, she refused to float students, as was done by the two other sophomore English teachers. She set real standards and gave real grades, even though she knew to do so would likely be to her detriment. In retrospect, the politically correct thing would have been to go with the flow, not taking any chances. After all, what did she have to gain? What she evidently lost was her job. But I and a few others gained much more – a real education!

As a sophomore, I likewise began taking Spanish. Transformational grammar brought Spanish to life like nothing else could have done. In short, all language is the same in deep structure. I was soon doing the trees in both languages. For a refresher, I took an upper level transformational grammar class at LSU. The College of Arts and Sciences required sixteen hours in a foreign language. Today, I converse in Spanish every day and attribute my comfortable use to the application of transformational grammar.

Transformational grammar didn't fare so well at El Dorado High School in the years that followed. Because of Cheryl Gregory's experiment, it became fashionable for teachers to say, "it is more of a mathematical approach to English and not really suitable for high school students." Almost nobody challenged that point of view. If someone did question it, they were immediately brought to heel.

Such has often been the case when a teacher stepped out of the box and questioned NEA's stand against merit pay for exceptional performance. As Morris adds in his book, many leaders such as Florida's Governor Charlie Crist made merit pay for teachers a central point in their educational program. But schoolteachers don't have the platform that a governor has. They are often bullied by this union.

A rival union such as the mythical AEA could completely change the thinking. Instead of keeping quiet because it is the safe and politically correct thing to do, teachers could begin questioning some of the stances that NEA has taken.

One example of this is teaching intelligent design alongside evolution. To be sure, not all NEA members are opposed to teaching intelligent design, but many are. Why? Because it invites cross discussion! So what is wrong with that? Isn't one of the goals of our public schools to teach students how to think?

British author Anna Benn, in her book *Insight into Russia*, states that Mikhail Gorbachev's introduction to a multi-party system completely blindsided the old guard. As the last general secretary of the former Soviet Union put it, "I see no tragedy in a multi-party system. We should not be afraid of it, the way the devil is afraid of incense."

The mere thought of a rival political party was revolutionary in itself. Anyone other the top man himself who proposed such a concept would have fallen under major scrutiny, if not danger.

It has to do with total control. When there is no rival point of view, it is easier to push anyone who may question the status quo into a corner and silently, quietly eliminate them. It happens every day.

The National Education Association has become more than an advocate for teachers to be fairly paid. Over the years, they have become nothing short of a political action committee. They regularly endorse political candidates. Because of their influence on teachers, who have a direct link with our children, many parents find their endorsing parties and candidates inappropriate. It is almost akin to churches being told that it is okay for them to endorse political candidates without sacrificing their tax exempt status.

These are some of the many reasons why an amendment to the Constitution such as what we are proposing will have more popular support than opposition. On the other hand, the establishment won't hear of it. Those in control will see it as a threat. But mainstream America might embrace it. And if they do, we can pass it. It will come down to identifying the opponents and confronting them. It will also require that we flush the snakes from the woodpile.

The snakes are those who will say that they agree in principle that we need to make English the official language, but will go no further than that. In itself, that point of view has no value. Without proficiency tests and immunity from legal challenge, it will be of mere ceremonial use and nothing more. But such a stance will be politically correct. Who is going to come out and be against anything that between 80% and 90% of the country favors? Not a smart politician!

The question becomes who is going to fight such an amendment? And the answers are relatively predictable.

We understand the trial lawyers and why they would oppose it. For them it's about money.

We understand the NEA and why they would oppose it. It's about control and accountability.

We understand the Libertarians and why they would oppose it. It's about big brother watching.

We certainly understand about the politicians needing the votes of illiterate masses. Never mind if these illiterate masses are clueless as to what they are voting for.

We even understand the mainstream media. They have gotten away from their Sigma Delta Chi pledge. Bias, which should never have entered into over-the-air federally licensed broadcast properties, has become a mainstay. Media partisanship is a growing threat to our freedom. Historically, the first objective of a government attempting to impose one way of thinking upon a people is to control the mainstream media. In our case, it is the over-the-air-broadcast media. This will be further discussed in an upcoming chapter.

The question is: can we navigate past the obstacles sure to be in our way and make this amendment a reality?

I think that we can.

Here's why.

America has realized that money doesn't grow on trees. We must find ways to reduce costs. This question is, "Who is *we*?"

Liberals will assert that *we* is the American people who have lived too well, most of them beyond their means. This argument would conclude that the answer is a long overdue sacrifice, as in accepting smaller entitlements while paying higher taxes. This is remarkably reminiscent of the Soviets telling their people, *"Vasha zhertvah bil dyealaht dlaya palooche zaftra"* (Your sacrifice will make for a better tomorrow). As sixty-somethings in Russia will tell you today, that better tomorrow never came.

Currently there is discussion that ranges from raising the eligibility age for social security to imposing a large gasoline tax on the American people. Of course, all are in the name of paying down the mounting U.S. debt.

Conservatives might agree to the reduction of entitlements. But raising taxes should be a last resort! The first objective should be putting all expenses under the microscope and asking the tough question: "Can we live without these expenses?"

The "E" Amendment brings about two hidden expense cuts that could be massive for the individual states and counties: Repeal of the *Voting Rights Act* and repeal of *Phyler v. Doe*. Without questions, liberals would scream bloody murder at the thought of either development! In later chapters, both will be fully scrutinized. The question that emerges is "would the American people prefer to keep these laws in force, even knowing that they are to the detriment of America, while happily accepting tax increases, OR would we be interested in examining the alternative?

In 1978 Democratic Senator J. Bennett Johnson of Louisiana sponsored a busing control bill. It proposed that the act of busing school children to achieve racial balance be limited to five miles and/or 15 minutes from their home. It was a moderate proposal, presented by a moderate member of the United States Senate. The reason behind the proposed legislation was simple: many of the rural counties could not afford to facilitate the court ordered mandate.

The bill flew through both the House and Senate and was included in a major appropriations bill. President Jimmy Carter threatened to veto the appropriations bill if Senator Johnson's busing control bill was not removed. The supporters acquiesced!

Busing advocates, including Carter and his newly appointed Health and Human Services Secretary Patricia Harris, defended the decision on the basis of constitutionality. After all, *Brown v. the Board of Education* translated to implementation regardless of cost. The problem was who ultimately would pay for this implementation?

The "E" Amendment would take the argument of both *Phyler v. Doe* and the *Voting Rights Act* out of the courts and put them into the hands of the American people.

From a constitutional standpoint, we only need three-fourths of the states to ratify the amendment. Alaska and North Dakota have the same vote as California and New York. For states such as North Carolina, South Carolina, Indiana, Oregon and Montana it translates into more representation in Congress, at the expense of California and New York. This will be the result of a census based on actual citizenship and not numbers.

Let us examine this question momentarily. Is it not fair to base congressional representation on the number of actual citizens legally residing in a state? Under the "E" Amendment, this will be the standard.

What about the president? Since a census based on actual legal citizenship versus total numbers might change congressional representation, he or she might oppose the "E" Amendment on these grounds.

It won't matter!

The *Hollingsworth v. Virginia* (1798) ruling concluded that a president could not veto an amendment and that it was not necessary to even place a proposed amendment before the president. That's huge!

The key to passing the "E" Amendment rests in our ability to bring about a paradigm shift in America. It amounts to the belief that the *Voting Rights Act* is an anachronism. We simply do not need it any longer because we are no longer living in the shadow and shame of *Jim Crow* discrimination practices. They were put to rest, once and for all, in the presidential election of 2008.

As a country, we must make a decision. Is unity through one language important and should it be made a priority? If so, then Section Five of the *Voting Rights Act* is anti-unity and must be stricken.

Regarding multi-lingual balloting, the *Voting Rights Act* requires "municipalities that receive requests for ballots in other languages to comply with the request."

Representative Dana Rohrabacher of California said of the request, "What unites us? It's our language, the English language," and that the *Voting Rights Act* is "hurting America by making it easier not to learn English."

There is another consideration: Cost.

The Tea Party, a non-partisan force, came on the national scene in 2009. TEA, the acronym for *Taxed Enough Already*, immediately positioned itself as a watchdog for excessive spending by politicians. Committed to pressuring politicians to live within their means, they launched national candidates in several states. Perhaps their poster boy is Kentucky's Rand Paul. Paul steamrolled past the Republican's establishment candidate in the primaries before hammering his Democrat opponent, capturing 56% of the total vote cast in the 2010 general election. Paul's Tea Party message was basic and simple: "Reduce the cost of government en route to a balanced budget. Don't leave the debt to our children."

Tea Partiers will quickly point out that this must be done on the state level as well as in Washington. When analyzing the costs of multi-lingual election ballots, the obvious becomes evident.

October 27, 2010, the Federal Justice Department forced Cuyahoga County, Ohio to make available bi-lingual services extended to 2800 Puerto Ricans. According to Mike West, Cuyahoga County's Board of Elections' Media and Education Specialist, the estimated cost was upwards of $289,000.

This will spawn a huge debate.

Should we amend the *Voting Rights Act* to include some of the provisions of the "E" Amendment? Should we repeal the *Voting Rights Act*? Should we pass the "E" Amendment with wording that stipulates that it deals with a completely different spectrum, superseding any and all previous legislation?

I would favor the latter.

The world has changed greatly since Lyndon Johnson's presidency. The Fifteenth Amendment made race a non-issue. The *Civil Rights Act of 1968* took care of discrimination based on race, color, religion, sex and national origin. Those issues are no longer on the radar. Section Five of the *Voting Rights Act* divides the country and creates a perfect landscape for reverse discrimination. It definitely must go.

Attempting to instigate a new standard requires a solid, new foundation. A separate amendment that deals with English as the one and only language *and* mandates literacy tests for (a) citizenship, (b) voting rights, and (c) eligibility for civil service and employment in certain professions is an aggressive objective.

America may be ready for it. Our use of technology has grown to a point where we are more knowledgeable and more up-to-date on current events, than ever before in our history. It will be increasingly difficult for politicians to keep the folks back home in the dark, as has all too often been the case in the past.

Constitutionally making English our one and only official language, with all of the listed provisions intact, is a bold attempt to create a stronger, smarter America that is safer and more unified than ever before. We have become a people without passion. Taking up the cause creates a new identity and a new purpose for all of us who love this country.

This writing defiantly steps on the toes of the status quo, in a manner than forces the average American to think. It could, and probably will, be a Constitutional debate for the ages, beginning with the question of the Fourteenth Amendment protection for children of illegal aliens. But consider the alternatives.

California is, for all practical purposes, bankrupt. Has anyone checked the number of entitlements such as Medicaid and food stamps that have been going to illegal aliens? For the sake of California alone, we must strike *Phyler v. Doe*. Adoption of the "E" Amendment intact might accomplish as much. We are faced with the question of, "Should this issue be decided by Congress or the Supreme Court?"

The entire topic of English comprehension is easy to understand. We must have an electorate capable of thinking for themselves. If they are unable to read what is on the ballot, they are prime candidates for manipulation. There are forces in this country which have made it their business to manipulate the poor and uneducated.

There are others who have used language as a mechanism to keep America from being ultimately united. They want to keep people from learning English, so they can better control them. Losing this leverage translates to a loss of power. Everyone here should have the opportunity to experience the American Dream. They should never be deprived of it due to something as basic as being unable to speak the language!

Issuing a call to those in opposition is nothing more than a challenge. The question is how much they love the United States of America!

We must get past this nuisance notion of political correctness and individually ask ourselves one question. Are we satisfied with what we have become or do we believe that we can be better?

It won't take three hundred million Americans to bring this off. It may not even take sixty thousand committed advocates, as was the case with the Bolsheviks. We have something that the Bolsheviks never could have dreamed of, the internet.

With the internet's advent, a new culture has emerged, the blogger. These are individuals who use the power of being online to communicate thoughts, ideas, and other pertinent information. They could make the difference in this quest to save and improve America.

How they will emerge, and the role they will play, will be defined in upcoming chapters of this writing. Above all, they will be the catalysts on achieving our objective:

The Measure Making English the One and Only
Official Language of the United States of America,
the Twenty-eighth Amendment to the Constitution.

I think that we can get it though the House and the Senate. That in itself will be some trick, to be sure! We can expect resistance. We can count on a lot of self-serving obstructionists who will do anything to impede it. Those opposed to it are about today. The "E" Amendment is about tomorrow and what kind of America we are leaving to our children.

Indeed, passage of the "E" Amendment will be a difficult objective. But not an impossible one!

Before us is a multi-dimensional question that is tied to one premise – our country is unique, different from every other country in the world. We are a people from a multitude of nations who came to this country seeking multiple freedoms. We were established as one nation under God. What has unified us has been the English language.

The decision Americans must make is whether we are ready to evolve into the smartest, best educated, most literate people in the world? Or, are we satisfied with the status quo of mediocrity, happily outsourcing brain jobs to smarter, more literate nations abroad?

Voter fraud is an issue that some choose to downplay. But nobody can deny that identity theft is an issue. ID cards will muzzle the former magnificently. The latter's demise will depend on two basic changes in the way America does business:

(a)   *We must make illegal the practice of outsourcing abroad any job that gives non-Americans access to American citizens' social security numbers.*

(b)   *We must instill tougher regulatory practices on the debt recovery industry. There are all too many instances where Americans have been victimized by aggressive, unscrupulous collectors, many of whom have criminal records.*

The latter two assertions are not the focus of *"E" is for English*. Nevertheless, they are interrelated. Voter ID cards can be the benchmark for addressing and correcting both concerns.

Setting a higher bar for professional licensing, civil service and the construction of multi-family housing just makes sense. Why would anyone be opposed to adopting such a standard?

It is probable that most of America will embrace the "E" Amendment. Those who won't will have their reasons, of course. Close examination will reveal that these opponents will lose something currently held, if "E" becomes the law of the land. The question is, "Can we overcome these self-serving insiders who are compromising our country?"

We most definitely can!
With the right approach.
And the right kind of advocates.

2 Welcome to Miami

The first time I set foot in Miami was in 1971. There was not much positive to recall.

There was traffic on top of more traffic with everyone constantly honking their horns. The city appeared to be inhabited by rude, surly New Yorkers. Everything for sale was more expensive than any place else I had ever been.

I wasn't impressed.

Ten years would pass before my return. This time it was for a business conference in the heart of downtown. It was fortunate that the conference was in a hotel. The streets were littered and abandoned. Many of the buildings were boarded up. In the evenings, the local residents gradually appeared. As the wee hours approached, we noticed the numbers increasing on the streets below. It wasn't anything to write home about.

Eighteen months later, when Al Pacino's cult movie, *Scarface*, debuted, I could only nod and agree that an accurate depiction of Miami had been presented.

Twenty-three years would pass before South Florida would beckon. It was another business conference. I got another look and this time Miami was a different place!

Perhaps the best way to really get a good look at the United States' southernmost major city is to see it from the water. There it was. Not the same grimy, boarded up reminder of a tourist boom gone bust. But a gleaming, sparkling gem that would make even the most critical eye take note.

Positively beautiful!

So what had transpired? The aftermath of two significant landmark influxes of newcomers – the evacuation of Cuba immediately after Castro's takeover in 1959-61, which featured the Peter Pan kids, and the Mariel boat lift in 1980.

Most Americans are totally ignorant of Cuba and Cuban history. Regretfully, most Anglos in America tend to lump Hispanics into one generalized classification. They would be hard-pressed to differentiate the vast numbers of Spanish-speaking people throughout the world today. However, spending time in Miami will change that!

In Ann Louise Bardach's book, *Cuba Confidential*, Cubans are described as the "Jews of the Caribbean." In actuality, more than 95% of Cubano's are Roman Catholic. This reference is made due to their nimbleness and ability to adapt to extreme and unexpected circumstances.

For America's part, Cuba remains our greatest foreign policy debacle. If there was ever a time when American common sense took a leave of absence, it was manifested in our dealings with Cuba.

American leaders, as far back as Thomas Jefferson have considered the advantages of annexing the Cuba. As Patrick Symmes recounted in his book, *The Boys from Delores*, America made a serious bid to annex Cuba in 1857 when the Buchanan Administration attempted to buy the island from Spain. This followed an similar effort made by the Polk Administration some years earlier. There was certainly support in Congress for such an acquisition, especially from the southern states who saw the island's fertile soil and slave-plantation culture as a natural extension.

Fifteen years later, the Grant Administration likewise offered to buy the island from Spain. American interest in the island, material and otherwise was great. There was also growing awareness of the struggles of the islanders to shed their Spanish overlords.

Spain turned down all offers. In 1898 they may have regretted it! A revolution had taken hold on the island. The Spanish-American War brought the United States in on the side of the revolutionaries. When the war ended, Cuba was an American possession.

Miami Downtown photo: *Totenkopf*

From the outset, the people on the island never received the acclaim and respect they deserved. It began with America's failure to recognize the bulk of the fighting on the island had been done by islanders, not Americans. This might have been because so many of the native freedom fighters were people of color. Still, Cubans were ready to begin the transformation from Spanish colony to American territory.

Most Americans are unfamiliar with the murky history of Cuba and her relations with Spain. Many at that time concluded that Cuba was the "ever faithful isle" because Cubans did not participate in Simon Bolivar's revolution that pitted the South American colonies against Spain. But discontent existed.

An incipient revolt in 1766 was ruthlessly put down. There were also revolts in 1794 and 1844, the "Black Eagle" rebellion and the ten-year insurrection that began in 1868. It was only through the efforts of then Secretary of State Hamilton Fish, that America did not become engaged militarily during the latter. In 1894-95, just as "Home Rule for Cuba" had become a burning issue in Spain, martial law was proclaimed in Havana, precipitating the final and successful revolution.

After almost a century of attempting to buy Cuba, it was suddenly an American possession. But America seemed no longer interested in permanent annexation. Some of the reluctance could be attributed to the concern that European states would form a league against the United States in favor of Spain. The fourth congressional resolution of April 20, 1898 gave the pledge as follows: "The United States hereby disclaims any disposition or intention to exercise sovereignty, jurisdiction, or control over said island (Cuba) except for the pacification thereof, and asserts its determination, when that is accomplished, to leave the government and control of the island to its people."

This "self-denying ordinance," likely had more effect than any official utterance in American history. It shaped the nation's behavior and long term outlook toward Cuba. There was strong opposition. According to Gregory Weeks, author of *U.S. and Latin American Relations*, The Teller Amendment, authored by a Colorado senator who wanted to make sure that Cuba's sugar would not compete with his state's crop of beet sugar, prohibited the president from annexing Cuba.

In the end, the Senate passed the bill in a 42-35 vote. The ordinance seemed unjustified in a time of triumph. Fresh from the massive gains of the Mexican War, it seemed natural for the United States to add Cuba as a new territory. Those who had actually served in the war returned with accounts of mutual respect between natives and Americans that grew daily.

However, the world had changed since 1850. The ordinance led by Colorado Senator Henry M. Teller, later known as the "Teller Amendment," laid the foundation for Cuba's disposition and future relationship with America. The intentions were eloquently stated by President William McKinley in his second inaugural address, "We remain accountable to the Cubans, no less than to our own country and people, for the reconstruction of Cuba as a free commonwealth on abiding foundations of right, justice, liberty and assured order. Our enfranchisement of the people will not be completed until free Cuba shall be a reality, not a name; a perfect entity, not a hasty experiment bearing within itself the elements of failure."

In reality, perhaps because the relationship was seen as temporary and not permanent, the overall attitude was different in the minds of Americans. Whereas California became an immediate target for settlement and development, Cuba was seen as something temporary. Some argue that it was all pre-conceived by business interests who might benefit more if Cuba was a sovereign Commonwealth. Others conclude that there was never a real plan for anything, it was just the "mood of the moment." It must be remembered, that President Grover Cleveland had advocated a comparable path for Hawaii a few years earlier.

In Clifford L. Staten, in *The History of Cuba*, explains "the U.S. occupation had three interrelated goals: to maintain political stability, to rebuild the primary economic infrastructure of the island to attract U.S. investments and to keep Cuba within the sphere of influence of the growing political and economic power of the United States."

The Platt Amendment, which became law, proved to be a bridge to nowhere for Cuban people. While it did give America the ability to supersede any foreign policy decision made by Cuban nationals, it did not give Cuba a direct path toward statehood. Nor was such a path discussed with any consistency.

Instead, our government took a *laissez faire* approach with big corporations. United Fruit Company purchased more than two million acres of prime farmland for a mere twenty cents per acre. Even though Cuba had excellent limestone for building roads, the government opted to take up the old stones from the streets of Boston and ship them south to use in the construction of streets in Havana and Santiago. While these companies did create thousands of jobs for the locals, the best jobs were always reserved for Americans.

Another source of tension was the American attempt to secularize the public schools. Prior to U.S. occupation, the Catholic church had played a dominant role in the lives of all Cubans. There were historical ties to Spain, dating from the days of Christopher Columbus. While many in Washington held to the conviction that modernizing the public schools was in the peoples' best interest, it generated resentment, both from the church and much, if not most, of Cuban society.

When the island was given her independence, a constitution was written and a bold attempt at democracy was made. In the end, it was concluded that the island didn't have sufficient experience at running a democracy, the government officials were too corrupt, and American interests would be better served by a friendly dictator, such at Fulgencio Batista.

This was the beginning of the end.

The United States was far too late in recognizing the truth about Fidel Castro. The unfortunate part of the story relates to the fact that two-thirds of the island's population was made up of a growing middle class. This was not like the Bolshevik Revolution where 1% of the population had 99% of the resources. True, there was immense poverty on the island. But there was more than equal prosperity.

Cuba was ready to depose Batista and his corrupt, ham-handed government. The longing for a 1940-style reform-minded democracy allowed Castro to attract and entice many. Later, they found that the wily Fidel had used their desire for a democratic government and hatred for Batista to, in effect, steal the revolution.

President Dwight D. Eisenhower and then Vice President Richard Nixon saw the danger of having a hostile government so close to our shores. At the end of their eight-year occupancy of the White House, they carefully instigated a plan designed to retake the island. Their successor, John F. Kennedy, picked up on the plan. He later botched it when he failed to provide air support at the Bay of Pigs.

Cubans were mercifully given political asylum by the American government – and they came. Often penniless. In most cases, without the language.

Eighty-year-old survivors tell of coming to the shores of the United States with nothing save the clothes on their backs and the keys to the Cuban residences still in their pockets.

Previously, it had often been difficult to get visas. Now, they were exiles. And, in their minds, they would always be exiles as described by Jorge Mas Canosa in Bardach's, *Cuba Confidential*.

Their children were Cuban, as well. As the years slipped by, they became Americans of Cuban descent. The children were native born Americans of Cuban descent.

These last two generations were doing something that had been in vogue in Cuba before and after World War II. They were learning English. This time, however, they were learning it, not because it might bring them better employment from an American-based company in Cuba. They were learning English in the public schools and being told not to speak Spanish. Period! It was not optional. There was no special accommodation for their circumstance. It was the law.

Recently, I had the chance to talk to a thirty-year-old, native born American of Cuban descent who had recently returned from an illegal trip to the island. The purpose of the trip was to see her eighty-five-year-old grandmother. After relating the islanders' day-to-day struggle to find enough food to survive, she turned to her parents' American experience. The woman spoke English as proficiently as she spoke Spanish. She remembered her mother and father's conclusion that, "learning English in a forced type of way was difficult. But it was a matter of survival." Twenty-five years ago they were told flatly not to speak Spanish, to the point of being reprimanded for doing so.

Today, obviously, it would be politically incorrect to issue such an ultimatum. There was even a movement to teach Hispanic children Spanish because they already suffered from poverty and discrimination. People would have laughed at such a prospect in 1960.

Due to their acquired mental toughness, Miami Cubans didn't complain – they adapted. The Cubans learned English. Then they gradually took over the city and county governments transforming it into one of America's premier cities.

It can only make Americans wonder what might have been if these same people had had the U.S. Constitution as law in bringing civility to their lush, Tennessee-sized island, best described as "a Florida with mountains as high as the North Carolina Appalachians."

The very strong argument for why America should again consider retaking the island is a topic for another writing. Without question, many contemporary Americans react the same way to Castro as a lot of Americans reacted to Adolph Hitler in 1938. Much, if not most, of this thinking can be attributed to general ignorance as well as indifference.

I recall my aunt's neighbor talking about his father's response to Hitler. "Well, 'ol Adolph's not that bad of a guy." He had defended. "Maybe we ought to give him a chance." To watch former President Jimmy Carter actually exchange cordial words with Fidel Castro confirms why he must be considered and classified as America's worst president!

Cuban Americans can only continue to do what they have done so well – survive. And thrive with the aid of the U.S. Constitution.

The problem afflicting America in so many instances is racism. Often people have never taken the time to learn about other people because they couldn't get past skin color, ethnic origin, language, religion or something else that might make them different. In reality, racism is a colossal waste of time and energy. It has made us lose sight of the big picture, the main objective, which is becoming one as a nation and a people.

Most people who have come to Miami have returned to their home town somewhere in America with stories that reflected the diversity of the city. Then their story would be relayed, often in distorted fashion. If the person who retold the story was not worldly themselves, their recounting would be received in a manner that was not always positive.

However, there are also stories from more open-minded Americans who, when visiting Miami find people just like themselves. It is often amusing to hear tourists revisiting Miami for the first time in three decades commenting on how much more courteous the people are today than in the seventies.

Perhaps the biggest surprise is the complete and total assimilation displayed by the Miami Cubans. Their English is perfect, often spoken with an ever-so-slight lilt, as pleasing as it is unique. Of course, they speak Spanish. And, to their parents' chagrin, it isn't always the perfect Castilian Spanish spoken in Madrid.

When the children went to elementary school, they were constantly exposed to two languages. Spanish was still spoken at home by their parents. English was taught in school. Since they grew up hearing their parents constantly conversing in Spanish, they learned the vocabulary from the earliest age. In school, they learned proper English usage. The end result is these children were conjugating English sentences with Spanish words. Hence, Spanglish.

Because most Americans, especially in the southwest have formulated Latino stereotypes, they are surprised to note that Miami Latinos do not resemble Mexicans. In fact, 95% of Miami's Cuban population is white. This is a stark contrast to the population on the island, which stands at 70% black. Visitors will naively proclaim their surprise to have seen blondes and redheads with blue and green eyes, among the Miami Cubans. As one Mexican national I have known for twenty years concluded, "The Cubans have a lot of pride. They are dreamers and have always seen themselves on top."

The pride of surviving and thriving is strong among Miami Cubans. Open? Yes. Expansive? Absolutely! Industrious? Cubans are as industrious as any peoples in the world. Clannish? Because of a legacy of being sold out, deceived, and treated as second class citizens by both the Spanish and especially, the American government, they have learned that sticking together has often been their only salvation. Corrupt? Corruption exists everywhere. Cubans certainly don't have an exclusive lock on corruption! Trusting? Not on your life. Why should they be?

The late Jules Mayeaux, a former general manager for WBRZ television in Baton Rouge, told me how he had hired a brilliant young radio programmer/sales manager from Miami by the name of George Jenne. Jules said, "George wanted to leave Miami because he just couldn't stand the Cubans."

"Why?" I had wondered.

Choosing his words carefully, Jules responded, "They were mutable."

In essence, they were adaptable, flexible and changeable.

The recipe for survival!

During the period of American ownership, the ready adaptation of American culture was prevalent on the island, but mainstream Cuban was never considered an equal. In knowing and working with today's Miami Cubans, it is easy to see how mistaken these Americans were. It was a time before television and civil rights. Sugar was king and securing maximum profit was the only thing that mattered.

Today, Miami is two-thirds Latino. The leaders of both the Latino community and the city are the Cubans. This is primarily due to two reasons. (1) They arrived first and in two great waves. (2) They totally mastered English while retaining Spanish.

The retention of Spanish made it possible to communicate with other newcomers from Latin America. Obviously, the advantage of being able to earn political asylum helped.

Miami has a large and ever growing Columbian population. Their influx was consistent and became more accelerated in the 90s. While the Cubans benefited from a hostile Castro government close to our shores, the Columbians benefited from a very strong relationship between governments.

While the young people quickly assimilated due to the teaching of English in schools, the pressure wasn't the same to learn the language as it had been for the Cubans in the 60s. Bill Clinton's administration ushered in the age of political correctness. Suddenly it became cruel to aggressively mandate the learning of English on the poor immigrants.

The Cubans were forced to learn English or forever be confined to manual labor employment. The first Columbians were pleased to note that the English-only standard was not as rigorous. They could attend insurance and real estate schools in Spanish. All the signs in public were bilingual. They could literally function without English.

Other South Americans were quick to take advantage of the live without English practice that was becoming the standard. In some cases, however, it worked to their detriment.

Ariel Menendez was a talented foreman in charge of an all Spanish speaking crew finishing the building directly adjacent to our condo building in South Beach. He was a wiry Argentine, with dishwater blond hair and blue eyes who explained that after living in Miami seven years, he still spoke no English. When I asked him why he didn't learn English, he said that he had never needed to.

Ariel also related that when a choice city job opened up that he would have otherwise been qualified for, he was ineligible due to the fact that he spoke virtually no English. It required "some working use" of English. He had never learned it.

Ariel ruefully admitted that had he been required to learn English, he would have learned it. Instead, he added, there were chicas and fiestas. Most men would admit that girls and parties are more fun than studying a language! Now, facing a construction slow down, Ariel has opted to return to his native Buenos Aires.

Today in Miami, landing certain jobs is often determined by language skills. Literally everyone prefers bilingual employees. However, the language proficiency required depends on the employer. In many cases it is similar to Hawaii.

I first visited Honolulu in 1987. Like many mainlanders, the beauty of the place so captivated me that I began interviewing for television affiliate sales positions. Those in hiring positions seemed to all be Japanese. Their interpretation of bilingual generally meant broken English and perfect Japanese.

Nine years later and three thousand miles to the north, I experienced an even more beautiful American city, Homer, Alaska. It was there that I met Warren Huff, a full blooded Inupiat Eskimo, originally from Nome.

Warren told a poignant story of how, at age six, American social workers took him away from his parents and placed him in a Homer orphanage. "They told me that my family was living in the Stone Age," Warren recalled.

Shocked, I couldn't help but ask, "When did this take place?"

"1960."

Recalling history, I responded, "Eisenhower was president but it sounds more like Khrushchev. Weren't you pissed?"

"Well, actually, we were living in the Stone Age," Warren mused. He explained how his family had lived in a little dugout and actually buried their greens and perishables beneath the dirt floor. "Yeah, you dig down two feet and you hit the permafrost."

In both the orphanage and school, Warren was told to forget his native language. He learned English and speaks it today with the same northwestern accent spoken by all Alaskans. He is married to a woman of Scandinavian descent from Minnesota. They have two grown children.

Compared to the disgraceful history of America's treatment of Native Americans, Warren's story is gentle and graceful. Especially, in light of the manner that he is respected and even revered by some of his fellow Homer residents today.

Yet, Warren's experience and immersion into English was very different than is practiced today. In retrospect, it was cruel. The government was determined to Americanize the Alaska natives as the practice had been carried over from the nineteenth century. By the time the Cubans came, the intensity of Americanization had lessened to a degree, but was still prevalent. By the nineties, it was becoming more and more lax. Today, it has reached the point that an English only speaker has a difficult time landing certain types of jobs in Miami. Especially in the service industry.

While it is politically incorrect to discuss linguistic preference, there are growing reports of employers opting for employees whose Spanish is their primary language. In reality, bilingual should mean being able to speak, read and write in two languages.

For example, I can comfortably converse in Russian. But reading anything of the least degree of difficulty is beyond my capability. I can write in Russian. But there are grammar mistakes and countless misspellings. If the Russian speaker is conscious of my limitations, speaking slowly with simple words, I can converse in a limited way. With a dictionary, I can produce a passable letter, in an hour or two.

With Spanish, I can read with total or near total comprehension. I can write without the aid of a dictionary. I can speak the language comfortably. I can watch Telemundo with almost perfect comprehension. Often, like so many Miamians, I lapse into Spanglish. But, overall, it is a fair statement to say that I have full use. With Russian, I have some working use.

This is often what the employer who is hiring is determining. Does the applicant have full use in both languages? Or do they have some working use in one of the languages? If the some working use is in English, they have hired essentially a Spanish speaker, in a country where English is supposedly the language.

In some areas of the country, the some working use of English hire usually involves a low paying, clerk or labor job. It's generally due to the lack of applicants. However, in a sluggish economy, this may change. Then what?

Sometimes we are not talking about only low paying clerk or labor positions. A Miami associate of mine told me candidly that he did not want to hire an in-house mortgage loan originator unless the person spoke, at least passable Spanish, good enough to take an application. He was obviously talking about more than some working use.

There are a lot of Latin American newcomers who arrive after high school graduation? Are we doing enough to aid their learning of English? Probably not.

Not that all Latinos want to speak Spanish! They don't!

Columbians, especially, are quick to tell their parents to speak English. In more and more Latino Miami households, Spanish is not heard.

Still, there are the newcomers who are finding it is easy to learn just enough English to function, as in to buy cigarettes and beer, while speaking Spanish 99% of the time. This is generally the case with those who come to Miami after they have passed high school age.

I love Spanish. I speak it. My five-year-old daughter is even learning it. But, as my Russian wife has made clear, "I learned English. So can everyone else."

Good point.

When you have a city filled with newcomers, it is important that they be included into our full economy and society as soon as possible. Florida Senator Mel Martinez, a Cuban national, pointed out the urgency for learning English. "Without it," he emphasized, "you have linguistic ghettos."

We are teaching it in schools. What else can be done?

For starters, we can mandate English only for literally every professional designation. Insurance classes, mortgage classes, and real estate classes typically offer the material in Spanish. If this is eliminated and the exams are English only, then those working in those fields will be forced to learn the language.

English, and only English, will be spoken in government buildings. No application for employment for any government position will be complete without an English proficiency test. This exam will be at high school level. Not the fourth grade level exam proposed in chapter one as a prerequisite for voting or naturalization.

Biscayne Boulevard, south end photo: Marc Averette.

Miami Highway Crossover photo: Kolossos

Doesn't this sound unfair?

Not really. It is the most fair and most practical path for the betterment of our nation. After all, there are a lot of smart, worthy people outside the country who want to immigrate to America and already speak perfect English. In an upcoming chapter, we will discuss this option. There is, without question, a strong argument to give preference to immigrants who are already fluent in English.

This past election, I noted that the ballots in Miami Beach were in four languages: English, Spanish, Portuguese and Creole. My wife was quick to question, "Why not Russian? Or German? Or Chinese? This is discrimination!"

Without question, she's got a good point. We must have voting ballots in one language. English is the language favored by the majority. And if a person can't read it, they should not be allowed to vote. That is what the "E" Amendment is all about.

Not that you will get much resistance from Miamians! These people are some of the most proud people in the country to be Americans. In fact, Hispanic surnamed Miamians will be some the most vocal and most supportive of the "E" Amendment. They see English as the glue which can bind us as one people. It is a binder that transcends race, color, religion, sex, and national origin.

In today's Miami, it is easy to see the end result – Cubans, Columbians, Argentines, Brazilians, Venezuelans, Peruvians and other peoples, representing the very best of their respective former countries. Many are marrying immigrants from France, Spain and Italy and all are speaking English. Their children are, in many cases learning only English. The second generation speaks our language with an ever-so-slight lilt. As has been the case with all immigrants from other countries, the heavily inflected accents subside. The new Miami is becoming an enclave of the world's Romantic elite. Speaking English.

Then there is the other Miami. These are Spanish speaking newcomers who aren't terriby interested in learning English. After all, nearly every sign in the city is bilingual. There are Spanish newspapers. There are Spanish television channels. Most employers speak Spanish. Learning a language is hard work. And, unlike during the 1960s, no entity, business or government is stressing the urgency to learn English. There is even some reluctance to encourage the use of English.

This is new and more and more commonplace in the business world. There are real estate agents in Miami, even office managers, who never utter a word in English from the time they enter the office in the morning until they depart in the evening. There are insurance agents who literally can't wade through technical documents in English. There are presidents of condominium management companies who can literally speak no English. There are countless stories of developers who have built and sold pre-construction condominiums without the ability to read titles and deeds in English.

So, what's the big deal?

It can be a very big deal, if you might have bought something from one of these individuals. So many buyers of real estate in Miami-Dade County have horror stores of developers not delivering on promises made. Some were intentional and flagrant. Others, however, stemmed from the sellers' not having a complete grasp of the English language.

An example of this comes to mind that ultimately cost several condo owners thousands, due to the developer's failure to fully understand a standard Fannie Mae condominium questionnaire.

A Columbian developer, who will remain unnamed, purchased an old South Beach apartment complex. With the help of a Bogotá investor, he converted the individual apartment units to condos. Contracting with an English speaking realtor, he sold 70% of the units pre-construction. The remaining 30% he retained, receiving premium rental income. He likewise retained control of the Home Owners' Association.

This wasn't a problem until some of the pre-construction buyers elected to flip their units. When the new purchasers began their financing procedures, the developer was confronted with the condo questionnaire, which includes the basic question, "Does any one person own more than 10% of the units?"

In defense of the developer, it is likely that he had pressure from the realtor to answer the question, no. Otherwise, he would have effectively killed the deal. No lender would fund a loan where 30% of the units were owned by one party. However, when confronted, he explained, "It is not one person who owns the remaining units. It is a corporation made up of me, my wife and our investor in Bogotá."

Somehow, the fact that a corporation is considered a person by the lender was lost in translation.

A banker had a solution to the quandary. Sell five of the units to FHA owner occupants and the problem would be solved. To the dismay of the remaining owners, the developer refused. His reasoning stemmed from a belief that FHA borrowers would bring low income people into the complex.

Where did he receive this information? He said his consultant advised him of this. The banker concluded that the consultant, like the developer, did not adequately understand English well enough to distinguish the difference between FHA and Section Eight, a HUD rental program designed for low income families.

The end result was his small condominium complex was classified as a cash only property. As would be expected, this was devastating to the values of the units.

Those who had bought pre-construction in hopes of earning a future profit were suddenly upside down, owing more on their property than could be recovered in a sale. To make matters worse, no lender would consider refinancing due to the high number of units owned by the developer.

It is reminiscent of an experience endured by a friend from Minneapolis who learned that in Hawaii good service is no substitute for good English.

Karl Edmondson, not his real name, landed a dream job in the television business. He was named manager of a branch of a Honolulu network affiliate. The branch was in Hilo, on the big island. Excited at the chance to live in paradise, he and his wife sold their home in Minnesota and ventured into the Hawaii real estate market.

Through a referral from the television station, they became acquainted with George Hiramoto, not his real name, a local real estate agent in Hilo. George was exceptional with his work ethic and propensity to go the extra mile. He was as punctual as he was professional. He spoke English with a heavy Japanese accent, but it didn't bother the Edmondsons. What was of greater concern was the astronomical price of real estate in Hawaii.

After three frustrating weeks, they came upon a real jewel.

George had located an old plantation house, some miles west on the Kona coast. The 3500 square foot home, originally built in 1906, was situated on a high bluff overlooking the Pacific. It had a deep porch, high Victorian style ceilings and crown moldings. Best of all, it could be purchased for $500,000. The Edmondsons were excited.

When they wrote the contract and told George they would need to borrow $300,000 to close the deal, he immediately referred them to a local bank in Hilo. The deal went smoothly and closed in less than a month. Almost a year later, they got the surprise of their life.

The house was leasehold. In other words, they had purchased the structure, but not the land. Originally part of an old pineapple plantation, the house was situated on 192 acres of land that were owned by a corporation headquartered in San Diego. Undisclosed by the real estate agent was the corporation's plan to build condominiums on the property.

Furious, Karl Edmondson called George only to learn that he had returned to Japan to attend to a dying relative. When Karl questioned the bank's loan officer and closing attorney, they could only refer him, in broken English, back to the real estate agent.

Did Karl Edmondson have recourse? No. He had signed the contract and the loan application and overlooked the fact that his purchase was leasehold. This detail was not explained with any clarity. Did his real estate agent understand the difference? It is possible that he did. But, the fact that he didn't disclose it was inconsistent with his overall service.

The Edmondsons concluded that George Hiramoto may not have truly understood the translation. It would have seemed unlikely that he would not have known the difference between fee simple and leasehold. But assuming that he did, he had not communicated this critical point to his clients.

Essentially, George had some working use of English. But, like so many professionals in Hawaii, while he spoke fluent Japanese, his English was rudimentary at best. Could he have passed a high school English proficiency test? Probably not.

The same held true for the Columbian developer in Miami Beach. Had he been required to pass a high school level English proficiency test as a prerequisite for obtaining his building permit, he would have been ineligible!

Would it be discriminatory to have denied the Hawaiian a real estate license or the Miami Beach developer a building permit? Under present law it would be.

However, with the "E" Amendment it would be the law of the land. And for good reason. Because neither the real estate agent nor the developer possessed adequate English skills, they brought harm and, in some cases, financial ruin to innocent, unsuspecting people.

This simply cannot continue!

As has been the case in Honolulu with Japanese speakers, there is growing evidence that in Miami there is a silent preference for first language Spanish speakers as employees. Generally occurring when the person hiring is Latino, many otherwise qualified applicants have been told, they needed some Spanish to be considered. In one sense, this is practical. After all, two-thirds of people in the county hail from Spanish descent. From another point of view, it is outrageous. Such a practice can easily become a tool of discrimination.

There is a code word used regularly by easterners who have departed Dade County in favor of Collier, Broward or Palm Beach counties. Miami had become "too busy." This description of too busy translates to too Latin. Sadly, this perception has been communicated to the extent that some newcomers from other states go so far as to avoid the city completely for this reason. This can have a negative impact on future growth and development, not to mention the impact on job creation by out-of-state companies. In short, the city is simply too attractive to lose the full benefit of America due to the resistance of a few to change.

Even more disquieting is the fact that this perception does nothing but fuel the fires of prejudice. Everyone should be proud of their heritage. We have stories of languages other than English being spoken in different parts of the country as we settled the continent.

French was the first language in southern Louisiana until the early 1950s. It was the preferred language in the smaller communities until they literally banned it. I have friends from LSU who tell me stories of elementary school students being disciplined for speaking French.

Russell Harrington, a longtime friend from Kaplan, Louisiana remembered, "We were told that if we ever wanted to go to anywhere else in America to get a job, we would find that everyone spoke English. This is what they told our parents. It wasn't optional."

Many can recount the stories of German immigrants who settled the Midwest in the late nineteenth century and taught German in the schools. These, however, were tiny farming communities in Iowa, not Miami in the twenty-first century. And that was before television. Today, learning English is as easy as watching the boob tube. But the desire to learn English must be there.

Humanity, as a whole, is lazy. Most will not learn a second language unless they are literally forced to do so. In Miami, the Spanish language is not only a cultural heritage but big business. There will always be a Spanish language alternative in books and the media. But, the more quickly the population learns English to the same proficiency as Spanish, the more quickly these prejudices and stereotypes will be eliminated.

Senator Marco Rubio stands as the prime example. The son of Cuban refugees, he is a native born American of Cuban descent. It might be mentioned that his parents departed Cuba with his grandparents when Castro took power. Forced to learn English in the public schools, they quickly assimilated. They later relocated to Las Vegas. Marco Rubio proudly professes to be the son of a "bartender and a hotel maid."

After graduating from the University of Florida, Rubio returned to Miami and completed his J.D. at the University of Miami. From there he entered politics as state representitive, quickly working his way to House Speaker. Today he is called the "future of the Republican party" and has even been touted as a possible opponent for Barack Obama in 2012! His overwelming victory over Governor Charlie Crist (the choice of the Republican establishment) and Democrat Kendrick Meek in the November 2010 election was proof that assimilation is the key to dispelling prejudice.

Like most Cubanos, Marco Rubio sees himself as an American of Cuban ancestry. He loves America and passionately describes the United States as the *only* country on earth where everyone can succeed, no matter how much money one has, who one's family and friends are, etc. Without question, he harbors a love for the Spanish language and culture. Still, he would likely admit that not all people are as motivated as his parents were in adopting their new country. In short, there needs to be a concerted effort to encourage assimilation. Miami must not Balkanize as has been the accusation of countless visitors.

Senator Marco Rubio (photo Gage Skidmore)

How can this be accomplished?

Simple, actually. The "E" Amendment will eliminate all public signs in Spanish. There will be no Spanish on any credit card machine or telephone voice mail. No professional examination will be available in any language other than English. As with civil service applicants, a high school English proficiency test will be a prerequisite for taking a bar, real estate, insurance, securities or property management examination.

Additionally, no multi-family building permit will be issued unless the applicant can show proof that the high school English proficiency exam has been passed!

Would this be unreasonable? Absolutely not. In fact, it would be a supreme kindness to those not convinced that it was in their best interest to learn English.

To come together, we must have the unifying ingredient of a common language. English is our language. Until the American people vote to make Spanish or any alternative the second official language, there can never be a substitute. Ultimately, when English replaces Spanish as the language of choice in Spanish speaking homes in America, an amazing phenomenon will take place. Latinos will become Americans of Spanish descent. In essence, most of the prejudice unjustly inflicted on these people will evaporate.

That in itself is sufficient justification!

3 English and Immigration

America's unofficial immigration policy can best be described with the quote often attributed to Rear Admiral Grace Hopper:

It is easier to ask forgiveness than it is to get permission.

Pavel Runochkin, not his real name, was twenty-five years old. He had a sister who had married an American. Back home in Russia, he had a twenty-two-year-old wife and two sons, ages four years and four months.

In 2007, Pavel came to America on a visitor's visa. This was his second time to visit the states. His first visit, in the winter of 2005, lasted six weeks. The papers presented to Homeland Security for his second entry stated four months.

Homeland Security tediously interrogated Pavel. In fact, they all but insinuated that he was not truthful regarding his purpose for being in America.

Their primary question was essentially what employer would hold a job for an employee for four months while he vacationed in America? Pavel worked for a bank. Undaunted, he explained that his bank had a liberal leave policy regarding employees visiting relatives abroad. This wasn't entirely true and the Homeland Security officials knew it.

Still, Pavel had visited America before. His visa was legitimate. In his previous visit, he had returned at the exact time that he had promised. With no concrete reason for denial, just general suspicions, he was cleared.

Pavel entered America through the Miami Airport. One of the red flags seen by Homeland Security was that his departure would be from Cincinnati four months later. When he explained that he had relatives living in both places, even more question marks were generated. Still, there was no reason to deny him. But, as he later confessed to his sister, "they may be watching me."

Was this entry extraordinary? Not really.

Pavel was a young Russian with a college education, he actually had two college degrees, a respectable job in banking, and a wife and two children still in Russia. His sister's paperwork was flawless. In fact, it could not have been done better by an experienced immigration lawyer. To make matters even more perplexing, Pavel had been granted two years on his guest visa. How had this happened? Homeland Security may have wondered if Pavel was actually serious about returning to Russia.

Two weeks later, after taking in some long overdue sunshine in South Beach, Pavel joined his brother-in-law, sister and niece in the nineteen hour drive to Lexington, Kentucky. When he arrived, he was greeted by the same neighbors he had met two years earlier.

Pavel had learned a little English during his previous trip to America. He had forgotten most of it in two years of disuse. However, when forced to speak English, he begin remembering and building on it quickly. Handy and innovative by nature, Pavel quickly went to work on his sister's large yard. It was badly in need of landscaping after the owners' winter absence. Slowly but surely, he made progress. While he continued to beautify his sister's yard, with base plants and mulch, he drew an audience from the neighbors.

Almost overnight, Pavel was being asked to perform landscaping work, ranging from digging holes to stacking stones. As he completed one job, another assignment seemed to always surface. He was a man in demand.

Pavel seemed to be able to do anything. He was an excellent landscaper. He likewise proved to be an immaculate painter. He even painted concrete floors with a flair that would have made the most discriminating Manhattan interior decorator take note.

Throughout the three plus months in Kentucky, he did more

Immigrants' Inspection, Ellis Island

than prove his worth as a painter and landscaper. He also made tremendous strides in learning English. In doing so, he came to realize how welcoming the people were with whom he came in contact. The most consistent question was "is there anyway you can stay?"

True, the people in Central Kentucky are some of the nicest people anywhere. They liked Pavel and appreciated his hard work and diligence. Their invitation was serious. When they learned how difficult it would have been for Pavel to have actually stayed in the country, legally, they were appalled.

It was not just difficult. It was close to impossible.

When Pavel's sister inquired about immigration procedures for Pavel and his family, she was told about twelve years, assuming everything was is in order and there were no problems. Twelve years. Why would it take so long?

The immigration system gives parents and children the highest priorities. Siblings of an American citizen are given a lower priority. Pavel's sister was actually told by an immigration attorney, that it would speed things up for her brother, if she were to sponsor their parents first, naturalize them and then allow them to sponsor Pavel and his family for immigration.

This was a setback. Pavel's parents were not interested in em-migrating. They were in their late fifties and confessed that at their age learning a new language would be too difficult. They also had friends and other children in their community who they didn't want to leave behind.

Pavel was disappointed. His sister checked on different visas, namely H-Visas. But those were as difficult to procure as any other type visa. It seemed to be a hopeless cause.

From an outsider's point of view, Pavel should have been a prime candidate for immigration. He was young. He was educated. He was married with two small children. He was a hard worker with an excellent work ethic. He was industrious. Most importantly, he embraced America.

In a country openly worried about its aging population and concerned with the overtaxing of social security, it would seem logical that we would be embracing, if not recruiting young people like Pavel Runochkin. But, we are not. For his sister to immigrate his aging parents it would have been as easy as buying airline tickets.

At best, Pavel's parents might work ten years before drawing social security. Pavel and his wife would likely spend forty years, paying into the system before drawing on it.

The question most would ask is why don't we give someone like Pavel a priority over his parents?

That is a question that is asked every day. And there still hasn't been a satisfactory answer given. Pavel would immediately join the work force. It might not be in banking. But, he was easily qualified for positions in home improvement and landscaping. He would have entered the workforce with energy and enthusiasm. Learning English would have been as natural for him as applying for an American driver's license. There would never have been any thought of retaining his old language in his new country.

The principal theme in *"E" is for English* is not about revising our immigration system. Still, there is no way to avoid some discussion. This writing's focus is on making English the official language in America. What can be emphasized is which immigrants will want to adopt our language with the greatest enthusiasm and the least amount of resistance?

Pavel and his family would embrace the language, if they were given an opportunity to immigrate. They would never think twice about the requirement that it be learned. In fact, they would likely scorn those who resisted learning it.

Which brings us to the next question. In addition to requiring a fourth grade level English proficiency test for naturalization, should there be a proficiency test for a green card? Why not!

After all, if half of the planet would like to live here, perhaps we need to raise the bar. Proponents of such a requirement would definitely have an argument!

Without a doubt, if Pavel Runochkin were given a chance to gain permanent resident alien (green card) status, he would be studying English six hours per day to make certain he passed the test. To him, English would be his key to staying in America.

You learn you stay, you don't you won't.

Is this being too hard on our immigrants? Pavel wouldn't think so. In fact, he expressed disgust when he observed the large numbers of Americans in Miami without any English. In broken English, he proclaimed, "No English, they should be kicked out!"

That may have been a bit strong. Yet, the question of English proficiency as a prerequisite for naturalization is not a topic that should be discarded. Requiring English proficiency for a permanent resident status carries some credence as well. Would this be asking too much from our immigrants? Probably not.

The big reason it isn't already in practice may be due to the ages of a lot of our immigrants. Many are past fifty, some past sixty. It stands to reason that learning a new language becomes more difficult with age. However, this fact is solid evidence of another reason the immigration priority system needs to be revisited. If siblings gained an equal priority to parents and children, there would be more people between twenty and forty entering the country. These immigrants would be quicker to learn English and enter the work force.

Could we do that and not flood our country with too many immigrants, too fast?

There can be an argument made to allow siblings the same priority level as parents and children. The United States needs younger, educated workers with at least working use of English when they enter the country. Most immigrants want to learn English as quickly as possible.

Many have entered the country on temporary visas and never left. Of these, a large number of people came in on religious visas.

How could this happen? Most of the time, it was because the sponsoring church either became defunct or lost funding. Sometimes, the deadline slipped by unnoticed.

Unfortunately, minor children who came to America with their parents don't learn until after the fact, after they are Americanized, that they are in the country illegally.

Such was the case with the Sosa family (names have been changed) in Flowood, Mississippi.

Alberto Sosa was born and raised in Madrid, Spain. After completing seminary in Seville, he traveled to Mexico. In Reynosa, a large city on the south side of the Rio Grande, he met and married Lucia Ortiz. There they settled and lived, parenting three children during the first five years of their marriage. Alberto had studied English while in seminary and spoke it fluently by this time.

Alberto was an ordained Assembly of God minister. Through a church in Brownsville, Texas, he arranged visas for his family and an assignment, several hundred miles to the northeast, in Rankin

County, Mississippi. In Flowood, they started a church. It thrived for several years but eventually folded.

During this time, Alberto's three children, Maria, Daniel and Linda, were enrolled in public schools. They fully acclimated to life in central Mississippi. Alberto's family visa was based on the church's existence. When it folded, his visa expired with it. The next step was somewhat tricky.

Some members of the congregation continued to attend services. As pastor, Alberto held services weekly and collected offerings sufficient to support his family. Any shortfalls were made up from money received for odd jobs that he performed for many members of the congregation.

Is this practice unusual in the rural south? Absolutely not. In fact, it is often typical of small, struggling churches. As has been traditional since the country itself was founded, bi-vocational pastors of small churches have other jobs to bridge the gap between church offerings and what is required to make a living. So, Alberto Sosa limped by, with the help of his church offerings and what extra he could muster from cleaning windows, digging postholes or selling firewood.

His children made out as well. Daniel mastered carpentry while learning the bricklaying trade. Maria taught piano lessons. Linda enjoyed being a straight A student. All three met local members of the opposite sex. Daniel and Maria married. Eighteen-year-old Linda had a steady boyfriend in Charlie Wheeler, a congenial, seventeen-year-old who played football and likewise made A's in school. Her parents adored Charlie, even when they learned that Linda was pregnant.

Having spent better than seven years in Rankin County, Mississippi, the Sosas were both adjusted and accepted. As has always been the case, the South has tended to be less focused on ethnic origin than the North. This little known characteristic goes back to antebellum days.

There has likewise been less religious prejudice and certainly less anti-Semitism. A prime example was Judah Benjamin, who was hailed as the finest legal mind in the south in 1860. A practicing Jew, Benjamin was the Attorney General in Confederate President Jefferson Davis' cabinet.

In the case of the Sosas, they were seen as hard working, God-fearing, people and that was the extent of it. Both Daniel and Maria had married Anglos. Linda was engaged to an Anglo. All of the Sosas, with the exception of Lucia, spoke perfect English. Their soft, drawling accent reflected Mississippi with virtually no hint of Spanish. In short, they were more Mississippian than Mexican.

Unfortunately, there are some bigoted southerners and Charlie's mother was one of them. Having divorced her husband eight years earlier, she still held many of the prejudices of her father, a 1930s throwback, who defined the substandard south.

When she learned that Charlie was dating a Mexican girl, she attempted to confine Charlie to the house. When this failed, she tried to prevent him from seeing Linda. After he threatened to seek emancipation, she forbade both from entering her home.

With nowhere to turn, Charlie joined the army.

Linda was horrified. The thought of Charlie moving to Fort Benning, near Columbus, Georgia was bad enough. Worse still, their baby was due after his departure.

But that, in itself, was part of Charlie's motivation to join the service. Like so many young recruits, he had been induced by the promise of the many benefits offered by the military. In most cases these benefits were real. There were exceptions, however as he would discover.

After his mother's cold dismissal of both he and Linda, Charlie sought other options. Linda's parents were strict fundamentalist Christians. That translated into Charlie and Linda needed to be married before they could live under the same roof. There was no compromise in their position. Whereas Charlie's mother was vehemently opposed to their marriage, they were wholeheartedly in favor of it. The Sosas wanted the child, while Charlie's mother expressed pure outrage that they had not aborted it. The two young people wanted to both marry and bring the baby into the world. But they still needed to find someone who would marry them.

Linda was of age. Charlie, still four months short of eighteen, was not of age in Mississippi. The states bordering Mississippi had similar standards. The army offered a way out. Not only would anyone approve the marriage of a service man, but there were excellent benefits available for both Linda and the baby. Charlie explained the scenario to Linda. While she openly preferred the care of her mother to an unfamiliar doctor in a strange city, she seemed to be more comfortable with the idea.

The baby was born. Charlie attempted to gain admittance into the military hospital only to learn the requirement of marriage. Still unmarried, he tried to remedy the problem by returning to Mississippi to marry Linda. There he got the surprise of his life – Linda had no social security card.

How could this be? Simple, actually! After his church officially disbanded, Alberto Sosa simply stayed with his congregation in Flowood, Mississippi. Most were from working class, blue collar families who knew nothing about immigration laws or visa procedures. What they did know was that Alberto was a man of God. They liked his family members. If they had learned he was in the country illegally, they would have probably said, "They're better than most of the people who are here legally."

Charlie, however, could not get Linda or his baby admitted to the military hospital. Nor could he legally marry her. In desperation, he called his father who had some limited experience with immigration.

What his father learned was both good and bad. Because Linda had come into the country at age ten and had mothered a child, she would be able to stay in the country legally.

However, in appealing her case to Homeland Security, she would be incriminating her sister, brother and parents. There was a probability that her siblings would be allowed to stay, since they were married to American citizens. Unfortunately, Alberto and Lucia would likely be deported to Mexico. To initiate and expedite the proceeding, the lawyer would charge Charlie $4000.

Some choice.

Charlie turned eighteen, but he felt much older. He suddenly was confronting a problem that much of America is starting to wake up to. There is a large number of shadow dwellers who have lived for years in America undetected. Maria, Daniel and Linda had come to the states as children of a minister. They had watched him establish a church. The church had officially disbanded, although the congregation was largely intact, due to the efforts of their father. Now, they were all nothing short of fugitives, evading the law.

In frustration, Charlie turned to his commanding officer who coldly reminded him that Linda's entire family was in the country illegally. His advice was to get custody of the child and let the chips fall as they would.

To Charlie, the Sosas seemed like anything but criminals. They were totally Americanized. They were accepted in the rural Mississippi community. He never thought of them as anything except fellow Mississippians and good, close friends. He had fallen in love with their youngest daughter. She had mothered his child. Now, he was being told that he could not marry Linda unless he dropped the dime on her family, potentially compromising their status in the country. He was even being told it was his duty as a law abiding American to do so. To magnify his dilemma, their son, James' disposition was totally in his hands.

In the end, Charlie did nothing. Linda wanted him to abandon the army and return to Flowood. When he patiently explained his inability to merely quit the military, she became irritated with him. She chastised him for joining and blamed him for running out on her and his son. With no retort available, Charlie became more absorbed in basic training and his life in the army.

Six months later, lonely and bewildered, he married another woman. Three months after marriage, he was in Iraq. His baby remained in Mississippi with his first love and her family. Nothing more was done.

Charlie Wheeler's experience and exposure to one of America's greatest problems lent insight on the failed McCain-Kennedy immigration bill introduced in 2007. Had it passed, it would have made it possible for the Sosas to come out of the shadows and take steps toward naturalization. Did they break the law? Technically, yes. Were the children at fault? No. Should Charlie have been allowed to marry Linda with the baby receiving benefits? A strong argument could have been mounted on their behalf. In all likelihood, he would have succeeded, at the expense of her parents.

What about Maria Sosa-Chambliss and Daniel Sosa? How were they able to marry? One reason was the laxness of where they lived. In Mississippi, many residents don't have social security cards. They are typically unnecessary. When Daniel and Maria married, they were over eighteen. Neither they nor their spouses were in the military. There were never requests for identification cards. Both had driver's licenses. In Rankin County, Mississippi, that was enough.

Perhaps the most noteworthy aspect about the Sosas case is that the people in their community both accepted them and wanted them. Alberto Sosa was a Spanish national. He spoke perfect English with a cordial Mississippi inflection. His profession depended on spoken English. His children attended the public schools in Rankin County. After several years, it was as if they had never lived anywhere other than Flowood, Mississippi.

Would their experience have been different if only Spanish had been spoken in their household? Probably. The fact that this family spoke English, living in a community where few Hispanics resided made their immersion similar to Russian immigrants. What is also noteworthy is how they were totally taken in by fellow Flowood residents. It provides evidence that discrimination against Latinos subsides when they adopt English.

Could English proficiency by illegal aliens be used as a factor in making deportation decisions? Certainly sounds ludicrous, but maybe some thought should be given to this question.

Through anchor babies, extended families, that entered the country illegally, have been allowed to stay legally, with the government's blessing. How could this happen?

The Fourteenth Amendment states that all persons born in the United States are granted automatic citizenship. However, historians reflect accurately that the Fourteenth Amendment was written with the freed slaves in mind. Prior to the Civil War, slaves were counted as three-fifths of a person when determining the states' numerical representation in Washington. After the war, the question was raised regarding citizenship and this standard was adopted.

When people began to trickle into the United States, one gleam of hope always beckoned. If a child could be born by parents on U.S. soil, the child would have automatic citizenship via the Fourteenth Amendment. Then, the parents, grandparents, brothers, sisters, aunts, uncles and cousins would have a case to remain.

Our country has always maintained a benevolent posture. The policy has been to unite and not separate families. Any difference or deviation from this standard has been considered cold, heartless and unsympathetic. Politicians who have spoken out against the practice have often been demonized. But the question remains. Is it fair to allow all of these relatives to stay, knowing that the original offenders, the child's parents, knew of the loophole in the law and exploited it?

Liberals are quick to say, "Yes. We cannot separate families, no matter what the circumstance. To keep children here and send their parents back to their native countries would be cruel, inhumane and heartless."

Conservatives counter in proclaiming that, "We cannot reward people for breaking the law. If they broke the law, they must be shipped back to their native countries, even if the children remain behind. They can, of course, take the children with them, if they choose."

This is a complicated issue. Especially in light of the looming specter of rationed health care. The actual thought of determining a preference between an illegal pediatric and a legal geriatric constitutes the ultimate universal healthcare nightmare. Proponents of universal healthcare say it won't come to this. But, are they 100% certain?

The wording of the Fourteenth Amendment is clear. But the circumstances of its inception must be evaluated, as well as other historical evidence of deviations, such as with Native Americans. There should never be a practice of rewarding manipulators of the law. Conversely, refusing to examine each occurrence on a case-by-case basis defies our greatness as a people.

The Development, Relief and Education for Alien Minors Act (DREAM) recently went down to defeat in the Senate. In many ways it has become a symbol of America's growing frustration with immigration control and the lack of a clear immigration policy that is favored by the majority. There were excellent reasons for passage and rejection presented by both advocates and opponents.

The "E" Amendment offers a compromise that takes the general idea of the DREAM Act and removes the "fuzzy outer garments" from it. In short, if any applicant can pass a 10th grade English proficiency test, they will be "given a path" toward citizenship. One of those pathways is the military, as outlined in the DREAM Act. Another would be the Peace Corps. There would also be community service projects such as "Big Brothers of America" that would be given as options. The biggest difference is that applicants under the "E" Amendment would receive *no* federal help such as tuition fee assistance, low income housing, food stamps, medical cards or any other federal entitlement. Their pathway would be probationary in nature, as it should be. At the same time, because of their circumstance, these applicants would have a chance to legally earn citizenship.

In an upcoming chapter, one of the greatest examples of the "E" Amendment's depth and timeliness unfolds. It potentially offers a bridge for the moderates on the issue of anchor babies and the dispositions of their families. In short, any anchor baby able to pass the intermediate English proficiency examination will be allowed to stay with an easy path toward citizenship. The same might hold true for the parents and any immediate family members. If they cannot pass the exam, they will return with their families to their native countries and proceed through normal channels.

There will be opposition to even this alternative. Suggesting the "E" Amendment could potentially override the Fourteenth Amendment is controversial. Still, would it be fair to deport Alberto and Lucia Sosa who came into the country legally, assimilated and contributed? Under the present framework, they only needed to parent a child and their residency was secure. To reward someone who enters the country illegally, knowing that permanent status is as easy as pregnancy, makes a mockery of the immigrants who went through the rigors and expense of naturalization.

What about the Sosa children. Obviously, Linda mothered a child of an American citizen and a DNA test could confirm it. But what if Charlie Wheeler had not been an American citizen? Under the present system, even without a DNA test, the anchor baby, James Wheeler, could be Linda's ticket to stay. What about Daniel and Maria? True, they married Americans, but that in itself is not a guarantee of permanent status. However, because the three Sosa children could obviously pass an intermediate proficiency test, the problem could potentially correct itself!

I met a career army man several years ago, to whom I posed the question, "Could we offer amnesty to any illegal who volunteered four years active duty and two years as a reserve in service to this country?"

He answered in the negative, citing reasons based on inabilities to use the English language. But what if they could speak the language to the degree of the Sosas?

That is a million dollar question. Without a doubt, this option might yield a lot of potential bodies for the armed forces. It might also produce numbers for peace corps type positions. It would be less expensive than deportations. Furthermore, it would be constructive and another motivation for learning English.

We have an estimated twelve million illegal aliens in the United States. Many have stories comparable to the Sosas. There are others, however, who are criminals from outside. Southern California remains an accident waiting to happen. We have children of illegal aliens with no status, no paper, no hope, nothing, save a place at the county hospital, at the taxpayers' expense, of course.

Recently it was reported that 40% of the Medicaid recipients in Los Angeles County are illegal aliens. This is a disgrace. How did it happen? Nobody can give a totally accurate answer. It may have started slowly. Then it grew. Then it grew more. Then it spread. Before we knew it, we now have a situation that is out of control.

Politicians have not come up with an answer. In cases where they've tried, such as with the McCain-Kennedy plan, it is opposed by 70 percent of the country. More of Middle-America echoed the words of Mitt Romney, "let them get in line and wait their turn." That straight shooting conclusion is revered by most Americans. But, from a politician's point of view, it is politically dangerous.

Most people in America associate illegal aliens with Latinos. This is incorrect. The majority of the people in the country illegally are not Hispanic. However, when politicians talk tough and propose decisive measures against illegal aliens, the first thing the media concludes is that they will alienate the Latino community with these views. This is an over generalization.

True, there are tragic stories like those of the Sosas. But, everyone, including Latinos, want answers, solutions and action. Making English proficiency a part of any illegal immigration bill would have support, as well as an impact. If we provide alternatives to deportation for English speaking illegal aliens, we might win on two fronts. What the alternatives would be and how those qualifying would be determined is another subject.

Beyond question, there would be support in the illegal alien community. This would translate to cooperation. The country is looking for both a solution and a positive outcome. With the requirement of fingerprints and photo ID card, control is assured.

Should people in the country illegally be punished? Yes, but it should be done in a positive, affirmating and forgiving way. Military service, community service or alternatives that benefit the whole country are fair. Most people in the country illegally would agree.

However, are we suggesting that we allow only those with the ability to prove their proficiency in English be given this option? Are we suggesting English proficiency as the mechanism separating those who could immediately become a part of the American family, and those who need to return to their native land and enter through the normal channels?

Yes, we are.

The purpose of the "E" Amendment is to make our country stronger, smarter and more unified! If these people in the country illegally can pass a high school reading proficiency test, they should be given a chance to remain. If they can't, they should be deported and required to go through the normal channels. Is this fair? Not entirely. And it certainly is not politically correct.

Critics will abound. They will stress that anyone already fluent in English will have motivation to come to America on a tourist visa and then stay. For this reason the price of amnesty will need to be significant. How significant?

This will be a tough, if not pivotal, question. It will be important that the price be constructive and not merely punitive. A measure designed for the overall betterment of both the country and the offending illegal alien will be optimal. The military is a great option and many offenders could be useful in the special services. The Peace Corps would likewise be a worthy alternative. There might even be merit in proposing a reduced pay, public works-type service where perpetrators could pay their debt to America. There will be thousands of ideas on this subject.

There are essentially two positions: (a) total unconditional deportation, and (b) amnesty for all. Conservatives favor deportation. Liberals favor amnesty. Can we not find a middle ground?

Amazingly, the answer is *Yes*, through the "E" Amendment. Tying English proficiency to naturalization and permanent status via an ID card, gives us better control of the immigration process. If a person cannot produce an ID card, it will serve as a warning bell. An ID card will be like a second driver's license. Without ID, it will be assumed that the person is unable to read at a fourth grade level and/or they are in the country illegally.

Better control can be further facilitated by requiring that all states implement English only written tests for driver's licenses. We could even go one step further, federally mandating the presentation of birth certificates prior to taking the written test.

Certainly there will be arguments against both stipulations, ranging from discrimination to an infringement on states' rights. But, an English only written test will remove many illegal aliens from the roads. With no birth certificate, there will not be the opportunity to take the test. People in the country illegally will therefore not have the right to operate a motor vehicle. This restriction in itself will discourage entry into America. It will also encourage departure. It will remove drivers from our crowded roads and freeways. It will force increased mass transit usage. It will be a deterrent to potential terrorists.

Over time, the system will begin to make its mark. In the end, the illegal alien problem will correct itself. It simply goes back to the central idea presented in this writing. The key to our nation's foundation is been the ability to unify all people under one language. We can continue this path, or we can become fragmented into many regions based on which language predominates in that area. The "E" Amendment provides the answer and, in doing so, preserves the country that we all love. Anything less and we have a cracked foundation. The "E" Amendment is the consummate mending of the crack.

Of course, there will be those who argue that this standard will result in many unlicensed drivers on the highways. This is a consideration, but of greater concern are the numbers of illegal aliens with driver's licenses who may be voting.

Can anyone remember going to the voting polls and being asked to produce nothing more than a driver's license? What if they are able to produce a fraudulent driver's license? Producing phony identification cards is becoming a growing business. The voter ID card, as specified by the "E" Amendment, will stop that practice in its tracks. Not to mention providing additional incentive for non-English speakers to learn English. The states can do their part in passing tougher laws and stiffer penalties for unlicensed drivers apprehended. There will be more use of mass transit, furthering the green cause. And, in the process, it might answer the thorny question posed earlier.

Could a smart, industrious, likeable guy like Pavel Ronochkin come to America on a tourist visa, learn English well enough to pass a proficiency test and live happily ever after? Sounds impractical, but in actuality, Pavel would study English diligently from the day he set foot on our soil. Knowing that his standard of living in America would be partially based on his ability to drive a motor vehicle, he would immerse himself in the language. And he would ultimately pass. The armed forces would be an advantageous means toward attaining his goal of eventual American citizenship. With his acquired English proficiency, two college degrees, and fluency in Russian, he would be an ideal recruit for our armed forces. Then, after four years in military service, Pavel would be ready to begin his pursuit of the American Dream.

What about Alberto Sosa? What could he do to compensate the country for his transgression? Alberto would have no problem passing an English proficiency test. In fact, English is the primary language used in his household. He broke the law. But, forgiveness is a characteristic of any great people. The proof that he had both assimilated and made a significant contribution would be taken into account. How Alberto came into the United States is light years away from the illegal alien who made a bold dash across the desert.

There would need to be a method for examining each applicant on a case-by-case basis. Alberto's situation would be deemed more circumstantial than Pavel's. Still, twenty-five-year-old Pavel might be considered more valuable to the country as an immigrant when compared to fifty-year-old Alberto.

America must never overlook any human resource. We must be proactive and not reactive when it comes to people desiring entry into our country. We must remember than the Fourteenth Amendment does not apply to those not Americans. The politically correct assessment is we cannot have different levels of expectations for different people, different sets of standards for different people and different rules for different people.

The politically incorrect assertion is the hell we can't! They broke the law!

In conclusion, the "E" Amendment creates a direction for our country that will ultimately formulate insight and a solution for a totally unrelated problem, the illegal alien question. The first step is control. We must be able to better account for all people in the country. Even though this goes against the beliefs of many good Americans, we must have a foolproof system of checking identities. Then we can examine the individual situation. We must not throw out the baby with the bathwater.

Requiring English proficiency, coupled with education, individual circumstance, and readiness to prove worthiness are the chief determinants that ultimately will answer the riddle.

American immigration policy has long been linked to family ties, accessibility, proximity, and luck. There has always been the benevolence of our government and a stubborn refusal to face accountability. Rather than confront the problem, we have shied away from it. The "E" Amendment will change that. Instead of looking at people in the country illegally with resentment and suspicion, we will see them from the standpoint of what can they contribute if given a chance to come into the family?

Without question, there are those who would like to keep things as they are. Inclusion of illegal aliens in census reports skews congressional representation in favor of the states harboring them. Proponents of the practice insist the Constitution requires that the whole number of persons be counted. Conversely, opponents correctly retort that during the time of our framers, Native Americans were not included. And, at a later time, slaves were counted as three-fifths of a person. The "E" Amendment provides a final verdict − only legal citizens are included in any census and every citizen must show proof of citizenship. If someone cannot, it is presumed that they are in the country illegally. This is the only fair way to insure equal representation for all states.

One accusation made by groups seeking election reform has been that illegal aliens are prime recruits for groups seeking to commit voter fraud. Considering the ease of obtaining a driver's license, this concern cannot be readily dismissed! Using English to lure illegal aliens from the shadows will be more easily accomplished if it is the only avenue for obtaining a driver's license. Then the path toward citizenship will be more tangible, more meaningful. How many illegal aliens are fluent in English? We don't know. But this could be a resource that we are not tapping for both the illegal aliens' and the nation's benefit!

To what extent are illegal aliens voting and how much emphasis are those groups putting on their recruitment? Probably not a lot, but maybe more than we think. A walk down Washington Avenue or through Lumus Park in Miami's South Beach reveals the large numbers of homeless. How many of these people are legal? We may never know.

What we do know is Miami's South Beach is an area historically stricken with identity theft. It would be here that the voter identification cards would be so welcomed. When you have practically everyone using plastic, it is easier than ever to run up huge bills with a stolen credit card. In many cases, the offenders are internationals. It would be in a scene like South Beach that the true depth of the "E" Amendment would be manifested.

4 Moscow

Moscow or MOCKBA (Pronounced Moskvah)

Just imagine… At age forty you awaken to learn that you have a fraternal twin, separated from you at birth, whom you never knew, but had heard mostly negative things about.

These were my exact feelings the first time I stepped off the plane in Moscow.

As in Russia.

Moscow and Russia may be a strange detour for a writing focused on making English the official language in America by constitutional amendment. But there are some amazing parallels.

Strength, unity and making Americans smarter individuals are the reasons for making English the official language in America. Perhaps the most telling evidence of why this should be done rests with how Russia was transformed from a disjointed, rambling, chaotic behemoth to a strong, unified superpower. This was accomplished after the Bolshevik Revolution. Amid all of the transgressions of Soviet dictator Joseph Stalin, his single greatest achievement was institutionalizing the Russian language.

Stalin's accomplishment ultimately made the Soviet people more cognizant of languages. It was common practice for Soviet school children to study a second language. As time passed, German was replaced by English as the number one second language. Then, as the Soviet Union gave was to the Russian Federation, it began to show signs that it might become more than a second language.

My first night in Moscow was spent aboard a boat anchored in the Moscow River. There, in the hotel bar, I was told by a Russian hotel manager that within fifty years English would replace Russian as the official language in Russia. Surprised, I casually mentioned that there were American citizens who were not interested in learning English. When I admitted that there were groups of people actually resisting it, he was astonished.

"How can they do this?" he demanded. "Your government allows this? How do these people find work? Do they not realize that English is the direction of the world?"

When I attempted to explain the concept of political correctness, he shook his head. "Your President Bill Clinton is a *gloopyetz*!" (the Russian word for fool) He meant it.

Moscow itself is strangely familiar. At first glance, it resembles New York City, with only white people. Then you begin to study the people themselves. They honestly look more like Americans than any other Europeans. After examining their history, there is an easily explainable, logical reason for this.

European Russian is composed of roughly 300 European nationalities. Over the centuries they have intermarried. And, there was the 250 years of Mongol occupation that took place between 1200 and 1450 A.D. When you think of our American melting pot and a tradition of intermarriage with Native Americans, the resemblance is perfectly understandable.

Often deleted from memory are the hundreds of different languages from various groups of people that were spoken as recently as the middle part of the twentieth century. My thoughts go to my father-in-law's family. His parents were Oodmoorts and Bashkerians. These are Eastern European cultures whose original homelands were near the Ural Mountains. The Oodmoorts were Islamic. The people could be described as sturdy, square-jawed people, of average to above average height, with ruddy complexions, light brown hair and blue eyes. Their languages come from the Uralic tree, as do Hungarian and Finish.

The Russian language is one of thirteen Slavic languages. It was actually not the language of choice for the Russian nobility

Moscow, the Kremlin

until the mid-nineteenth century. Up until then, Russian gentry often spoke French. Russian was spoken by the common people in much of the country. More often than not, peasants spoke the same language that their ancestors had spoken depending on which part of the huge country they lived.

When Joseph Stalin institutionalized Russian throughout all corners of this huge country, learning Russian was not optional. In other words, only Russian was taught in the schools and permitted in society. Government, *kolholz* (collective or communal farm), schools, the military, there were no exceptions. Past the Urals and into Siberia all the way to Kamchatka, there were no exceptions. In the traditionally Islamic regions of central Asia from Tashkent to Baku, only Russian was allowed. The same held true for the ancient Christian lands of Armenia and Georgia (Stalin's home country). Only Russian was acceptable.

Although it may have imposed the Russian culture on multitudes of ethnic peoples, it did bring the country together. And ultimately made it stronger. When the Soviet Union collapsed in 1991, many of these lands returned to their original languages. Many did not.

In one sense, imposing a language by force robbed many small countries and peoples of their national identity. But, there is no argument that the language brought the people together. The end result was the entire region enjoyed more peace than times before. People became more mobile. They became more cosmopolitan. They became better educated. There were so many more books written in Russian, that the average person became better educated. Discrimination patterns were greatly diminished because more people spoke a common language. The people became more unified.

Today there are probably twice the number of books written in Russian as are written in English in America. It is also easy to see how much better educated the children are in Russia. This in spite of difficult economic times in recent years.

Could America experience a comparable result if English became our one and only language? Would we become as proficient with languages if, like the Russians, it became mandatory for our children to learn a second language, with study beginning in the seventh grade? It is a mathematical certainty.

In fairness, America is not and never was as linguistically diverse as Russia was in 1920s. English is the language of choice. But, our command of the language is not as good as it should be. We have many Americans who can speak broken English, but are opting for another language out of habit. We have others who are from English only homes who have never truly mastered the language. Requiring a second language will force any student to spend more time reaffirming their knowledge of English.

So why are so many Russians learning English? Practicality.

In Europe, English has replaced French as the second language of choice. It is commonly referred to as the international language of business. English is so prevalent in Moscow today that one can literally live there without the ability to speak Russian. The *Moscow Times* is an excellent English language tabloid published daily. CNN is available twenty-four hours per day as are Sky News and BBC America. Bookstores are flooded with English language magazines and newspapers. What is especially interesting about the *Moscow Times* is the lack of an American filter. This is the case with numerous Spanish language newspapers available in Miami as well.

Thus, you can get the official American line from CNN. Then you can read the *Moscow Times* and get the Russian take on the same issue. In many instances they confirm that our countries are not always on the same page. Exposure to the other guy's point of view heightens geopolitical understanding.

In August 1999, I had the pleasure to meet a wealthy, sophisticated British citizen of Indian descent. He spoke perfect Oxford

Moscow, Tverskaya Boulevard photo: *Dimitrij Smirnov*

Jeff and Olga Willis

English and I later learned he spoke less Russian than I did at the time. He was representative of many foreign business people who had come to Russia, established businesses, and thrived. His company had brought quality small appliances to all parts of Russia.

When circulating throughout the huge Russian capital (Moscow is larger than New York City), I continued to be amazed at how reminiscent of the United States it was. In parts of the city where buildings were erected during Stalin's time, you would think that you were in Chicago. The people could have been in any large American city. I was equally amazed at how many Muscovites spoke at least some English. Some spoke it with shy modesty. Others spoke it was well as I did. You could generally tell who had studied formally. They spoke a version more akin to Oxford English, as my wife, Olga, did.

English was everywhere. From T-shirts to the license plates on automobiles! However, there were notable differences. Observing McDonalds and Pizza Hut restaurant signs in the Cyrillic alphabet would make most Americans proclaim, "Hey Dorothy, this sure ain't Kansas!"

Over the years, as my Russian improved, I realized that I could communicate with about 75% of the residents. Usually, I would speak Russian. They would speak English. Communication, real communication, took place. I learned a lot.

I came to understand that so much of what the American media has said isn't entirely accurate. The truth is, while curious about us, the Russians hold no ill feeling toward Americans. If anything, they embrace a lot of things American, ranging from cars and clothing to music and food. Especially, the English language. This has changed somewhat due to Putin's anti-American influence on the broadcast media.

In November 1998, fate gave me the opportunity to have adjacent seats with a U.S. State Department official on a return from Moscow. During the nine-and-one-half hour flight, she opened up, allowing me to go behind the scenes in American-Russian relations. As she surmised, "There were people on both sides still living in the 70s."

She painted a picture of the official world and the real world between Russians and Americans. The official world was still laced with caution, mistrust, and decades-old stories of bygones. To appear too friendly to the other side was considered politically incorrect. The real world reflected people who genuinely liked each other and enjoyed the other's company, but could not figure out how the leadership on both sides had managed to screw things up for the sake of continuity. As she concluded, "We were trapped by own stigmas and illusions."

Did Mikhail Gorbachev single-handedly end the cold war? Ronald Reagan haters thought so; giving the ex-general secretary 100% of the credit. That is naïve, if not purely stupid.

Both American and Russian insiders concluded that communism was already dying and Gorbachev was trying to put a human face on it, as a last ditch effort to save parts of it. Thanks largely to the failed communist system, his country was going broke.

When Reagan committed America to investment in the Strategic Defense Initiative (aka Star Wars), he effectively upped the ante. It was as if the United States had invoked a high stakes poker game. The Soviet Union couldn't continue. In the end, it folded.

There were several other key points that came out of this nine hour conversation. While many Russians eagerly aspired to learn English, feeling it was the future, Americans had little interest in learning Russian. When I recounted the advice my Alaskan Eskimo friend had given me, "to know a people is to know their language," she concurred.

"But Russian is such a difficult, confusing language," she professed. "Everyone in the embassy either speaks English, or wants to speak English. Everybody in Europe is learning English. Americans don't realize how lucky they are to grow up with English."

She applauded me heartily when I told her that I was attempting to learn Russian. Unfortunately, to say Russian is a difficult, confusing language is entirely accurate. When I began studying, I was doing it in an attempt to better learn the Russian culture. To Russians, learning English was a practical decision based on futuristic application.

To start with, Russian is one of the most highly inflected languages in the world. You think that you have a word down perfectly, only to find that the Russian speaker doesn't understand due to your failure to stress the correct syllable.

There are no "be" verbs in present tense. There are no articles. While the tenses are not that difficult, the noun cases are extremely difficult. In English, we speak only in the nomitive case. In Russian there are six noun cases.

As I began learning the language, I found myself conjugating English sentences using Russian words. As my Russian wife, Olga, put it, "it is like a little child, learning the language." People would hear it and either thought it was funny or cute. But they generally understood. As I began to go deeper and deeper into the language, I realized how patient and good-natured most Russians were with a foreigner's clumsy attempt to speak their language. They were keenly aware that it is a difficult language and fully appreciated someone's desire to speak it, even if it sounded strange and comical.

This largely self-taught version of an old, complex language gave me added insight into the culture. The Russians are practical, cut to the chase, people. Although there are occasional streaks of opulence, as a rule they don't believe in waste. Whether it is food, time or words, there is no tolerance for waste. The language reflects such a point of view.

There are many words and expressions that don't translate. There are expressions that both people have that are meaningless to the other. Often, because Russians look so similar to Americans, we have a tendency to forget that they are not the product of western civilization. They did not grow up with *Aesop's Fables* and *Canterbury Tales*. Theirs is a history of separation from the west. Initially, it was the Russian Orthodox Church. Later it was the Communist Party.

Russians, in general, think Americans smile without sincerity. To look at the facial expressions of most Russians, you would think they had lost their best friend. When an American refers to an extenuating circumstance, the Russian's retort is that it is an excuse for breaking a promise. Many Russians simply categorize Americans as bullshitters. There is certainly a feeling of shallowness and insincerity. A lot of these misunderstandings are derived from the differences in language.

Germanic and Slavic languages are decidedly different. The application of transformational grammar was infinitely valuable in this case. Because languages are all the same in deep structure it made it possible to complete the most accurate translations.

Accurate language translations can be critical in relationships. Americans who have spent a lot of time in Russia and with Russians will quickly label Russians as literalists. In other words, if you say you are going to do something, do it. No gray areas. Many American diplomats have secretly admitted that Russians would quickly say *nyet* to an idea or proposal, only to come back with an alternative that might be even more favorable to the American cause.

Unlike some languages, it is difficult to speak Russian without thinking in Russian. Have you ever watched a Russian speaker, even one with perfect English fluency, attempt to give directions to an English speaker in English? It is as if they are giving instructions in shorthand. Russians don't use as many words. The English speaker listens to what often amounts to abbreviated instructions. They are confused. To the Russian, they appear to be inattentive, simple-minded and even stupid!

Some Russians, including former president and current Prime Minister Vladimir Putin, think Americans have the idea that Russians are dirty and live in trees. Yet, for the life of me, I can't imagine what Russians he is talking about. The Russians I have known have been a lot cleaner and better educated than Americans. It is highly likely that President Putin had a translator who misunderstood or lost something in translation and shared the mistake with his boss. Putin is learning English and may gain the opportunity to alter this mistaken notion.

There has been some resentment over how difficult homeland security has made it for Russians to get American visas in the past, but that is changing rapidly. There are now more millionaires in Moscow than in New York. Additionally, the emergence of a new bourgeois class has resulted in an ever growing demand for Russian tourists to spend their dollars stateside.

You still meet Russians who have come on work and travel visas and stayed past the expiration dates on their visas. With their propensity to quickly pick up English, their educations and overall attractiveness, most are reporting Americans are actually encouraging them to stay, permission granted or not. Assuming this is true, it may be a protest due in part to the American government's perceived leniency for illegal aliens entering the country from south of the border.

British movies such as *Birthday Girl* and *Eastern Promises* have illustrated a corrupt, mafia-infested Russia that may have limited validity. But, all in all, the people have impressed me as warm, hospitable and genuine.

The word *friend* in America is often synonymous with acquaintance. *Friend* in the Russian sense, is something very special. Such as someone you call at 3 A.M. on a Tuesday morning, after your car broke down thirty miles away, and he comes to help. Or someone who lends you their last five dollars, so that you can buy your child a train ticket to attend summer camp. That's a friend in the Russian sense of the word.

Journeying deeper and deeper into Russia, I gradually saw the numbers of people able to speak rudimentary English diminish. To my surprise, I could not find any English publications in the Novosibirsk international airport when I last visited in 2004. Nevertheless, there continued be a smattering of English speakers in this city of 1.5 million. The familiarities and similarities to America and Americans were overwhelming. I may as well have been in Cincinnati, although the landscape resembled Dallas. When confronted by a host of curious youngsters, I heard a number of English words. I seriously doubt I would have heard many Russian words in Cincinnati or Dallas. I was later told that the schools in Novosibirsk are exceptional.

A few years ago, in Anzhero-Sudgensk, a coal mining town of about 75,000, five hours north of Novosibirsk, I had the opportunity to attend a middle school recital. In many ways, it was like a time warp. The children were very respectful of the teacher. While the building was old, it was warm and clean. There was perfect order and a feeling of unity and purpose. When I voiced these observations to my wife, she readily admitted that teachers were held in the highest esteem. It sounded similar to the way teachers were looked at in America in the mid-sixties.

When I admitted to this Russian educator that schools in America had a common practice of floating children who proved incapable of learning, she looked at me with shock.

"Poshemoo?" (Why?) she questioned.

I had no ready answer. Olga was forced to translate for me, explaining that in America it was considered dangerous and politically incorrect to fail children. Better to float them and not make waves. Unlike America, Russian teachers have less fear of lawsuits and firings over aggrieved or estranged parents. Unlike Russia, American public schools are generally supported by a powerful administration and an activist union. The general focus tends to be on what the teacher, rather than the student, did wrong. It is preferable to float the student than to hold them back until they learn the required material.

American children eat more, read less, and watch more television. While American schools typically have more resources, such as computers, there is less of an emphasis on physical activity. While there have been recent efforts to set some sort of national minimum standard, our school children are probably doing less with more than any other nation in the world. Although some insightful American politicians have indicated the need for reform, it is a long treacherous endeavor.

Instilling respect for the teachers is not a paramount priority in America. The prestige held in American schools pales when compared to the respect enjoyed by Russian educators. As a result, there is no need for teachers to be policemen in Russian schools.

The problem may stem from the unwillingness to admit that our schools are underachieving. The National Education Association is quick to remind the country how underpaid our educators are. And they are. But, when the idea of merit pay enters into the discussion, it is greeted with hisses, boos and thumbs turned downward. Teachers are often told they are victims.

What we see in Russia is something comparable to what we had in the past; before the NEA. It is called national responsibility. The Russian educators feel it is their duty to make certain each child entrusted to them gets everything they can possibly give them. Not because they are being paid to do so, but because they have been entrusted to do it, by the parents and by the nation. It comes down to two simple words that begin with the letter P – PRIDE and PASSION.

It could be argued that there have been negative offshoots of a more free Russian society. Some of the traditional discipline has broken down. There have been growing problems with drugs. That notwithstanding, the commitment to teach on the part of the teachers has not diminished. Even during certain periods where they worked literally for months without paychecks. The same held true for state medical workers and some government administrators. The transition from a command economy to a market economy was often painful. Regardless, the esteem for teachers, especially from parents and students, in Russia today is far greater than in the United States.

Many Americans hold the somewhat superficial opinion that most, if not all, Russians would prefer to live in America because Americans live better, as a whole. It is true, for some like Pavel Runochkin, when they have relatives already in America. The same might also hold true for a professional with excellent English skills. But, for the most part, Russians love their country and their countrymen. There are unstated reasons for this.

By Russian standards, Americans are somewhat reclusive. It comes from living in houses and not apartments. In January 2001, I had the unique experience of staying in a Stalin-vintage apartment house, courtesy of my wife's friend. She shared a large, one room apartment with us. When she gave us a tour of the building, Anatoly Rybakov's perestroika classic *Children of the Arbat* came to life.

Essentially, there were four fourteen by fourteen foot rooms on each floor. There was a common kitchen and a community bathroom on one end of the floor. On the opposite end was a double wash basin. This was the epitome of luxury living in 1930s Moscow.

Fortunately, my wife, my wife's friend, Tanya, and I were the only inhabitants on the floor. It was a strange sensation to look out this fourth floor window and watch Muscovites queue by the bus stop amid the falling snow. I could only imagine the days when as many as twenty-five people had lived on this very floor, happy that they had a roof over their head. Not to mention an indoor toilet.

It has been said that children actually raise each other. Perhaps living more closely together with fewer luxuries has contributed to Russians being more avid readers than Americans. While the

Russian language had been institutionized throughout the Soviet Union and promoted heavily, it still remained a vehicle of separation for many Russians. English represented a departure. Hence, the interest and enthusiasm in learning it.

When Gorbachev introduced glasnost to the Soviet people, a flood of western magazines and newspapers found their way to Moscow newsstands. It brought about a desire like never before to learn English.

Russians are typically happy when a friend or acquaintance drops by their home with a without invitation. Especially when they are accompanied by a bottle of vodka. With the exception of Alaskans, Americans are usually uncomfortable with such a prospect.

Russians find Americans sober, somber and more preoccupied with work than anything else. My wife's Indo-British boss warned her that she would find America boring. Most Russians would agree.

There are, however, distinct advantages in becoming American, especially for a woman. As my wife recognized, while Russia is a man's country, America is definitely a woman's country. Help wanted ads for secretaries in Moscow request help that is twenty-five years of age, tall, slender, blonde and pretty. We can only imagine what would happen to an American employer who advertised such a preference. Especially through the mass media.

Spousal abuse in Russia typically draws less attention, repercussion and fallout from authorities. I have heard men tell stories of their friend's wife reportedly being beaten by the husband only to have the police shrug off her accusation and saying she likely needed it.

Russian's who have studied English extensively, usually beginning in the fifth or sixth grade, find emigration easier. The language barrier is real and it is difficult. Coming to America can be a lonely, burdensome experience for Russian immigrants with no previous

Vladimir Putin, Prime Minister of Russia

exposure. Americans without the Russian language rarely emigrate to Russia.

Because the languages come from different trees (Germanic versus Slavic), there is little similarity. An American emigrating to Russia without the language would likely be lost for several years. Part of the problem rests with the scores of expressions that are constantly used in Russia.

When Olga motioned to a server in a restaurant with the single word, *Devooshka* (young girl), I asked, "Isn't she offended that you address her like that?" Her answer was no.

Later when I heard the expression, *ochen nraveetsa*, (very like) in conjunction with a certain American chocolate bar, I again saw the dissimilarities in the two languages. An American would say "I like Snickers very much." Or "I really like Snickers."

The Russian speaker would proclaim, *"Mne ochen nraveetsa Snickers."* (Me very like Snickers.)

Russian expressions such as *"Ee dee soo dah?"* (Come here) or *"Tee koo dah?"* (Where are you going?) are even more confusing. When I said, *"Pahdaytee zdest?"* (literally "Come here") Olga hooted with laughter. She, like most Russians, thought it was hilarious. But she acknowledged that she understood what I was trying to say.

The answer I received that was most memorable of all was *"Dahnyet."* *Dah* (Yes) *Nyet* (No) What was it, "yes or no?" Olga explained that the literal translation was "well no." But it was not a strong no. In other words, with adequate persuasion the "no" could be turned into a "yes."

Conversely, Russians coming to America find learning rudimentary English rather easy. The problem begins when they learn that to get a professional job the use of technical English is often an unwritten stipulation. Then it becomes a major hurdle.

Some years ago, I made the acquaintance of a former Moscow videographer who had married a Russian professor at the University of Kentucky. Igor Sverdlov recalled his first year in America when he had no English, not enough to even go to the store and buy cigarettes. It helped that his wife was perfectly fluent in Russian. He ultimately learned English from watching horror movies on television.

Television is a powerful language tool, if used for that purpose. Unlike Latinos in Miami who may have a dozen Spanish language channels to choose from, Igor and other Russians were fortunate to have one or two Russian channels obtained through pay per view offerings. The end result is a more expedient transition to full time English use.

Igor explained he was fortunate in that his profession did not require immediate technical use of English. He told me he had advised Russian hairdressers in Moscow to attempt to emigrate to America because English was not immediately necessary for them to make a living and there was a huge demand for hairdressers in America who wanted to work.

Naturally, those Russians who begin the formal study of English at a young age have an advantage. My wife began taking English classes at age ten. The study continued through college, ending with her earning a bachelors degree in English. As a result, she was able to immediately assimilate. Her third full year in America saw her earning high six figures, in the banking industry no less. It might be added that the Russian language was never used along the way.

Another young Russian, twenty-seven-year-old Inessa Kirov (name changed), told me she had always dreamed of learning English and living in America. Learn English she did, she even learned French along the way. However, she quickly found that America had iron doors for anyone wanting to immigrate, who did not have family already in America.

The quandary became real as she explained her countless efforts to obtain a tourist visa. After several unsuccessful attempts, she went to work for a Russian-American businessman in Moscow.

Her boss had originally gone to Chicago with his parents while in high school. Never hearing all the details, it sounded like so many stories of university professors who had fallen out of favor with the Soviet government. His parents had evidently been granted political asylum and allowed to immigrate. Nineteen years later, he returned to Mother Russia. Through work, Inessa finally reached the shores of America. But to gain permanent status, she had only one alternative – marry an American.

Not that this route was distasteful. Thousands of Russian ladies have married Americans. What seemed unfortunate to me was how an educated, multi-lingual professional, such as Inessa Kirov, could not be given a priority for immigration over some of the new Americans who were entering the country with neither the language nor an education.

In September 2008, my wife naturalized in Miami. It was a moving experience. But when I saw the scores of newly naturalized Americans at the swearing in ceremony, I was shocked at how many still spoke no English. Amazing. How could this be?

Ed Burney (name changed), a veteran immigration lawyer, headquartered in Charleston, Illinois and specializing in the former Soviet Union, put it bluntly. "Half of the planet would love to immigrate to the United States. Determining who gets pretty subjective."

In the case of the new Americans without English, they likely entered America through some sort of family connection. Burney, and others, suggested that America was definitely in a position to examine other criteria for entry – such as education and English proficiency.

Without question there are thousands upon thousands of people living outside the United States who are fluent in English. In Moscow alone, there are scores of trained professionals who would love to become Americans. We are talking about doctors, engineers and scientists, not clerks and day laborers.

I recently read an article bringing to light the fact that almost half of the PhD candidates are internationals. The writer went so far as to suggest that each graduate be issued a green card. It makes sense, doesn't it?

The problem with such logic is its lack of political correctness.

To suggest that America base its immigration quotas on education and English proficiency will be greeted with howls and protests. The opponents will suggest that such a policy is inhumane and discriminatory. They will cite the numbers of families that would remain separated due to changes in the immigration priority system. And we still haven't gotten to discussing children of illegal aliens living in the U.S.

Most Russians could care less if we change our immigration system or not. The pan-Russian point of view has been ingrained in them and is supported by centuries of accomplishments and achievements. In many cases these came at a tremendous price. Once I ventured on the other side of the mirror and saw how Russians really are, I began to see America from a different perspective.

No doubt we are the greatest nation in the world, simply because we are a mixture of all nations. Unfortunately, we place political correctness above what is truly in the best interest of the country. Especially when we determine who is given the right to enter our land. In essence, when determining who enters our country, we don't emphasize such things as education and the ability to speak English. If naturalization and permanent resident alien status hinged on passing a fourth grade proficiency test, learning English would become a matter of life and death. Maybe it should be that way.

Contrary to the opinion of some Americans, we are not the only great nation. The Russians would be quick to remind us of this. There is an arrogance in Americans as seen by other nations that reflects, not the American people but our government and some of our companies. A decisive remedy for this would be to place education and English language proficiency on a higher plane than family connections.

A lot of this perceived arrogance may stem from our unwillingness to see things from the other person's point of view. Russians like things American, such as music, clothing, art and food. At the same time they disdain us and silently cheer when we do something wrong.

Ten years ago, I had the pleasure of meeting Elena Tsigelnitskaya, the general manager for the large television station in Krasnoyarsk. When she learned about my background in the industry, she opened up and proudly showed me their facility. It was superb. Then I met her production manager, Andrei. In great detail he explained their operation, equipment, scheduling, even revenue. I was amazed at their openness.

Elena spoke impeccable Oxford English. Andrei, her production manager, spoke only in Russian. Elena told me that he spoke English, although not perfectly. As our meeting continued, Andrei told me of his desire to shoot a documentary on location in Alaska. When I mentioned that I had been to Alaska, not once but on four separate occasions, both he and Elena were intrigued.

From reading James Michener's epic, historical-based, fiction offering, *Alaska*, I was aware of the American mismanagement that followed the original Russian settlement. Carefully recounting these incidents, I saw Elena swell with pride. I could tell they both liked me because I was portraying American miscues, shortcomings and failures. Humility from an American was evidently rarely seen by Russians.

Much of it is the result of decades upon decades of negative Soviet propaganda. Even though Russians today acknowledge the lies and failures of the Soviet regime, many of its teachings are still ingrained in their collective consciousness.

One of the most outlandish things I heard came from two American couples, who were staying in the same Krasnoyarsk hotel

I stayed in. Like many American families at that time, they were in Russia to adopt children. One couple hailed from St. Louis. The other couple was from Denver.

After relating the problems with paperwork, bureaucracy, expense and inconvenience, they told me that old Soviet propaganda described Americans who came to Russia to adopt Russian babies, just so they could take them to America and sell their organs. This claim had been discovered buried in an old Soviet periodical.

Krasnoyarsk had been a closed city until 1995. Few Westerners had set foot in it. But, like Novosibirsk, there was a fair number of Russian residents who spoke English perfectly.

To hear the baby claim was shocking, but it lent insight into what kind of regime we dealt with over the years. Even well meaning ex-communists such as Boris Yeltsin, could only cry in shame when he learned the truth about American bounty.

On a trip back to Russia, following a tour of a Houston, Texas supermarket, Yeltsin could only blubber, "What have we done to our poor people?" He had previously concluded that the well-stocked supermarkets he had toured in Washington and New York had been staged. When he realized the truth, he was humbled and later angry.

Boris Yeltsin's discovery, and the revelation that followed, had a profound impact on all Russian reformers. English became the language that symbolized information. Increased and enhanced information translated to freedom. More and more Russian people wanted to learn it. And they were learning it, word by word.

Copiers, which had been seen as mini-printing presses and forbidden during Soviet days, became more commonplace. Computers and cell phones became available. Internet cafes sprang up everywhere. Everyone was learning some English.

Gradually, after visiting several parts of Russia, I began to finally believe that what the gentleman at the hotel had said might have some credence. With the interest in English and things American,

English might actually replace Russian as the official language in Russia fifty years in the future.

For convenience, if for no other reason.

Russians are very practical. They see themselves as number one and possess an inner pride that can be felt. Seizing an opportunity to bond and not scold Russians would be beneficial to both of us. Some politicians and members of the media remain naïve on the subject of Russia's progress. These skeptics typically are those who haven't ventured on the other side of the mirror. We who have ventured know the truth, and we laugh at their ignorance and naivety, knowing that it is only a matter of time before they figure it out.

Russians don't care. They don't need us and never did. But every time a Russian comes to America and sees how we live, we all take one baby step in the right direction. Making it possible for well-educated young people, fluent in our language to immigrate without marriage is in the best interest of our national security.

There would be enormous advantages in forming a deep alliance with Russians. For starters, there is the security issue. Most young Russians see Americans as potential role models. They are better educated and in many ways every bit as entrepreneurial and industrious. Still, they are relative novices with regard to experiencing democracy. Swapping ideas can benefit both peoples.

A great starting point would be with the space program. There is huge interest in the space program and it has been through partnerships in space that friendships have been kindled. Combining technology could be a win-win scenario for both countries and for the world. It can become even more attainable if Russians continue to learn English at their current rate.

America has better farmland and more agricultural capabilities. Russia has huge reserves of oil and natural gas. A strong alliance would be advantageous to both countries. The military aspect goes without saying. Not to mention, theoretically mining helium 3 on the moon and jointly exploring Mars.

With a language barrier that erodes with every waking hour, in a world that grows smaller with each passing day, anything is possible!

In the end, the fraternal twins unite, combine their resources and talents. Then they begin the huge, but not impossible, task of bringing peace and order to a world that desperately needs both. It can and will happen. It is merely a matter of how long it takes for English to become familiar in 50 percent of the Russian homes. Fifty years? Forty years? Maybe even less.

This is all the more reason for Americans to become the masters of English. Nobody wants to be left behind due to laziness. The "E" Amendment will insure that this won't happen.

What about breaking up the continuity, referred to by the state department official? True, there are entities on both sides that might stand to lose something in the event practicality and common sense take hold. What could be lost? A number of things ranging from defense contracts to consulting arrangements. There are always losers as well as winners with every change that transpires.

Proponents of gay rights would be dealt a mortal wound, if America suddenly became cozy with Russia, openly touted as one of the most homophobic countries in the world.

Environmental activists, aka Greens, would shudder at the thought of a large oil and gas contract that would insure America's use of those energy sources for years to come.

In Russia, multilingual advocates of democracy, such as Boris Nemsov, would find numerous kindred spirits in America, much to the chagrin of Putin and his cronies.

Russian industry would be forced to raise their standards, as their people would demand relief from high tariffs.

The bar would be raised regarding corruption.

Most significantly, both countries would begin a more free

exchange of peoples and ideas. With television and the internet, the walls of separation have come tumbling down. Beginning with the language!

There are still challenges. In the early days of the Russian Federation under Yeltsin, practically anything went with regard to the media. In Putin's presidency, Russia's national media has shown less and less independence. His 70 percent plus approval rating reflects a one-party system. Today, objectivity is not a hallmark of the Russian broadcast media. The constant portrayal of one point of view, the official government line, has resulted in a population that is more apathetic, with fewer objections.

Many Americans predict that an American media – long on bias and short on objectivity – is a threat to America's freedom. The domination of Putin's broadcast television and his squelching of any and all opposition lends credence to these concerns.

Because Russians have minimal experience in setting standards for a free press, they can benefit from a close friendship with the United States. Media should be free. But it must also be responsible. Government should never use the media, especially the broadcast media, to advance their agenda. The First Amendment is the key to democracy. But if government manipulates any part of it, our freedom is at risk.

The lack of a free media kept the Russian people in the dark for as long as democracy was throttled. As technology increased, the suppression intensified. Then, there came a point that traditional suppression became impossible. Glasnost allowed the genie to emerge from the bottle and there was no putting it back in. Part of glasnost included allowing Russia's fraternal twin to come across to the other side and see for themselves.

For now, we can only reflect from our venture to the other side of the mirror. Unlike in America, Russian schools begin teaching a second language as early as the fifth grade. One hundred twenty-five years ago, the second language of choice was French. Seventy-five years ago, German was preferred. Since the fifties, English has replaced all other languages as the favorite secondary language, as it has in most parts of the world. As time passes, we will see more and more instances where English will be utilized as the primary language as the economies of the world globalize.

What about the many highly specialized, well educated English speakers in Russia and other countries? Should they be given a preference over poorly educated, non-English speaking immigration applicants? This is a question that we seriously need to ask ourselves. Whatever the verdict is, it should be a decision that is made by all Americans, not merely those who are active in the immigration process.

Without question, Russia is a highly advanced country with a proud tradition. Stalin saw a danger in allowing his countrymen to exit the country. The government even imposed stiff penalties for unauthorized departure, both to the perpetrator and their families. Nothing of the sort exists today. Tough American immigration laws make it difficult for foreigners without families currently living in the United States to enter permanently. But, that could always change.

Current immigration policy can be described unofficially as, "It is easier to get forgivenness than to get permission."

When the standard changes to, "We want the best, the brightest, the most educated immigrants, from the most highly developed countries, already fluent in the English language," expect Russians to be at the front of the line.

5 The Education Trade-off

Pillaging through some old records and papers with my eighty-three-year-old mother, I came across a memento, one of my first grade reading tests. The four words we were tested on were "A," "I," "To" and "Do." The test was dated September 17, 1962.

The memories flooded back – the school, the smell, the baby blue lockers, milk period, recess, the lunch room, the classmates. It was somehow, more personal and intimate than when my children attended the public schools.

The public schools I was exposed to through my children in the 90s were some of the best in America. They were professional. They were orderly. The subject matter was solid. From the viewpoint of most contemporary educators, they were outstanding. Still, something was missing.

What could it have been? The cities were slightly different in size but the states were similar. Maybe it was merely the differences between schools in the mid-60s and the mid-90s. To be sure, it was less intimate. Perhaps the biggest distinction was the way the teachers carried themselves. They were more confident, more authoritative in the 60s.

A lot of change has taken place over the past forty to fifty years in American public schools. My father was a schoolteacher, as were his mother, two sisters and brother. They talked about the changes that took place, especially in the 1960s.

Some historians now refer to this time as the second reconstruction. Prior to the sixties, public schools in the south were, for the most part, segregated. There was the much publicized Little Rock Central incident. There were countless episodes of resistance to *Brown v. the Board of Education* throughout America. After years of protests, reprisals and public outrage, the stronger hand, the federal government won. Change came.

Resistance to racial integration was exaggerated. True, there were some ugly moments. And, in many cases, these moments were not restricted to the south. Most baby boomers were of the opinion that the time had come. There wasn't hatred to speak of between races. The media sensationalized a lot of it. The part of the story that is only now beginning to surface was the brutality of the methodology and how it actually demeaned the African American children.

Separate but Equal was, in retrospect, a crock. It sounded good. At the time it was coined, it was the politically correct point of view. In practice, while the separate was accurate, the equal wasn't.

The deficiencies in black schools as compared to white schools have long been debated. Some argue that while the resources given were comparable, black children never had the in home attention that white kids enjoyed. Others concluded that economic inequalities between black and white families played a role. Still others proffered that the tradition of unequal opportunities in a bigoted world contributed to the minority children giving up early.

These were insights held by academicians.

Were they accurate? Yes. But there were other factors as well. The country could not get past segregation. For a politician in the south to advocate it was, in many cases, political suicide. Only through an activist Supreme Court did full-scale integration happen. Certain cities and parts of the country were handled with a lighter hand than others. The tool utilized was court ordered busing.

Was this necessary? For decades the politically correct response was yes. Last year, this ruling was overturned. How could this happen? And, why did African American Supreme Court Justice Clarence Thomas vote in favor of its overturn?

Justice Thomas voiced an opinion that many insiders in the public schools have quietly murmured for years: Black students

Supreme Court Justice Clarence Thomas

were demeaned by a 1950s Supreme Court that was made up of well-meaning, but largely out-of-touch elites. They understood that integration had to end. But their methodology employed a "coal shovel when a scalpel and tweezers were called for."

To say black schools were inferior merely because whites didn't attend them was an insult. When full-scale integration took place, black schools were often closed, or they became middle schools, administrative offices, technical schools or something unrelated. Prior to their closings, these schools had been central to a community identity. While the action was meant to promote equality, it sent a signal to the black children that they were attending sub par, inadequate schools that were deficient and no longer acceptable. The community connection and identification were largely ignored.

When full-scale integration began, it was largely determined that white children were slightly ahead in the classroom. Later conclusions confirmed this was primarily due to better in home support, better economic conditions and better overall living conditions. As economic conditions improved for blacks, so would the performances of the students.

Or so the theory went.

What actually happened was something totally unintended. Busing to achieve racial balance caused many white families to take their children out of public schools and place them in private schools. Many of the private schools were nothing short of segregation factories. While some were strong academically, others were mediocre.

Some families went so far as to relocate altogether. In the smaller cities and towns, integration proceeded without much incident. In the larger cities, all too often, what remained in the public schools were minority students with a few of the poorest white students.

Did these all knowing elites understand this? Probably not. Their children didn't attend the public schools. I recall Senator Edward Kennedy locking himself inside a public school after he was physically threatened by an angry Boston mob over the busing issue. Senator Kennedy had voiced his accolades for the program, but became uneasy when taunts echoed the fact that his children attended exclusive private schools that were not only expensive, but as segregated as any school in America.

What they likewise didn't predict was the outcome after the neighborhoods integrated naturally. It was likened to a train that was unable to stop. Three examples of this unpredicted end result come to mind.

A well known Baton Rouge surgeon told an emotional story of how his seven-year-old daughter was bused from south Baton Rouge to the inner city. The public elementary school, which was close to his new affluent home was 38% black. The order sent his child to an inner city school which was 58% black. His problem as he pointed out, was his child's acclimation and lack of exposure to inner city children. He himself had attended that same public school as a child. At that time, it was an all black school. Being black, he wanted his children to go to a suburban school. He confessed that he had worked his way through medical school scrubbing toilets, so that his children would not be forced to attend that same inner city school. He described it as dangerous. His children were not street smart, the way he had been forced to become as a child. The doctor angrily took his child from the public schools and placed her in a parochial school.

A year later in Nashville, an affluent African American lawyer learned that his two high school age children would not be allowed to attend Hillsborough High. Hillsborough High was located in an upscale south Nashville area, near the Williamson County line. Instead, they would be bussed to an inner city school very near the neighborhood where he had grown up. He was outraged. He made an appeal to the school board. Hillsborough High was predominantly white and they were busing black students to it from other parts of the city to meet the racial balance requirement set by the court. It seemed to be a winnable argument at the time. Not so. They said there was nothing that could be done. Why? The school board was nervous about the idea of tampering with a decision that had been handed down by a federal judge. They feared any extra tweaking or requested change might cost them a concession elsewhere that they otherwise would not have to make. Ultimately, the Nashville attorney sold his home at a loss and moved across the county line to Brentwood, four miles to the south.

Another example, also from Baton Rouge, when Judge John V. Parker mandated a new busing plan in 1981 for the parish, a biracial committee at Lee High went to him and asked to be excused from the order. They had a good argument. Lee High was roughly 40% black. The parish, at that time was 39% black. They based their request on togetherness and good race relations at the school. All students, black and white, identified with Lee High. Nobody wanted to travel far to another school due to the price of gasoline. The biracial committee's position was very simple. The purpose of the busing order was to achieve racial balance. Based on the percentages of white students and black students, they were perfectly desegregated.

Judge Parker's comeback took everyone by surprise. He reminded these students that their school was one of the most affluent, if not the most affluent, public high schools in the parish. He referred to their school as elitists.

Elitist? Maybe, I missed something somewhere. Wasn't *Brown v. the Board of Education* about race? As the Lee High students and the African American surgeon concluded, Judge John V. Parker was not merely busing to achieve racial balance. He was busing to achieve social balance.

Our Constitution is a piece of art, but even it may have some weaknesses. The judicial link has been described as a potential liability. Obviously, the Constitution, namely the Fourteenth Amendment's equal protection clause, does not protect people from being poor. For a federal judge to interpret the Constitution in this manner is cause for deep concern.

John V. Parker was out of touch in many ways. Yet he wielded a tremendous amount of unrestrained power. His tendency was to legislate from the bench. People in East Baton Rouge Parish felt he overstepped his bounds and actually trampled on their overall rights. This is definitely the classic argument for appointing judges who interpret the Constitution and nothing more.

"E" is for English will be one of the first writings that cuts directly to the heart of the public school issue, even though to reveal these findings is painful. Not to mention, politically incorrect.

Back in the mid-60s, prayer was banned in the public schools. Of course, the argument was that the Constitution guaranteed separation of church and state. But, did they really understand the founding fathers actual intentions when they coined that phrase?

Many Americans left their native lands and came to America to escape religious prosecution. We can begin with the Pilgrims. The Quakers? They were actually old time Pentecostals. They spoke in tongues and literally shook or quaked when they uttered prayers in these tongues. William Penn was owed a large sum of money by the King of England. He took land in the new world in lieu of payment. The King had an abundance of land and was happy to get rid of the Quakers. So much for the establishment of Pennsylvania.

We could write a book filled with stories of people leaving their native countries for America because America meant freedom to worship as they chose. When the framers of the Constitution re-ferred to separation of church and state, their meaning translated to the government not imposing a state religion on the people as had been the case in many countries in Europe. Consider the "Church of England," we will not have the "Church of the United States."

I remember reciting the Lord's Prayer every morning in school. Now it is banned.

So, why was the Lord's Prayer considered offensive to the point of banning it from our public school children? And what does that have to do with the learning curve of African American children?

Everything.

As former president Ronald Reagan bluntly put it, "There are people on the very fringes of society not believing in anything, who are the primary opponents of prayer in the public schools. They are assaulting our traditional values."

Of course, there are those who don't hold Ronald Reagan as high in esteem as others do. But, we need to take a look at the public schools before and after prayer was banned. Prior to the ban, there was a much stronger Parent Teacher Association. There was more discipline in the classroom. There was much more personal accountability from both teachers and students. There was less violence. There were fewer drugs. There were fewer teen pregnancies. In general, there were better moral standards.

Where we had prayer before, we now have the National Education Association and their doctrine of secular humanism. What they brought to the table was representation of the teachers; a true advocate for increased pay and benefits for the public school teachers. What remained unanswered was what trade-off was it for the teachers?

Whereas before, the teaching profession attracted some of our brightest and best people, teachers are now leaving in droves. Fifty years ago, teachers were held much higher in esteem than today. Fifty years ago, teachers were given much more authority. Fifty years ago, teachers had the latitude to exercise discipline when necessary. Fifty years ago, teachers were more respected by their students and this respect was ingrained in the students. Fifty years ago, teachers were also given the task of preparing students as if it were their duty, as Americans.

The National Education Association, the larger of the two teacher's unions, has linked most of the shortcomings to compensation. The membership of the American Federation of Teachers is mainly in large urban areas. As Dick Morris identifies in his recent bestseller, *Fleeced*, the NEA "has derided merit pay based on evaluations of teacher performance, whether through their students test scores or by using other criteria, as inappropriate."

Did integration have anything to do with the decline of the public schools? No. That is a myth.

Busing was an expensive plan that not only cost taxpayers, but added to the financial woes of countless lower middle class families, in the name of desegregation. Additionally, because they often had a bus to catch, minority children lost the priceless opportunities to participate in afterschool programs. These ranged from sports to dancing to science-based activities. There were even free tutors and enrichment classes available at some of the schools.

True, there were some older teachers who retired at the time of integration. But, many of these sixty-somethings had contemplated retirement for years. Any big change would have done it.

Did they retire because school prayer was banned? No.

When school prayer was banned, most Americans took it in docile fashion. There was some splashing around, by some special interest groups, but America was surprisingly submissive. Churches especially, were silent, as if their only thought was potentially jeopardizing their tax exempt status.

It was coincidental that forced integration happened at the time that prayer in schools was banned. There have been attempts to resurrect school prayer. But, as always, there is opposition from such groups as the American Civil Liberties Union. The NEA has made it fashionable to conclude that separation of church and state is the way. People of all religions have adopted it.

What nobody wants to correlate is the rise in violence, drugs, teen pregnancies, and dropout rates since prayer was banned in the public schools. To utter that would be politically incorrect. Yet, it is true. It has all contributed to moral decline in America.

Black families have been hit hardest of all by the decline of moral values in America. There is an alarming ratio of single parent households in the black community. Many kids in cities are on the streets at early ages. They are often told to look to government for answers. But, the real fact is, government can't solve the problem.

The public schools, which historically were a rallying point and a place where they could establish identity, are much colder and more impersonal than a half-century ago.

Teachers in inner city schools today are often so consumed with keeping order that it is difficult to teach. There isn't that bonding or sense of responsibility. The one-on-one relationships are not as prevalent as they used to be. A lot of this stems from the fear of a lawsuit. But, more than anything, teachers just aren't respected by the students the way that they used to be. More and more, the teaching profession in inner cities has become not much more than a hazardous duty paycheck for daycare.

Does everybody see it this way? Absolutely not. Could it be improved? Definitely. Are we willing to try? I think so. But, schools must again become the rallying point; the place of identity.

To fail these children can lead to problems, both for the school and the administration. The accepted practice is to float them. In essence, process them and make room for the next group. It is a sad but true reality that many of our children graduate from high school unable to pass a *fourth* grade English proficiency test, let alone a *tenth* grade equivalent examination.

The National Education Association will be horrified at the thought of a fourth grade proficiency test as a requirement for a voter ID card. They will be absolutely terrified at the thought of a high school equivalent, proficiency test as be a prerequisite for employment in government or selected professions. And they will fight it. Aligned with the ACLU, the NEA will be a formidable adversary. So do we fight them?

No, we compete with them.

We can literally beat them at their own game.

There is nothing wrong with teachers having a union. However, monopolies are bad. The NEA is big and powerful and, with few exceptions, such as the aforementioned, American Federation of Teachers, has few alternatives. Could we not have a rival union that will compete with NEA for membership on a national scale? Similar to Republicans versus Democrats?

The quickest way to recruit out of NEA is to convince its members that it is essentially dishonest. The Achilles' heel of the NEA is its annuity.

Annuity? Could a retirement fund provide recruiting material for a rival union? Most definitely. Here's why. The NEA has roughly 3.2 million members. They have actively, aggressively induced their members to invest in overpriced annuity policies. Then, they have blown their savings and eaten into their retirement accounts in exchange for millions of dollars annually that have been paid to the companies offering these plans.

In turn, the union receives cash back from the annuity companies. They receive contributions to NEA causes. They pay excessively for exhibitions at union events. And, they provide other cash incentives that may be good for the union, but not necessarily in the best interest of the teachers who invested in the annuity.

Most teachers are not experienced investors. They are convinced they can trust the union with their life savings. Never would they imagine that as much as five percent per year is taken off the top for administrative costs.

Most teachers buy in to the promise that the power of the union will result in their getting the best deal. Nothing could be further from the truth.

When a rival union breaks down the NEA endorsed annuity scam, they will immediately begin the erosion of the organization. It is a left field approach. But, the quickest way to destroy loyalty

New Jersey Governor Chris Christie, (photo Luigi Novi)

is to eliminate trust. NEA members will be angered when they learn their beloved union is cheating them monetarily. That will provide the perfect opening for the rival union's pitch for membership.

This new union will support the "E" Amendment. They willbe some of its chief advocates. In addition, they will promote other badly needed measures.

Let's begin with some of these differences. The NEA opposes merit pay for teachers. As Morris put it, "hard-pressed school districts have to dole out their pay increases with a thimble. Why? Because they cannot raise some teachers' pay; union rules mandate that any pay raise must apply to everyone equally."

This new union will support merit pay for teachers. Actually, we are seeing more and more evidence that the concept of merit pay is catching on. Such has been the case in the Denver public schools. In Minnesota, Governor Tim Pawlenty has made great inroads with teachers' unions. But those isolated cases have been the exception and not the rule. More often than not, the proclamation by New Jersey Governor Chris Christie is: "I support the teachers but not their stubborn, self-serving union."

The new union will support making the learning of a foreign language mandatory in American public schools. Beginning in seventh grade, all students will be required to choose a language and spend six years becoming fluent in that chosen language. Why? One proven method to master English is to learn a foreign language. Where will we get the teachers and the money for such a directive? We will focus on learning to read and write first in the language. This will require less technology and therefore be less expensive. The teachers can be produced overnight, if we waive the requirement of an education teaching certificate for foreign language teachers.

The new union will support a starting pay scale for English teachers that is 20% higher than all other disciplines. This has never been proposed and may actually face legal challenge.

When you think about it, these measures are revolutionary. The "E" Amendment's adoption will put so much pressure on the NEA that they will naturally be forced to fight it. A rival union, we'll call them the American Education Association for illustrative purposes, will blindside them. Teachers have been bullied into adherig to the NEA for years. This union has instigated a silent, but effective campaign of brainwashing our public school teachers. To them, the answer is an all powerful, secular humanist government lighting the way. Teachers today are grunts compared to the teachers of fifty years ago.

The "E" Amendment will bring prestige back into the profession. After all, schoolteachers are trusted with our greatest single resource – our children. We need them to be more active, assertive and accountable. They need to be paid better. Why not make their compensation performance based? Many other professions are performance based. Why shouldn't good grades by students put bonus money in a successful teacher's pocket? The NEA is opposed to it. To them, seniority is the only measure for compensation. True, there have been signs of softening. But, there is simply too much inertia. A rival union would siphon away membership.

We need to give our teachers more latitude. They must be allowed to make decisions without fear of reprisal. We must instill respect for our teachers in all of our students. More than anything, we must instill pride in our teachers. They need to be better appreciated. They have a very difficult, critical task in preparing our children for the future. We must promote the idea of respect for our schoolteachers.

English is one of the most difficult subjects to teach effectively. Our children must be able to read and spell. They need to write with correct grammar. Teaching English grammar is not easy. In fact, it is one of the hardest subjects to teach. That's why teachers aren't exactly lining up to teach it. It's not always interesting. At times it can be tedious and boring. But it is absolutely necessary. That's why English teachers should be paid a higher wage.

Will our proposed amendment improve accountability? Nothing will make teachers more accountable than knowing their graduates will need to pass a fourth grade proficiency test in order to vote or a high school proficiency test to get a job for the government.

Are we being unrealistic?

The question is not political correctness? We know we are being politically incorrect. After all, we are openly discussing an amendment to the Constitution that will supersede the *Voting*

*Rights Act.*The question is, are we being unrealistic in setting this standard? The opponents will say we are. They will say requiring a proficiency test in order to vote will be disfranchisement. Will that be their greatest fear? I don't think so!

Perhaps the opponents' greatest fear will be the loss of influence and control over segments of the population previously unable to properly read. The better educated a person, the more they will think for themselves and make their own decisions. It will be more difficult for a political action committee to tell them how to think and who to vote for. It is all about loss of control.

Minority children will be the biggest winners if the "E" Amendment becomes law. Not just children speaking a language other than English in their homes. We are talking about children from homes where English has always been spoken. Because, it will force the schools to be more accountable. Never, has there been a stress test of this magnitude enacted on our public schools. With a rival union surfacing to harass the power structure of the National Education Association, it's likely that we will see big changes in the public schools.

No. We are not being unrealistic. In fact, we are doing something that should have been done a long time ago. We are cutting to the chase and identifying the real reasons why all our kids are not performing to the level they should. We are finally discussing problems that we have for years attempted to sweep under the rug.The realities aren't pretty. In fact, some are discouraging. But, we must face them, politically correct or not.

We must make certain all minority children, especially those in inner cities become masters of the English language. This is an achievable goal. But, it will come only after some of the inertia is overcome. To do this, we must bring back prestige to the teaching profession. We must resurrect moral values in our public schools. We must entice the best education students to become English teachers. We simply cannot have any barriers, even constitutional theory to thwart our efforts.

What about *No Child Left Behind*?

Morris considers it "the most important advance in public education in fifty years."

Some credit does need to be given for at least trying something. Was it perfect? No. Did it have flaws? No doubt. Could it have been improved? Certainly. Its future existence may come down to Congress if they water down *No Child Left Behind*, as many want. It is not perfect. But it's as good as anything else that has been put forward.

No Child Left Behind was never properly funded. It had merits. But a national standardized test will always have critics. The National Education Association opposed it. But, they have been against everything that has bucked the status quo. So why was *No Child Left Behind* expected to be greeted with anything other than criticism and contempt?

More concretely, what is needed is more of the old type of schooling. Reading, spelling and grammatical usage should be emphasized. Knowing that students will be expected to pass a proficiency test to become voters should raise expectations immediately. But, passing a test is only the beginning.

When our schools become referred to as the first stop for future realtors, insurance agents, securities dealers and building contractors, our English teachers, especially will see a rise in both prestige and esteem. And it will be justified.

We need to put lawyers, judges and administrators in the end zone and get our teachers back on the sidelines. We need to wrest control from this powerful union and return it to the parents and the teachers.

In many ways managing our public school system has similarities to a running a business. In the corporate world, when a

The infamous "Scopes Monkey Trial" in Tennessee in 1925 is an example of teacher reprisal. It pitted famous lawyers Clarence Darrow and William Jennings Bryan against each other over a teacher who had taught evolution.

The teacher was found guilty but never punished in this world famous court case.

John T. Scopes, the unfortunate teacher.

policy stands in the way of doing business, it is time for that policy to be re-evaluated.

The same holds true in educating our children. Our entire educational system needs to be re-evaluated. We cannot have any deterrents. None whatsoever. These children are our future. If any of our children are graduating without the ability to pass a fourth grade English proficiency test, we have major problems.

These schools are being funded with our tax dollars. Yet, we often feel powerless to identify problems. The ideas and doctrines that have been promoted by the National Education Association have become so ingrained in our psyche that we sometimes find ourselves apologizing for suggesting alternatives. This must end.

A rival union might do the trick. Members of this rival union can actually be catalysts for making the "E" Amendment a reality. The first step is to pass the "E" Amendment. This will give our public schools the necessary direction and bring about the kind of change that will keep us competitive on a world scope.

We will have opposition, but we have a just cause. And we have millions depending on our victory.

I speak of our children. Especially, our minority children.

There is an ancient philosophy: divide and conquer. America's elites have flawlessly executed this principle. At the first murmur of an opposing viewpoint, they historically play the race card. By stimulating hate and resentment, they have maintained influence. Lives of underprivileged children are sufficiently challenging. They need attention, compassion and an invitation to truly come into the family. Most importantly, they need a catalyst to help them get there.

The "E" Amendment insures a true ticket to equal opportunity. By striving to be nothing less than masters of the English language, they will become part of an idea that transcends race, religion, ethnic origin and the past. This is the true essence of the "E" Amendment – creating unity through an idea that supersedes every dividing characteristic.

Are we up to that challenge?

I think we are.

Everything entailed in the "E" Amendment is about creating a smarter, stronger and more secure America. And it begins with the creation of a more unified America. We cannot sit back and focus on resentment. We must be proud of who we are and where we came from. We must constantly be aware that each and every one of us has something to offer. We must be suspicious of those who attempt to stimulate hate and resentment. To be sure, they always have a motive.

Any entity who attempts to throw roadblocks in our path is against improving literacy in America. After all, a more literate electorate is a more knowledgeable one. This makes them much more difficult to control and manipulate. Sure the opposition will play the race card whenever convenient.

The idea is to teach our children how to think. Any organization attempting to impede such a goal should be questioned.

The ACLU has used the court system, under the guise of separation of church and state, as a vehicle for suppression and sedition. In today's world, the shoe is now on the other foot when reviewing the infamous "Scopes Monkey Trial" that took place in Tennessee in the 1920s. Then, it was evolution on trial and its supporters made the case that creationists were attempting to enact sedition on them. What a difference a day makes!

The thought of merit pay for teachers' performance will be scorned. The NEA has made their position very clear on performance-based teacher compensation.

The idea of paying English teachers a premium is new. Literally nobody has proposed simply paying English teachers 20%

above the normal pay scale. There are many who would argue that other disciplines merit the same treatment. However, the need for better English efficiency begins with more and better motivated English teachers.

The ambitious objective of all students being exposed to six years of a second language is equally novel. Yet, when the requirement of an educational teaching certificate is removed as a prerequisite for instructors, we will have the numbers. To many educators, this objective may sound totally unreasonable. But, we can try. What do we have to lose?

In short, facts are facts: We are not making the grade as a nation. It is time to get back to the basics. The "E" Amendment will force our public schools to do just that.

6 The Heart of It All

If America was looking for the ideal place to move the nation's capital, it would be difficult to find a better place than Lexington, Kentucky.

First, we journeyed to south Florida. Then, we abruptly turned east to the tune of sixteen time zones. Now we return to whence we came. Back to where it all began, in the heart of it all: Middle America.

Lexington, Kentucky occupies a unique part of America. Squarely between the Sun Belt and the Rust Belt, it is, to quote a former WTVQ general manager, "comprised of Southerners with a Midwestern mentality."

This beautiful place exemplifies the Native American name *Kan-Tuk-kay* – the land of grass. Commonly referred to as the "Bluegrass Region," the grass is not really blue. But, the land is covered with a thick sod, known globally for it value of creating strong, light bones in world class race horses.

Looking closer, a visitor will note a big sky. There are grass covered knolls divided by thick hardwood hollows. On an annual average, Lexington receives roughly fifty inches of rain. As a result, it is green for most of the year.

Lexington is English. In fact, according to a friend who hails from East London, Darryl Wiggett, it looks "bloody similar to parts of England." Darryl talks in a typical East London fashion. If you were monitoring the 2008 Geico Insurance commercials, you would think that Darryl's voice was the gecko's himself. It was he who noted that the number of English people who had come to central Kentucky was largely due to the horse industry and the similarity of the place to England, in general.

This is probably the least ethnically diverse region of America. If one were to ask people here what they thought about the idea of making English the official language of the United States, more than half of the Lexingtonians would proclaim, "I thought that English already was the official language."

This is no joke. Most people in places like Lexington, Kentucky would be shocked if not angered over the fact that some might resist using English. To the average Lexingtonian, speaking English is as natural as launching the stars and stripes with the sunrise. Who could possibly think of existing in this country without it?

Under their breath, some would sigh, "Well, I guess they must be referring to Cardinal Valley."

Cardinal Valley, in the western part of the city, is comprised primarily of Mexicans. Most came in with the horse industry. There are billboards in Spanish. There are ethnic restaurants, bookstores, video stores, grocers and even drug stores that cater to Spanish speaking clientele.

While awareness has been raised, like most everything else, people in Lexington are tolerant, which isn't surprising. People in central Kentucky are simply nice. In fact, they are some of the nicest people in America. Throughout history, people from this region have been peacemakers, conciliators. The Civil War was a prime example.

The economy today in central Kentucky draws many similarities to the economy of 1860. While education, technology and medicine have become major players, the old agricultural standbys of burley tobacco, Bourbon whiskey and thoroughbred horses still are benchmarks.

What also remains constant is the mentality.

Border state Kentucky has always been a place where all regions of the country, Midwest, South and East joined. It was here that Henry Clay engineered his American System. It was the home John C. Breckinridge, the king of compromise, and John Hunt Morgan, the merciless marauder. But, all in all, Lexington is a city that stimulates a love for America like no other place I have lived.

It is likely that 90% of the people living in the Bluegrass Region would favor the "E" Amendment in it purest form. Selling the "E" Amendment in Lexington would be as difficult as selling college football to Tuscaloosa, Alabama. People would find the proposal to be both moderate and reasonable. They would also say, "Why haven't they done something like this already?"

One on one, from the sanctity of their homes, Lexingtonians, like Americans throughout the country are quick to be kitchen table politicians. They will tell their families and friends what needs to be done and what should be done. But, when it comes time to get active, they are busy with their day to day activities. This is not to say that they are lazy. They aren't. They are as involved as their next door neighbors. Which translates to work, parenting, church and occasionally a little recreation – such as horseracing, tailgating, going to the mall and, of course, basketball.

The quality of life in Lexington is excellent – good public schools, excellent medical facilities, a wide range of choices for higher education, reasonable housing costs and a temperate four-season climate. People here are some of the most content in America and for good reason. Only, when something begins to trickle down that may interfere with their world do they become active.

Voter fraud is one issue that is a hot button in central Kentucky. There is something anti-American that is exemplified by cheating in an election. When this reality is exposed, people become irritated and ask, "How can this be happening?" Or, more specifically, "who is allowing this to happen?"

Will people here be opposed to abridging the *Voting Rights Act?* They will need to hear a reason. But if someone stated that *Jim Crow* is dead and the world has changed in the past forty-five years, they would give countless examples of how that is true. Starting with the 1966 University of Kentucky basketball team.

Lexington is high tech. It is a sophisticated upper south city that has been at the cutting edge of technology in several industries. When I visited Veterans Park Elementary in 1996, I was amazed at both the facility and the tools at their disposal. They had everything. And best of all, the school was situated on a beautiful rolling, former horse farm in the midst of an up-and-coming, middle class neighborhood in south Lexington. The children had everything, including computers.

When my six-year-old son showed me the computer he and a classmate shared, I remember commenting how great it was to see our tax dollars used in such a productive way. His teacher was quick to remind me that Veterans Park was a magnet school. Other schools were not so lucky.

The thought that came to mind was how young children were starting with computers. Today's teenagers cannot remember a time without computers. The internet came into heavy use in the late 1990s. Fifteen-year-olds were not in school when internet use became a day-to-day thing. Now, it is part of their lives as much as their cell phones. Who would have believed it?

I was amazed one day to see my wife talking online to a friend in Moscow. From Lexington! The significance of that conversation was that we were looking at her friend on the monitor as they spoke. To today's fifteen-year-old, this isn't that big of a deal. But, when I think about the total absence of communication with someone in Moscow, when I was fifteen, it's like a dream.

What do these teenagers talk about? Fun. Fashion. Movies and movie stars. Vacation places. Music. Gossip. Good stuff. Are they apathetic? Not really. Shallow? I don't think so. Bored? Definitely. Are they candidates for a cause? If it is a cause they believe in and can become a part of.

Sociologists have concluded that most teenagers merely want to belong, to be a part of something. They are becoming cognizant of a world that is changing constantly. It is beginning to sink in on some that their own futures may be on the line. Watching young people between eighteen and thirty-four participate in the 2008 election may have been a sign of things to come. There is concern and even anger in these ranks. What is happening to their America? Is it being compromised?

When you think of flashpoints for our proposed Twenty-eighth Amendment, you think of Miami and Los Angeles. In reality, it will be places like Lexington, Kentucky, Madison, Wisconsin and Austin, Texas that will lead the way. It will be small- to medium-sized cities with large, state universities that are hotbeds for middle America reform issues.

A Constitutional Amendment calling for English proficiency tests won't get a lot of resistance in Lexington, Madison or Austin. Neither will voter ID cards. In fact, most young people would say, "It's about time somebody had the guts to propose such."

The next questions will be, "What can I do to help? How can I get involved?"

Here is where it begins. With the question, "How can I be a part of something? What can I do to help my country?"

President John F. Kennedy's famous proclamation, "Don't ask what your country can do for you, ask what you can do for your country," is manifested.

Young people love their country as much as anyone. They are growing up with technology their parents could not even dream about. They are also seeing a world that is growing more and more complicated. In the past, if you were fortunate enough to live in a beautiful, garden like city, such as Lexington, trouble was far away. To worry about the rest of the world was an unjustified exhibition of stress. You watched your local television stations, read your daily newspaper and that was the extent of your information. It was all that you needed or wanted.

Not anymore.

With cable television and the internet, people of all ages are becoming more attuned to the nation and the world. We are more mobile. We are better informed. Many are awakening to the reality that we live in a global economy. People shopping for colleges are growing increasingly concerned about both tuition costs and the number of American jobs that are being shipped overseas.

These are the people who first asked the question, "considering the problem of identity theft, is it safe for someone in New Delhi, Manila or Bombay to have access to my social security number?"

When you are competing for a place in the classroom and workplace, it can be a cold realization that we may be losing our country. Have we lost America? Maybe not yet, but we are well on our way. The key to arresting that erosion is to make our kids smarter. It begins with making them the masters of the English language.

People in Lexington Kentucky will be the first ones to say, "Amen brother!"

Lexington isn't a high crime area. It has good public schools. It has excellent race relations. There is probably less discrimination in Lexington than any other place in the country. You don't see vagrants on the streets. You see beautiful parks, clean streets and well fed people.

Wouldn't this city be the last place to find discord with national problems such as illiteracy, voter fraud and discrimination?

No. It will be the beacon. It will be the place where the rest of the country looks to.

Kentucky has always been the glue holding America together. Abraham Lincoln, a native of Kentucky, said in 1861 that "to lose Kentucky would be to lose the war." He proved to be correct.

This was a state that had ties to both North and South. Kentucky had always been and still is, southern. Yet, many Indiana and Illinois residents could trace their history back to Kentucky in 1861. Taking sides was difficult. Most Kentucky politicians did everything they could to keep the country together. When the guns at Fort Sumter sounded, people were forced to choose sides. It often came down to the individual counties in determining who was with the blue and who went gray.

Appalachia was solidly pro-Union as were the Western Coal Fields. The Bluegrass Region and the Purchase region, far to the west, were mostly secessionist. Louisville, with its growing merchant class was mixed. The state could have gone either way. In the end, the indecisiveness of Confederate General Braxton Bragg and his inability to execute a brilliant strategic plan, he himself had devised, kept Kentucky in the Union. There will always be the question of "if." Evidence suggests that had Bragg completed his quest as designed, we might be two nations today.

Did Kentucky want to break away? Most did not for economic reasons. Life was too good. As Bragg put it, "the Kentuckians' hearts are with us but their Blue Grass and fat cattle are agin us!"

This summed up Kentucky life in 1862, and it pretty much summed it up in 2007. But, as times changed, people began to look around and take note of places outside their beloved Bluegrass. They could quickly surmise that other Americans didn't have it as good as they did. This was unfortunate, of course. But, when the realities of college costs, that they could no longer afford health care, and banks that wouldn't lend money sank in, they realized, they too, were affected.

Does illiteracy have anything to do with health care, college or banking? Not directly. But, they came together to slow America to a standstill. When people have less opportunity, they have more time on their hands. When they are frustrated, they become activist. When they are from a traditionally prosperous part of the country, all of these frustrations are magnified.

What are people in the heart of it all, as in middle America, looking for? Results. They have learned that it often begins in their back yard.

Kentuckians are getting better at penetrating politicians, learning what is underneath the good old boy exterior. Running on image is becoming increasingly difficult. More and more, politicians are being asked tough questions and being forced to provide real answers.

One story that unfolded in the summer of 2009 was the question of whether written driver's license tests should be allowed in languages other than English. Kentucky State Police Commissioner Rodney Brewer decided that it was a luxury the state could not afford in the midst of across the board budget cuts in a recessed economy. He was overruled.

Governor Steve Beshear stated the decision was incorrect. Defending his position, he added that the idea to offer the written test in English only, did not reflect the values of his administration. He described Kentucky as "a state welcoming people to do business here." He cited Kentucky as an increasingly diverse state with a growing population of people from other countries who are business executives, students and legal workers.

Did the governor's point of view hold merit? Certainly. In his mind the fact that Kentucky had attracted billions of dollars in foreign investment from around the globe, justified it.

Currently the written test for a driver's license in Kentucky is offered in twenty-two languages. I recall my wife's astonishment when she was asked if she preferred to take the test in Russian. Her answer was no. But, a girlfriend from the former Soviet Union told a story of having her international license accepted by the state police. Because the international license was in Russian and the woman there said that she couldn't read it, she issued my wife's girlfriend a valid Kentucky driver's license, no questions asked. Perhaps this is what the governor meant when he described Kentuckians as a welcoming people.

Sounds really benevolent. But, what if this immigrant had been a terrorist? It's a disquieting thought.

Governor Beshear is not a simpleton. He is a smart lawyer, turned multi-millionaire. Without question, he was thinking about the upper echelon executives from countries such as Japan who had settled in Kentucky with employers like Toyota. Certainly, the inconvenience of being forced to learn English well enough to pass a written driver's license would not be popular in some circles. But where would the average Kentuckian stand on this question?

Kentucky Governor Steve Beshear (photo Gage Skidmore)

Often immigrants who come to the state are poor. The inability to drive a motor vehicle would make earning a living that much harder. Unlike the majority of the state, Lexington has a good mass transit system. There is growing interest in bicycling. Overall it would take people out of certain job pools. Immigrants would face a decision, learn English or settle for employment that does not require the ability to operate a motor vehicle.

Would this be cruel? No. It would force everyone to learn the language, ultimately improving their chances of success in America. Allowing any official use of another language would slow their assimilation into American society.

What if their stay in America is only temporary? Wouldn't this stringent standard discourage foreign investment and settlement in the state as the governor suggested?

We are likely talking about less than 200 people in a state of 3.5 million. These are simply insufficient numbers to allow for a lessening of a standard. We must encourage all people to learn English. For their own sake. Any compromise in this standard invites division in our country. We cannot allow any citizen to be left out of the American Dream.

Would Governor Beshear settle for a fragment of the population to be destined for second class citizenship status? Not intentionally. His point of view may have actually reflected the local newspaper's opinion that it is safer if people driving on our roads are licensed. That allows law enforcement to track individual driving records and protect us all from persistently dangerous drivers.

Unfortunately, this logic is one-dimensional. Giving non-English speakers a pass on the driver's license exam increases accidents due to their inability to comprehend certain words such as yield and pass. Not to mention heightening the chance of issuing driver's licenses to an Al Qaeda terrorist.

There is another consideration. Should passage of a written driver's test in English become a prerequisite, people will be more motivated to learn the language. True, there will be those who break the law. But more will study the language well enough to pass the examination. In the end, the state would be doing them a kindness, while promoting unity. What Governor Beshear may be advocating and the Lexington *Herald Leader* may be seconding is giving immigrants a crutch, in the name of political correctness.

There is another consideration underlined by Tea Party activists: the question of cost. Commissioner Brewer projected that using only English for written driver's license examinations would save the Commonwealth of Kentucky more than $200,000. In a state that is being forced to raise taxes to cover budgetary shortfalls, this is no small thing! As Commissioner of Agriculture(and lengendary *unforgetable* basketball star) Richie Farmer coined, "While I'd love to drive a Range Rover, if all's I can afford is an S-10, I guess I'll drive the S-10."

Richie Farmer, basketball hero and Kentucky
Commissioner of Agriculture

Finding people more fair-minded than central Kentuckians is no easy trick. Their patience and tolerance for people of different races, colors, religions, origins and creeds should be seen as an example for the world. But even these patient, good-hearted people have a limit. Making exceptions and allowances for immigrants because it might be deemed the politically correct thing to do, doesn't hold water. In short, their stand might be summarised as: "we will welcome you. We will accept you. But, we are not going to bend the rules for you."

The issue of immigration proved to be a sobering point for many politicians such as John McCain. McCain understood the problem and brought a good case before the American people. But he learned his point of view is in the minority. As with the majority of America, Lexingtonians echoed Mitt Romney's, "get in line and wait your turn."

There is a strong resentment for illegal aliens in Kentucky. There are a lot of people who would be classified as the working poor, making up the population. To them, it's simple. "If I can pay for my doctor visit, they can too. If I can buy my groceries, so can they."

There is no hatred in these words, but the resentment is growing. A typical example is Martin Mason (name changed), who resides in Madison County, Kentucky.

Martin has three jobs. He landscapes, he owns a small nursery, and he is a stone mason. His work is somewhat seasonal. He earns about $40,000 per year. His wife works part-time taking care of children. His son helps him in the nursery and is starting a small lawn mowing business.

On the question of health insurance, Martin says, "The name of my insurance company is Martin Mason Insurance." In other words, Martin doesn't have health insurance. What happens if Martin becomes sick or hurt and can't work? Sorry about his luck. He just sucks it up and gets by.

In analysing the newly passed Affordable Health Care legislation, Martin reveals that his daughter-in-law, who works for a large national bank in Richmond, just received a 21% increase in her health insurance premiums for 2011. The bank cited *Obamacare* as the reason.

"I would like someone to explain *affordable* to me," he muses. "Maybe I'm just not smart enough to know what's what! But it sounds like a bunch of bureaucracy." He describes the young woman who keeps his daughter-in-law's small child. "She has a medical card that pays everything. Everything! While my son and his wife are paying about $250 per month for something that won't pay until they hit some gosh awful amount. They just better not get sick!"

Of course, health insurance is not in the budget for Martin Mason. "However, if two companies didn't have a monopoly and we could buy health insurance like you buy auto insurance the way that Rubio fellow from Florida said, that might change," he says hopefully. "It's like buying goats at an auction. If there are 2000 goats to be sold, you'll get a better price than if there were 200 goats for sale. It doesn't take a Philadelphia lawyer to figure that one out!"

Retirement? He owns the six acres he lives on. He has quite a garden. He is buying the modest house he lives in and hopes to have it paid for in six more years. That's it. He and his wife are thinking about buying her brother-in-law's adjoining five acres and raising goats. They have even discussed planting vineyards and starting a wine distillery.

Is Martin happy? Yes. But, he resents someone getting something for free that he is paying for, especially, if that person is not in the country legally. In fact, this practice infuriates him.

What about someone who is voting illegally? This is very personal to Martin Mason. In his eyes, one man, one vote should be the law. If someone breaks it, they are spitting on the entire country. A support group who facilitates voter fraud is the ultimate crime against America. His attitude on this is that they should be punished severely and with no quarter. If told the only way to prevent voter fraud would be to use voter ID cards, he would say, "Let's do it."

When asked, "Is it wrong to expect people to be able to read at a fourth grade level in order to cast a vote?"

His answer is simple: "No, otherwise, they would be voting someone else's mind. Not their own."

Posing Martin the follow-up question of, "What if they told that person how they wanted them to vote?"

His answer would be, "How could you trust someone to vote your interests? You couldn't. This is how the little guy always gets short-changed. By trusting someone who is supposedly helping them but is really feathering their own nest. Better not to vote than to not be able to read what you're voting for. Or letting someone tell you what you're voting for when you can't see for yourself."

Can Martin read at a tenth grade level? Yes. A high school graduate himself, he is very strict with his three children about their schoolwork. He is quick to say, "Learn while you can because there'll be a day when you'll wish you had. We have paid for these schools. Make the most of them." To his children, especially his twenty-year-old son, he instills the mindset of "save your money and buy a piece of land. They are not making any more."

He always has his eyes open for bargains. Whether it's a used garden tiller, last year's vegetable seed priced at ten cents a pack at Fayette Garden Center, or even a Jack Russell mix puppy that nobody wants, but might make a passable squirrel dog, he is always on the lookout.

Some would classify Martin Mason as working poor. But, in his eyes, he is not poor. He is blessed. When asked the question, "Would you want to be anywhere else?" His answer, "Not on your life." as looks at his home and the beautiful place that he lives in.

This is the essence of America.

Needless to say, we have experienced millions of Martin Mason's throughout the nation's history. They have built our country. They have bled for her and they have died for her. The only difference today is Martin Mason is online.

That's right. In his modest frame house in Waco, Kentucky, Martin Mason is surfing on the internet. Like so many seasonal workers, he has downtime during parts of the year. This means more time online. And he makes the most of it. He chats with people all over the country and the world. This isn't the 60s when Martin would have retired to his easy chair to watch Earl Scruggs pick his banjo on CBS's *Hee Haw*. He has better things to do. Such as converse with Hans Stroebner (name changed), who lives on a farm north of Munich, Germany. Or talk to Ben Brock (name changed) in Clovis, New Mexico, who is attempting to convince Martin to raise goats on his land.

How much time does Martin spend on the internet in a given week? Maybe ten hours. What does he do besides chat? He reads news headlines. He reads advertisements. He watches breaking news stories. He is learning the joys of YouTube.

And how old did we say Martin is? Actually, we never disclosed his age. But, here's a hint. His son is twenty. He has a fifteen-year-old daughter and a three-year-old son. His wife is thirty-eight. He was her age when he bought a computer and first got online. That was five years ago. Martin Mason is typical of the millions of new internet users. Unlike his children, he did not grow up with the internet or computers. In fact, his daughter has taught him more about computers than anyone else, and he has relished the experience.

His wife and son have their own computers and spend their fair share of the time online. Surfing and blogging have become the number one pastimes in the Mason household. Tonight, Martin is finishing up his first YouTube video and anxious to return it to Hans, who sent his YouTube message just two days ago.

What does Martin Mason's surfing and blogging on the internet have to do with illegal aliens getting free health care and food stamps? Think about it.

Up until very recently, you would never talk about a rural, working poor, forty-something man like Martin Mason sending YouTube messages to a guy in Germany. Now you are. As his technical comfort with the internet grows, so will his ability to communicate with other Martin Masons in America and the world. It is free. He has the time. All that he needs is an issue.

This is the difference between 2008 and 1968. Cable television and the internet have made information available to all parts of the country. Previously, rural America was often unaware of changes being made in Washington that directly affected them. The internet especially, has leveled the playing field.

For years, there has been discussion of abolishing the electoral college system. The 2000 election created a solid argument for its abolition. But there is another aspect to consider. Do we want to give seven or eight states the ability to speak for the remaining states?

The small circle of elites representing America's ruling class are mixed on this question. Those counting on the inner city vote definitely court the idea. For their purposes, it ties their task in a neat little package. It is easier to induce illiterate people when they are more concentrated. There are difficulties with dispersion.

The electoral college forces national office seekers to travel the country, hearing a variety of voices. No electoral college would mean no need to go to places like Lexington, Kentucky. Or, Tulsa, Oklahoma. Or Columbia, South Carolina. If you carry California, Texas, Florida, New York, Pennsylvania, Ohio, and a couple of other states, who cares?

Obviously for states like Kentucky, abolition of the electoral college is a step toward silencing them on the national scene. How could anyone advocate a measure that would disfranchise their own people? The founding fathers saw this danger. They wisely predicted that if elections were based solely on popular vote, it would be easy for politicians to concentrate their efforts in the larger urban areas, with little regard for the rural areas. That would equate to doling out the spoils in a few metropolitan areas while the remainder of the country went begging.

This couldn't happen. Could it?

Look at Russia. The power is centralized in Moscow. St. Petersburg, the second city gets its share, largely due to the fact that it is Putin's home town. Some of the secondary cities get their pieces of the hegemony.

The small cities get little in comparison. The standard of living is greatly dissimilar in cities of one million plus compared to cities of less that 100,000. Why? Because the people in the smaller towns have little voice. The votes are cast on a popular basis and, with few people braving the rural areas, they are easily outvoted by the city dwellers.

It is reminiscent of country singer, Jerry Reed's song, "You Got the Gold Mine and I Got the Shaft."

This is what some politicians have in mind for our heartland.

The "E" Amendment takes the wind from their sails, once and for all. By putting a focus on making these urban dwellers masters of the English language, they become weaker candidates for pawn service for the ruling elites.

Wouldn't these urban dwellers benefit from having more money pumped into the urban areas and less into the rural areas? What they need most is the command of the language. That will only come through legislation that will not allow them to participate in the election process, if they fail to learn how to read English on a fourth grade level. That can only happen if they know that unless they can pass a high school proficiency test, they can never work in government or selected professions.

The "E" Amendment allows everyone to trade a few bones for a better, well rounded education. Only by becoming masters of English can they escape drone duty, actually a form of slavery to these elites.

For too long Middle America has sat back and allowed this tiny group of insiders to determine their fate. It was virtually unnoticed. Through the middle part of the last century, mainstream America was manipulated.

The internet has emerged to give them a chance to regain their country. This movement won't be led by Harvard lawyers and MIT graduates. Nor will it be initiated by insightful opportunists boasting their own agenda with powerful lobbyists to back them. The people who will bring about this change will be people like Martin Mason.

Grassroots people, who truly represent all of us.

With the powerful tool of cyber communication at their disposal, people who have been traditionally shuffled to the rear by the powers that be, will elbow their way back to the front of the line. There will no stopping them. Once the bug bites them, they will cease only when America has been retaken.

This is truly, the heart of it all. Mainstream America. Kentucky is where it converges. It is a place that has historically represented the absolute best qualities of our country. Ranging from hard work, tolerance, acceptance and open-mindedness. By the same token, there is a strong sense of fair play here. Nobody has room in their heart for cheaters, swindlers and people thousands of miles away saying "we know what is best for you."

Do you want to know what the majority of people would think about adopting the "E" Amendment? Go to a Lexington, Kentucky restaurant, or bar, or maybe Keeneland, assuming the horses are running. Ask them. They'll tell you.

"Way past due!"

7 Eagles to the Rescue

"I know thy works, that thou art neither cold nor hot; I would thou wert cold or hot. So then because thou art lukewarm and neither cold nor hot, I will spue thee out of my mouth."
— Revelation 3:15-16

We began our journey at the southern tip of the eastern seaboard. We then took a detour to the far reaches of Asia and returned to where it all began, the American heartland.

The question under consideration is "What would be the ultimate fallout if the United States of America were to adopt English as the official language by constitutional amendment?"

In an earlier chapter, we looked for possible opponents of such an amendment. At first glance, they appeared to be few in number, but heavy in influence. Furthermore, because details such as a required English literacy test would be portrayed as radical, many Americans who might normally think it was a good idea, would be discouraged from even making the attempt.

This is the area where we must bring about a paradigm shift in the minds and attitudes of the American public. Our people must stave off the notion that a tiny ruling class will prevent them from having a voice and do their part to make the "E" Amendment a reality.

Could we actually pull it off? Absolutely! It will be difficult. Yet, when more than 80% of the country is in favor of something, it will eventually get done. Make no mistake, however. The opponents will do everything in their power, fair and unfair, legal and illegal, courageous and cowardly to thwart our noble and timely endeavor.

What is needed are visible advocates. These visible advocates will acknowledge their love for the United States of America to the extent that they will devote five minutes per day to doing something for the cause. We are not necessarily talking about money. The other side has money and a lot of it. We are talking about something much more personal – LOVE and PASSION.

Love for the United States of America and passion to do what it takes to preserve her and, if necessary, to die for her. These ingredients have always been the hallmarks of true patriots. These patriots do exist, still. But their love and passion for their country has been assigned a lower priority of late. In today's America, power, greed and corruption have gradually replaced patriotism, nationalism and honor.

How did this happen? Nobody can say for sure. It might have begun with the advent of television. Some would argue it was when the government decided that *it* is the only thing people need to have a meaningful life. Others argue that excessive materialism is the culprit. There are still others who say that our Constitution contains flaws, that it was created for a rural society and now, 225 years after inception, we are an urban society. Some favor doing away with the electoral collage system. Many make a case for term limits for both congressmen and senators. Still others feel that some small states have too much power while large states have don't have enough based on their population. There are many theories and all may hold some credence.

What is certain is the fact that America is very diverse. We have literally every type of landscape and every representation of humanity on the globe. Bringing it all together has been the greatest miracle of all. But we did it. And the basic, single unifier has been the English language.

Therefore, making it the official language by constitutional amendment should be a no-brainer. Right? The careful, politician's answer would be "within reason."

But what is within reason? Continuing to do what we are doing now, which is keeping it as the predominant language, but allowing other languages to co-exist in the back alley? This practice would seem to be the safest, most politically correct avenue. But is it the best avenue?

Eagles for America will say, "no, it is not!"

So, who are these Eagles?

They are any American who loves his or her country so passionately that they will take on anyone who seeks to bring it down. That means anyone, who would do anything, that will threaten the existence and security of the United States of America.

Anyone can be an Eagle. In sociology terms, it is an anticipatory reference group. If you want to be an Eagle, you can be. All you must do is love your country to the extent that you will declare anyone who might threaten it, the enemy.

So who is the enemy?

Anyone who opposes the "E" Amendment, no matter who they are, is the enemy.

So, in other words, anyone who is opposed to making English the official language by constitutional amendment is the enemy?

Yes.

But what if they like the idea of making English the official language but are opposed to a literacy test and a voter ID card?

You can't be half-pregnant. They are with us or they are against us. There is no middle ground.

Here's why. We have large numbers of Americans who are voting and can't comprehend what they are voting for. We must find a positive, affirmative way to motivate them to learn to read. We have others who are actually resisting the use of English in favor of another language. This must stop. We have still others who are voting multiple times. This is a crime and must be stopped at all costs. Identity theft is the fastest growing crime in America. There must be a decisive plan to deter it.

Obama speaks to Joint Session of Congress, 2010

So few of them and so many of us.

Wouldn't many legal experts argue that the "E" Amendment, in this form, will violate the *Civil Rights Act of 1968* and certainly the *Voting Rights Act?*

Sure they will. It doesn't matter. The "E" Amendment will supersede the *Voting Rights Act* enacted in 1965. It is visibly an anachronism. *The Civil Rights Act of 1968* was created to eliminate discrimination based on race, color, sex, religion, national origin, etc. It was not designed to include illiteracy. Depending on who interprets this law, it is probable that some loose constructionists could find a way to include a chimpanzee under its protection.

More precisely, politicians dependent on illiterate masses for re-election will fight to their last breath to oppose such a standard. Let's face it, if a fourth grade English proficiency test is required to obtain a voter registration card that stipulates the holder undergo a fingerprint test and a retinal scan, many will not even register. Then these politicians depending on their votes will be hard pressed to get re-elected.

What about federal judges? Won't they do everything in their power to prevent even a vote on such an amendment? Some will, unfortunately.

Introducing a constitutional amendment that will be immune from further constitutional challenge will be unprecedented. There will be every type of resistance known to mankind to keep Americans from exercising their right to vote on it. But what if four out of five Americans want the "E" Amendment added as the newest constitutional amendment? Doesn't majority rule?

Now, we are getting to an ugly part of our argument. True, most Americans will be in favor of the "E" Amendment. But, those opposed will be the ones who will lose the most. In short, while they may profess a love for the United State of America, they love their power and fortunes more.

Most politicians and judges are wealthy people. They are on top, America's ruling class. To have the political landscape so disturbed could cost them everything. For them, it will be better to leave things as they are. Even if, in their hearts, they know adopting such a powerful, pivotal addition to the Constitution is in the nation's best interest.

So how can these Eagles make a difference?

Very simple. They will start the process of instilling a premise in the American psyche – *If you are opposed to the "E" Amendment, you are anti-American, unpatriotic and unfit for leadership in this country.*

Sounds intimidating, doesn't it? Yes, but after all, it is our country we are fighting for. We can't do things halfway. If anyone, from the president down is opposed to the "E" Amendment, he or she is "anti-American, unpatriotic and unfit for leadership in the country."

That's fairly black and white. As it should be. Think about it for a moment. The "E" Amendment is calling for a higher standard of literacy in America. Along the way, it is attacking voter fraud and identity theft. It is likewise offering the first real middle ground alternative for immigration control. It is stating that our minority children are being short-changed in the education process by a system that makes socializing them a higher priority than educating them.

This will be the message of our Eagles.

Eagles will wage a tireless assault on anyone opposing the "E" Amendment. They will launch a cyber campaign that will position opponents to the amendment as individuals who are unconcerned with literacy in America, unconvinced that voter fraud exists in America, insensitive to the horrors of identity theft, and oblivious to a positive, constructive solution to immigration control.

The "E" Amendment offers all. Those opposed will be labeled obstructionists, opportunists, and out of touch elitists, who stand ready to compromise the country in favor of their own power and influence. Eagles will remind people that while they themselves are volunteers for the cause, these obstructionists are compensated collaborationists. Eagles will point fingers at "E" opponents as individuals who seek to undermine the country and deny many Americans their shot at the American Dream. The appeal will be an emotional one, designed to arouse the deepest sentiments in Americans.

One aspect, however, must be stressed. *Our passion must remain non-violent.* Under no circumstances can there be any physical intimidation. Anything else will be seen as mob methodology.

We must remember that we are advocating a higher standard for education in this country. Our ultimate goal is a smarter, better educated America. We aspire for Americans to be the masters of the English language. We see a future America that is multi-lingual. We cannot deviate from this path. We can win this war because our people will be more driven. The other side represents largely arrogant opportunists with socialist leanings and no real substance. Besides, the pen is mightier than the sword. We will accomplish our goal by advancing the idea and then winning the war of words.

So, in other words, will we instigate a letter writing campaign?

Yes, in a manner of speaking. The internet has become a powerful tool of modern communication. More and more households are getting their news and information from the internet. Unlike twenty years ago, scarcely a home is without a computer. Internet communication is quick, easy and inexpensive. We can use the internet, not only to send messages, but to glean pertinent knowledge about every single figure currently in a decision making capacity. Best of all, we will make our message more powerful and personal with the use of another contemporary tool, YouTube.

How will it begin? We need one congressional candidate to run with a pledge to sponsor the "E" Amendment.

But that could take forever. Especially if that person, assuming they are able to get elected, is in the minority party. The majority party might not take kindly to anyone who will actively be suggesting that opponents of this amendment are un-American, unpatriotic and unfit for leadership in the United States. Of course they won't.

It will start with a partisan media that will ridicule, chastise and attempt to defame and degrade every person who voices support for the "E" Amendment. No worries, however. Many of these media representatives are likewise, anti-American, unpatriotic and unfit for leadership in the United States of America. Media moguls occupy a critical position of leadership in this country. Unfortunately, there are many who have betrayed the trust given to them. They ultimately proved too irresponsible for their position. A possible remedy to this reality will be discussed in an upcoming chapter.

How do we get through to the masses with only the internet? Won't it be like attempting to assault a cannon with a popgun? Imagine a piece of bread lying under a slowly dripping faucet. What happens to the bread after an hour or two? Get the picture?

At first it will be difficult to gain a lot of penetration from internet text messaging and blogging. Then it will begin to pick up steam because this kind of message goes far beyond the airwaves.

Here is how. The media representatives, like judges and politicians, have lives outside the media, legislative or judicial chambers. They have lives and they have families. When their preference for opposing such an amendment becomes fixed, then it may be time for them and their families to begin questioning whether they truly want to stay in America. After all, nobody will stay in a place where they are demonized to the point of being declared outcasts and traitors. And that would be the ultimate goal.

When opposition to the "E" Amendment is deemed politically incorrect, we will have won.

Won't harassment of judges' and politicians' families be considered cruel? Yes. But with America's future at stake, it must be done. This is war. All is fair in love and war.

What about big money and influential businessmen?

Same thing. Nobody is bigger or more important than the nation. It doesn't matter who it is or how much money they have. Don't think there won't be intimidation attempts either. Economic intimidation can be counted on. When people can use the power of the purse, they will use it. Remember this is one of the ailments of the country today. Greed and corruption have polluted our system to the point that the entire country is run by lobbyists and special interests. Does anyone think for a second that these entities will go down easily? It will be a fight. At least, at first.

Then, when the tide begins to shift and it becomes evident that more than 80% of the country is in favor of this amendment, many who were originally opposed to it will rethink their positions and get on board. That is a mathematical certainty. The "E" Amendment is not anti-business. If anything, it is extremely pro-business. Think about it. Isn't it in the best interest of all businesses, large and small, to have a better educated America?

That is the ultimate goal of the "E" Amendment. We are merely employing a different kind of motivation to insure that every student who attends our public school system graduates with at least a fourth grade reading capability. Is that asking too much?

We likewise want all residents of the country to use English, not an alternative language in both their home and their day-to-day business practices. For the sake of unity in the country, we can settle for nothing less.

Furthermore, working for the government should be perceived as a privilege, not a right. This is precisely why a government worker's English should be better than average. The ability to pass a high school proficiency test is not an unreasonable stipulation. The same will hold true of someone seeking a professional license. To whom more is given, more is expected. These should be every politician's watchwords. Without fail. Without flinching.

This sounds fascinating. But what about HR 997, the *English Language Unity Act*. This currently proposed legislation will make English the official language. With its passage, won't our mission be accomplished?

Make no mistake. This is great legislation. But, it is only the beginning. Currently there are fourteen senatorial and 109 congressional co-sponsors. The passage of this legislation is only a matter of time. However, HR 997 is only the first step.

We must not only make English the official language in name but in actual usage. This translates to Americans being the masters of it. When virtually every high school graduate is able to write a grammatically correct business letter, we will have accomplished our objective. HR 997 is great but it is only the beginning.

We must make English the official language by law. But we must likewise make literacy a part of the equation. This is where there may be differences, even with those who favor HR 997. The "E" Amendment explicitly states that "if you can't pass a fourth grade English proficiency test, you can't participate in the electoral process. If you can't pass a high school proficiency test, you are ineligible for jobs in government as well as certain types of professional licenses and designations." To some, these requirements will be deemed radical. But are they?

Let us look back. Historians will recall that the idea of allowing women to vote was considered radical by many. What about during Reconstruction? There were Northerners as well as Southerners who considered the idea of suffrage for freedmen totally out of line.

But those were arguments for increasing the voting universe. We are now talking about potentially reducing the numbers of voters?

Our goal is the betterment of America. The "E" Amendment does not discriminate, exclude nor favor any segment of the population. The entire thinking behind the amendment is a unified America. We need a rallying point; a central idea that transcends all differences and brings us back to why we are Americans and why America is different from any other country.

The objective is to improve America. In an effort to protect our country and promote improved education and literacy, we are attempting to alter the Constitution.

Protect the country from what?

Actually, the question is from *whom.*

There is a tiny group of leaders who are dependent upon the continued ignorance of certain segments of the population. If they can't read, or if they are unable to read English, they will be much easier to control. These leaders will do everything in their power to keep things as they are. They will even use divisive methods, such as racial or ethnic differences within our peoples, to keep us distracted. The specter of a population where every single adult is capable of reading at the fourth grade level rivals their worst nightmare.

But shouldn't everyone have the right to vote, even if they cannot read and write? No doubt there are many good Americans who feel that voting is everyone's God given right.

This is where the paradigm shift must take place. Up until now, the answer has been *yes.* Eagles for America say, "No, those days are past. If you are to participate in the election process, you will present a voter identification card. To obtain the voter registration card, you will be required to pass a fourth grade English proficiency test."

Okay! So we find a congressman who is willing to sponsor the "E" Amendment. Congress moves very slowly or not at all. How can we ever get such an amendment out of sub-committee?

This is where our Eagles begin to fly. Getting names of the committee members will be easy enough. The key rests with the chairman. Once we learn the chairman's position we can immediately begin an e-mail and blogging campaign to his or her constituents. When more than 80% of the populace is in favor of a measure, it is dangerous for any politician to go against it. They may drag their feet. But, when it becomes potential material for an opponent in an upcoming election to use against an incumbent, look out!

The specter of a legion of Eagles supporting the opposition will chill any incumbent. Organization is the key. We are talking about a nationwide movement. In effect, Eagles in Springfield, Missouri and Medford, Oregon will be communicating with Eagles in Mankato, Minnesota and with the constituents of their hostile incumbent congressman. His or her, "E" advocate opponent, attempting to unseat him will be joined by Eagles nationwide, echoing the mission statement. The momentum will build under the banner of who loves American and who loves themselves? The incumbent will be positioned as self-serving, out of touch, unable to relate to America's most pressing concerns. Their defeat will be an Eagle obsession.

As the organization grows, we can continuously keep Eagles informed regarding the positions of congressmen in their districts. As the numbers of Eagles grow, so will the barrage of daily e-mails and blogs politicians receive. They will not be the sole recipients. Their constituents will likewise be included in the message.

It will go something like this:

Congressman Joe Blow of the Fourth District of Pennsylvania has voiced partial support of the "E" Amendment, although he doesn't like it in its present form. However, Jim Wind, of the opposition party likes the "E" Amendment in its present form and urges its passage.

Because Congressman Blow doesn't truly have a grasp of the breadth of the amendment, he must be voted out of office. It doesn't matter what he has done for the district in the past. Since he doesn't like something about the proposed amendment, it has to be concluded that he is opposed to it. This makes him "un-American, unpatriotic and unfit for leadership in the United States."

Jim Wind, by the same token, is a true patriot and de-
serves to represent the Fourth district. Therefore, we urge
you to disregard party, disregard everything else except the
preservation and security of the United States of America
and vote for Jim Wind for Pennsylvania's Fourth Congressional District.

We are not necessarily talking about just writing letters. These
words will be presented in both text and in the form of personal
audio-video messages. In effect, our Eagles will be bloggers for
the "E" Amendment. Their weapons of choice – YouTube and
Facebook.

Did you notice the appeal to disregard party? This is a non-
partisan proposal. The objective of the "E" Amendment goes far
beyond party lines. It has to. This is not an amendment to give either
party an advantage. In fact, 20% or so of the populace who will oppose the "E" Amendment are composed of Republicans, Democrats,
Independents and literally every party registered in the country.
The "E" Amendment is about America, protecting, preserving and
improving her. Support transcends party affiliation.

Regarding Congressman Joe Blow and his opponent, Jim
Wind, did you also notice how cut and dried it is? There can be
no middle ground where the "E" Amendment is concerned. A
watered down version, which Congressman Blow obviously favors,
will be meaningless. Unfortunately, we can expect to see a lot of
Congressman Blows. Politicians typically look for every side of an
issue. To be confronted with proposed legislation this black and
white is frightening.

To be sure, there will be politicians who will support the "E"
Amendment intact. There will be others who will say that getting
something this decisive passed through both houses and signed
into law will be next to impossible. But don't kid yourself. When
five out of six Americans favor something, eventually, they will get

their way. It may take a generation, but it will happen. And it must happen. Our country is at stake. Nothing matters more. If there is a politician who will knowingly use their influence to block it, they must be removed from office.

At this juncture one might say, "Okay. So there might be a few congressmen who will support this "E" Amendment. And, you've put together a grassroots lobby capable of getting the word out, even raising a couple of bucks in the process. You might even get it out of committee. There have been House Speakers in the past who would never allow such an amendment to come to a vote. There are many baby boomers who remember the '80s. It is possible for a House Speaker to ignore the will of the people in favor of their own agenda. What then?"

With the Republican takeover of the House of Representitives, the dynamics have changed. Essentially Republican, John Boehner and Democrat Nancy Pelosi have swapped places. John Boehner is now Speaker of the House. But who is John Boehner and what impact, if any, will he have on our cause?

Essentially, John Boehner can be described as the "embodiment of Middle America." The second of twelve children, the Ohio Congressman is the consummate story of the self-made American. Growing up in Reading, a blue collar suburb of Cincinnati, he was the product of a conservative, Roman Catholic family that placed responsibility on him at an early age. Boehner is remembered for his willingness to take on any low paying job, because "it had to be done and was a step toward something better." Many of today's political leaders have roots in some of America's most prosperous families, literally born with a silver spoon in their hands. Boehner remembers having a spoon in his hand too; a soiled one from his days as a dishwasher in the Boehner's family tavern!

Boehner has his critics. Opponents have accused him of being chummy with certain special interests, such as the tobacco lobby.

Certain columnists have hounded him mercilessly, accusing him of flaunting his newly acquired affluence. All notwithstanding, the question posed is "would John Boehner intentionally block legislation of this sort?"

Speaker of the House, John Boehner

We must return to the Speaker's roots. His family could be categorized as working class, John F. Kennedy Democrats. Boehner has always been a proponent of hard work and entered the work force early. However, when he came to grips with how much money was being deducted from his paycheck (sometime in the mid to late seventies), he began to question both the excessive spending and welfare culture that was a product of Lyndon Johnson's Great Society. Echoing Ronald Reagan's allegation that, "I didn't leave the Democrat Party, they left me," he voted for the former California governor and has been solidly Republican since. He is a classic Reagan Democrat. It should be a certainty that he would never impede any proposed legislation that reduces the cost of government.

Without a doubt, the House Speaker will be pivotal in allowing such a proposed amendment to come to a floor vote. This is why the party leadership must be placed under the microscope. Unlike the previous Speaker, Boehner is attempting to do a balancing act, between the establishment of his party and the emerging Tea Party Republicans. This is where it gets even more complicated.

The Tea Party is made up of fiscal conservatives, but some have Libertarian leanings, while others actually resemble Populists. What unites them all is the disdain for out of control government spending. To Tea Partiers it comes down to government living within its means."

The *Establishment* Republicans may be dwindling in numbers but they remain a force. There is likewise a shrinking number of Blue Dogs, such as North Carolina's Heath Shuler who have demonstrated their willingness to cross party lines.

A twenty-year veteran of the House, will Boehner be classified as establishment? An interesting question! He has experienced a roller coaster ride during his tenure as a congressman. He is pragmatic and would immediately point out the need to prioritize between the most pressing concerns and other items on the wish list. The "E" Amendment's place in line would come down to how much noise Eagles could make! The quickest way would be to link the "E" Amendment to the guaranteed savings at the state level. This savings would come from "E's" override of the *Voting Rights Act* and repeal of *Phyler v. Doe*.

Additionally, "E's" focus on curtailing identity theft would create thousands of low paying service sector jobs, making it possible for the chronically unemployed to re-enter the work force. Furthermore, "E" brings forth the most fair, practical and comprehensive plan for immigration reform yet.

Those opposed to overiding the *Voting Rights Act* and repealing *Phyler v. Doe* would immediately label proponents as villains! Especially those from hostile districts such as the former speaker. The difference between January 2011 and October 2010 is we now have a speaker who would at least review the proposed legislation without prejudice. As Boehner's Press Secretary, Cory Fritz reminded, the speaker is multi-diminsional. My guess is that if Speaker Boehner fully examined the "E" Amendment and realized how much good it would bring to America, he would not only allow its floor vote, he might even sponsor it personally!

The "E" Amendment is non-partisan. Unfortunately, our legislative system frequently creates partisanship and there is nothing we can do to correct that, no matter how noble our cause. It might even require that some congressmen committed to our cause change party affiliation.

I can recall this happening in numerous instances, when moderate Democrats in the South were forced to switch parties because House Speaker Thomas P. "Tip" O'Neil was considered too far out of the mainstream. It was an example of ideas transcending people and party affiliation.

Even though more than 80% of the nation will favor the "E" Amendment, there will be rogue districts made up of Americans so far out of the mainstream that they may be able to withstand even the heaviest of pressure. A House Speaker hailing from such a district exposes one of the few flaws of our Constitution. The 2010 Congressional Election may have temporarily eliminated this impediment!

Never forget the fact that we are in the current predicament because a few, well-disciplined fringe elements hammered home their objectives while the majority sat idle. A House Speaker opposed to allowing democracy to run its course can be perhaps the greatest obstacle. Especially if it is someone from the fringes of political opinion. Be warned. They won't go down easily, no matter how hard we target their district and their constituents. Politicians possessing this kind of arrogance infuriate most Americans.

Unfortunately, this tiny group of ruling class elitists are riddled with such characters. They honestly don't think that mainstream America is smart enough to make such a decision. In their minds, we lack the intellectual tools to vote on a measure carrying consequences this far reaching.

They will want to protect members of their party from being pressured into casting a vote. The thought of cyberspace being saturated with bloggers pushing this amendment and identifying those opposed to it will be seen as nothing short of undermining their authority. The specter of the Eagles for America using YouTube, Facebook and Twitter to force a floor vote will infuriate them. Still, in the event we somehow get the "E" Amendment out of committee and get it to a floor vote, will it pass?

This will actually be easier than getting it out of committee. Because of the huge numbers of Americans who will be on fire to have the "E" Amendment become part of the Constitution, many politicians will be afraid to vote against it.

The Senate might be a bigger hurdle. Throughout history the Senate has changed, altered or simply refused to pass legislation approved by the House. As Dr. Tomas F. Mauricio, Jr. surmised, we have *Republicrats* and *Democans*. Mauricio said, "when you get comfortable in a positon of power, you don't want to do anything that would jeopardize it." Even if they were convinced that the "E" Amendment was the right decision, it would be viewed as politically risky. He described Senate Minority Leader, Mitch McConnell as a *Republicrat*, using his endorsements of Trey Grayson (the unsuccessful opponent of Senator Rand Paul in the Kentucky GOP primary) and Governor Charlie Crist, Marco Rubio's victim in the Florida Senate primary, as evidence for this assertion.

This is why our Eagles will employ a work down approach. Without question, there will be a significant number of friends of the "E" Amendment in the Senate from the outset. We will start with senators who currently favor HR 997.

Now, let us add those who favor voter fraud reform. There are a number of senators who have already come out in favor of proactive measures to eliminate voting discrepancies. The "E" Amendment's requirement of voter registration cards utilizing fingerprints and retinal scans will be the perfect deterrent for election fraud. Obviously, "E" Amendment advocates will find powerful allies with both the election fraud reformers and the supporters of HR 997. I cannot think of one senator on either side of the aisle who would argue that identity theft is not a critical issue. Voter ID cards will not totally eliminate identity theft. But, they will prevent a large percentage of it.

Better than that, it will be easy to brand opponents of the "E" Amendment as both proponents of election fraud and unconcerned about identity theft. Certainly no lawmaker cares to be associated with criminal acts. But this is possible.

The "E" Amendment's main provision is the passage of a literacy test in order to receive a voter identification card. Those favoring increased monitoring as a method of preventing voter fraud and identity theft would see the Eagles as their greatest allies. Certainly, there might be some temporary hesitation toward the requirement of a literacy test. Then, the concept of a smarter, more unified

America will gradually take hold. It's no joke. Literacy is a critical issue in America. Sure, a proficiency test might be perceived as drastic medicine. Still, the elimination of illiteracy is imminent, if we raise the bar, significantly and decisively. Ultimately, after thorough examination, those seeking to end voter fraud and deter identity theft will see their objectives met.

There is still another group of purposeful Americans who will be on board with the "E" Amendment – immigration reformers. Many politicians would rather defer, sidestep or simply put off the need to fix our broken system. Even though most Americans were opposed to it, Senators McCain and Kennedy should be credited for their attempt.

The "E" Amendment proposes a bridge to deal with the Fourteenth Amendment's assumption that anyone born in the country is automatically a United States citizen. After thorough examination, I believe most Americans would concur that the authors of this amendment did not intend for it to be used as a loophole for lawbreakers.

With its thoughtful compromise, the "E" Amendment lays a foundation for future interpretation. This coupled with the requirement of English only driver's license testing allows the system to correct itself, without the use of fences or storm troopers.

Tea Party members would be quick to note the potential savings that would come from elimination of both *Phyler v. Doe* and the *Voting Rights Act*. Both measures have cost the states millions in legal fees alone. Implemention costs amount to even more money that America doesn't have to spend! The "E" Amendment takes the decision away from the courts and places it in the hands of the voters.

Finally, the ban on oursourcing of "any job that required the social security number of an American" would not only reduce identity theft, it would result in domestic job creation.

Could this amendment get through the Senate intact? Maybe not on the first try. Originally the *Dillon v. Glass* (1921) ruling determined "Congress could impose voting deadlines" for constitutional amendments. Some years later *Coleman v. Mullen* modified *Dillon* leaving further decisions of timeliness to Congress.

We must remember that many senators are dependent on the illiterate masses for their very political futures. There are well-organized, well meaning foundations who will call the "E" Amendment a mechanism of disfranchisement. And, from a certain point of view, it is. It is clearly the choice between "universal suffrage versus a stronger, smarter more secure America."

All twenty-seven amendments have been approved by a two-thirds vote of each house of Congress. But Article V, an obscure section of the Constitution allows states to offer amendments without Congressional consent.

The framers anticipated that the federal government might grow too powerful and require future reform. As a safeguard, they created a second way to offer amendments.

In the event that two thirds of the states submit petitions, Congress must call a convention to propose amendments. From there, any amendments adopted must be forwarded to the states for ratifcation. Article V has been referenced by Kentucky Senator Rand Paul as a path for bringing about Congressional term limits. It could likewise prove to be an alternative avenue, in the event the "E" Admendment was held up by a few stubborn, dogmatic senators.

Evidently the framers had a notion that this measure would guarantee state sovereignty. Up until the final days of the Philadelphia convention, the only way to amend the Constitution was through the petition and convention process. Congress could not propose amendments itself. Or, call a convention.

On September 10, 1787, a week before the Constitution was signed, both Alexander Hamilton and James Madison objected. Hamilton quipped, "the State Legislature will not apply for alterations but with a view to increase their own powers. The National

Senator Rand Paul (photo Gage Skidmore)

House Majority Leader Eric Cantor with
President Barack Obama (White House photo)

Legislature will be the first to perceive and will be the most sensible to the necessity of amendments." In the end, the delegates reached a compromise. Congress was given the power to offer amendments but not to call a convention on its own. The states were granted exclusive right through the petition process.

Can the states instigate a petition to bring the "E" Amendment into law? Under the Constitution, they can. And this little known, vaguely referenced Article V may already be coming into play!

Following their success in the 2010 mid-term elections, Tea Party movement members and others disgusted by an arrogant, unaccountable federal government have been promoting the "Repeal Amendment." It would essentially nullify federal laws if two-thirds of the states agreed. Twelve different state legislative bodies support it currently. It is supported by House majority leader, Eric Cantor, a well know advocate of states' rights. In unison with Paul, Cantor is doubtful that Congress will propose an amendment that would curtail its power.

With a House Speaker who will likely be more "friendly" to our cause, the "Article V option" may not be necessary. However, the current composition of the Senate and the need for two-thirds of its members' support suggests a "front door, back door" approach.

The world has changed since those muggy, late June days in 1776 when the framers hashed out what would ultimately be our Constitution. We cannot have totally illiterate people voting, any more than we can disfranchise female voters! Too much is a stake. We have a complicated world and even more complicated voting ballots. They are certainly more comprehensive than the ballots seen in the days of Thomas Jefferson.

The question every American needs to ask is, "If people cannot pass a fourth grade proficiency test, do they truly understand what they are voting for?"

There are some who will say, "It doesn't matter. Everyone has the right to vote, even if they cannot read the ballot."

This, in itself, is a self-righteous argument that has served the ruling elites well. But think about it. Is requiring passing a fourth grade proficiency test for a voter identification card unreasonable? "E" Advocates say, "If this is what it takes to eliminate illiteracy in the United States, NO IT IS NOT."

It is all about a paradigm shift in America. In essence, what is proposed is a change in the traditional point of view. The law now reads everyone has the right to vote. Period. What is proposed is only those who can read at a fourth grade level are capable of interpreting the ballots. Those desiring a stronger, smarter country will see the wisdom of it. This will ultimately benefit the country and her people, by providing the necessary motivation to force people to learn to read English. Those satisfied with the status quo will say it doesn't matter.

This is where the Eagles can effectively use the internet to convince cyberspace that, unlike in 1776, we have a country that is not based almost solely on farming. Illiterate voters being used by powerful special interests to sway elections are a dangerous liability to the country. Only through insuring every American's ability to read, and base their vote on their own interpretation, are we guaranteeing to all full membership in the family. And a real chance to experience their American Dream.

Obviously elevating America to this standard will drastically change the electoral voting landscape, especially in states where the elections are decided by the closest of margins. The thought of literacy tests, fingerprints and retinal scans will spell doom for many incumbent politicians. They will fight it to their deaths. True, it might take an election or two to get the necessary votes. However, attempting to administratively kill an amendment with a deadline won't happen.

In the closely contested states, politicians facing removal, are certain to reverse their positions. Common sense will dictate it. After all, when voters are given a choice between a candidate who advocates election fraud and a candidate who wants to stop election fraud, they naturally will vote for the latter. Can a candidate who opposes making English the official language, and opposes a smarter, more unified America, have a chance against a candidate who campaigns for both? Why wouldn't constituents want to remove that incumbent from office?

Being for or against the "E" Amendment creates the perfect litmus test. Voters have a tendency to vote for politicians they like, even if they are unclear on the candidates' political positions. An "E" Amendment litmus test will be easy for the average voter to understand. Either the politician loves America and is a true American patriot and supports the "E" Amendment or he or she does not support the "E" Amendment, thus making them un-American, un-patriotic and unfit for leadership in the United States of America.

There is no middle ground here. You are or you aren't. You are in favor of a smarter, stronger more secure America, or you are satisfied with the status quo. You want to improve literacy in this country or you don't. You want to better control immigration or you don't. You want to deter identity theft or you don't. You want to stop election fraud or you don't.

The "E" litmus test will be a death sentence for the image and sound byte campaigns preferred by today's politicians.

Eagles can actively flood cyberspace with this litmus test and they can be effective. Worded correctly, the correspondence can position any politician opposed to the "E" Amendment as someone who is attempting to undermine the country and manipulate the people for personal gain. Of course, there will be howls and cries of foul from certain special interest groups. In the end, politicians will be afraid to oppose the amendment. To do so will be giving a signal that there is something dark and sinister with both their lives and their candidacies.

Judges, however, might be more of a problem.

The *Voting Rights Act* came during the Johnson Administration and was the result of the infamous *Jim Crow* laws that existed in the South. Literacy tests were used as a tool to disfranchise African America voters. The tests were ambiguous. They were often administered randomly. Those administering the tests could do it on a selective basis. No test was the same. There was no structure, only an objective of discouraging African Americans from voting. In 1965, the year of the Act's inception, it was seen as a necessary measure.

It is possible that opponents of the "E" Amendment will attempt to correlate those bigoted *Jim Crow* literacy tests with the proposed test discussed in a later chapter. Unlike the *Jim Crow* tests, these tests will be standardized on a national level. They will be consistent. They will not be ambiguous. Everyone, regardless of region, will receive the same test.

The literacy test that the "E" Amendment advocates will be determined by a non-partisan commission and will be designed to make certain that the voter has at least a fourth grade reading comprehension. To many, this will not be radical at all. But to certain judges, it will be disfranchisement and a violation of the Constitution. Their argument will not be a weak one. That is why the amendment is necessary.

Standing squarely in the way of the "E" Amendment is this same *Voting Rights Act*. The primary purpose of the *Voting Rights Act* was to outlaw literacy tests. However, those literacy tests were based on disfranchisement of a specific segment of the population. They were race based. The "E" Amendment does not discriminate against any of the protected groups detailed in the *Civil Rights Act of 1968*.

Section Five of the *Voting Rights Act* allows municipalities to place alternative languages on the voting ballots. This is quite simply bad for the country. It discourages Americans from learning English. It creates division within our people. It creates a landscape for reverse discrimination. It ultimately weakens the country.

As recently as June 2009, this argument was heard by the Supreme Court of the United States. The court elected not to rule, exercising judicial restraint to the relief of those in favor of leaving it untouched. But the next challenge may yield different results. There is growing momentum for English only voting ballots.

There are many judges and politicians who will scoff at the idea of any literacy test on constitutional grounds. That's why we must have a constitutional amendment legitimizing it. We likewise need to make certain that we are not constantly flooded with lawsuits once the "E" Amendment gains passage. Making this amendment immune from legal challenge will save millions in legal fees.

How will such a test be prepared and who will appoint those preparing it? First and foremost, test preparers must be professionals in the field, not political appointees. There are a number of companies nationwide who might submit bids to be the official providers. These preparers need to have educational backgrounds. They absolutely must be non-partisan. The tests should be done on a federal level to insure uniformity. They will be updated annually.

There will be two levels of tests. The primary test will be a prerequisite for a voter registration card. Candidates for naturalization and permanent resident alien status will receive the identical exam. It will be structured so that anyone having at least a fourth grade reading comprehension can easily pass.

The secondary test will be designed for (a) anyone seeking a job in federal, state, county or local government, (b) a prerequisite for any professional licensing test such as securities, insurance, real estate, property management, and (c) the seekers of any type building permit involving commercial and/or multi-family properties. The secondary test will be structured at the high school level.

I can hear it now. In Des Moines, Iowa, this concept might be an easy sale, but in Miami, it might be an uphill battle.

This is where our Eagles must demonstrate not only persistence but compassion. Sure, it might be difficult for some to comprehend the importance of requiring more advanced English skills for certain jobs or licenses. For the sake of America, for the strength and security of America, we must be one people with one common tongue.

Surprisingly to some, Latin surnamed Americans might be some of the greatest advocates of the "E" Amendment. Victims of discrimination in previous generations, they have watched and witnessed the dissipation of prejudice in passing years as English replaced Spanish in their homes and communities.

Rightly, finally putting prejudice in its grave is as simple as leading the charge to confirm the "E" Amendment. Make no mistake, Latin surnamed Americans will be some of our strongest and most active Eagles.

We have discussed a grassroots movement that will begin with congressional sponsorship. We have discussed the pitfalls of getting such an amendment through a congressional subcommittee. We have addressed the problems potentially possible with a hostile House Speaker who refuses to let the amendment come to a floor vote. We have likewise discussed the difficult process of getting such an amendment in its original form through the senate. We have conceded to the reality that it might take a senatorial election to ultimately get the numbers necessary for passage. We have addressed concerns equated with federal judges who may aspire to block the message due to constitutional concerns and current laws.

We can almost certainly expect every sort of legal challenge due to the complexities of introducing a literacy test. I can hear some suggesting that a literacy test might compromise the Four-teenth Amendment's equal protection clause. That is all the more reason why this question must be addressed in the wording. These are considerations that will be turned over in every legal mind in America.

In short, no matter how much passion, persistence and perse-verance our Eagles may have, they still must face the reality that under current law, many legal scholars will conclude that what they are promoting is currently unconstitutional. Strict constructionists could methodically concur that "while we certainly see logic in your argument and merit in your cause, we can't change the Constitution to accommodate your idea."

This will be a hurdle that we must clear before we can move to the final steps. Not that it is impossible.

We already know that a huge majority of Americans favor mak-ing English the official language of the United States. We know English as an official language is gaining support with every pass-ing day. We are aware that a growing number of congressmen and senators favor some kind of resolution to curtail voter fraud. Without question, the "E" Amendment's provisions will represent the most decisive and proactive attempt at curtailing identity theft.

A literacy test has negative connotations, but when fully ex-plained, most Americans will conclude that it is in the best interest of the country. We don't have any other option. The world is chang-ing and we cannot cling to the status quo. America, as we know it, is at stake. We simply do not have time to be dogmatic over a past principle that is holding the country back.

Nationalism and patriotism are two esoteric qualities that can be called upon to advance any cause. When our Eagles begin ad-dressing the need for this amendment in its undiluted form to be adopted on the basis of nationalism and patriotism, we bring forth another ally: EMOTION.

Emotion may be a poor friend in the courtroom, but it is a valuable companion on the street.

The greatest defense Eagles may use against anyone who raises constitutional concerns will be their association with the status quo. After all, Chief Justice Roger Taney argued the status quo point of view in handing down the *Dred Scott Decision* in 1857. Was he correct in his assessment? Abolitionists didn't think so, but an astoundingly large number of congressmen and senators concurred with the Chief Justice.

In short, just because it may involve a paradigm shift amongst some of our people, doesn't mean it should be dismissed. Enacting a fourth grade English proficiency test as a prerequisite for a voter identification card is a departure from past practices, but it is clearly necessary. Our society is much more sophisticated than it was in 1776; or in 1976 for that matter. If we do not adjust accordingly, we face the danger of compromising something far greater than the universal right to vote, literate or not. The question becomes is eliminating voter fraud as critical as making certain that every soul, literate or not, votes? That is the choice. Three pivotal benefits come with a yes answer: improved literacy, protection against identity theft, and better immigration control.

It is clearly the status quo versus a smarter, stronger, safer America. This will be our Eagles' tireless, unrelenting argument.

Historically, a dry, logical argument based on current fact has been an outmatched adversary for an argument, dripping with emotion that espouses both nationalism and patriotism. When you have an angry populace, tired of the status quo, ignited by the mystique of nationalism combined with the emotional appeal of patriotism. it should be enough to make even the staunchest advocate of the status quo recoil.

Nationalism and patriotism are fine words. But the question remains, if you could evade all of the obstacles named, will it be possible to get the president to sign off on such an amendment?

We don't need his signature or approval.

Based on the historic case of *Hollingsworth v. Virginia* (1798), it is not necessary to place amendments to the Constitution before the president. Nor can the president veto any proposed amendment.

How difficult will it be to get the necessary number of states to ratify the amendment? This might actually be easier than getting the "E" Amendment to a floor vote in the house.

To a number of states, ratification will translate into more representation in congress. Because the "E" Amendment will require proof of citizenship as a prerequisite for inclusion in any census, states that have included large numbers of non-citizens in their census counts will stand to lose seats in the House of Representatives. Certainly South Carolina and Oregon will not have any problem picking up a congressional seat at the expense of California.

State ratification will be discussed in a later chapter. As far as the president's opinion of the "E" Amendment, Barack Obama is living proof that perception of race has changed since the inception of the *Voting Rights Act*. While he enjoyed solid support from African Americans, it was non-African Americans who voted him into office. He is actual evidence that the *Voting Rights Act* is an anachronism.

Most Republicans will suggest that President Obama will never compromise his pals at ACORN. In their view, ACORN is a prime perpetrator of voter fraud. On the contrary, the president has been a strong advocate for accountability in the public school system.

Will he openly endorse the "E" Amendment?

In an upcoming chapter we will discuss the multi-dimensional quandary created by the "E' Amendment and how it may yield insight into Barack Obama's character. Logically, he knows that his very election is evidence that the *Voting Rights Act* is no longer necessary.

Yet, from a personal sense, he will probably acknowledge that had the "E" Amendment been law, he might not have won the election.

We must never forget that Obama is not part of the same generation as Jesse Jackson or Al Sharpton. His pre-*Civil Rights Act* years were spent in Honolulu, Hawaii, arguably the most cosmopolitan city in America. He never attended segregated schools. He has no Black American ancestry. He is African American, in the true sense of the word.

The current reality that was spawned by the *Voting Rights Act* is another thing altogether. Even though it might be in the best interest of the country, Barack Obama will have strong opposition from many of the people who elected him.

With the status quo comes inertia, all too often it is tied to self-interest and self-preservation.

To conclude that Barack Obama might catch some friction from members of his party is an understatement. But, George W. Bush would also have had constituents who would have discouraged him from endorsing the "E" Amendment. We must remember, the status quo, regardless of party, will be skeptical and nervous regarding any measure, this decisive, this black and white, that will force them to take a position.

Certainly it will be easier to hide behind lawyers and official spokespersons.

However, it might become the decisive issue in a future presidential campaign. There is no question that if the "E" Amendment makes it this far, it will be on the lips of every American. And, if Eagles are true to form, any opponents of the "E" Amendment will be labeled as "anti-American, unpatriotic and an advocate of voter fraud." Not to mention being "unfit to lead in America."

8 The Power of the Internet

So, the internet will be the primary transmission vehicle for our message. Fine. Elaborate.

Our Eagles can communicate quickly, easily and inexpensively via the internet. But do people honestly read text messages to the degree than we can bring about a paradigm shift in America? Maybe. Don't forget, we are not limiting our communication to text messages. Hello, YouTube!

For those not totally familiar with YouTube, let's talk.

"E" is for English is a book for everyone – whether you are an expert with computers and the internet or an average user. What is most important is that you love America and want to save her. To save her, we must make use of what may be our greatest resource at hand – the internet. To use the internet to the fullest extent translates to becoming the masters of YouTube, Facebook, Twitter and any other tool which may aid our communication effort. We can do it and have a lot of fun in the process.

Here is how it will work. Our Eagles will introduce themselves to cyberspace. With a personal message that will speak from the heart, they will tell a little about themselves and why they are an Eagle for America and then proceed to focus on their specific message. The internet user will, not only read their words, but see their faces, expressions and zeal for the task at hand – to save our beloved country.

Here is an example:

Hello, I am Rick Stick and I live in Lafayette, Indiana. I love my country because it is the only country that makes it possible for everyone to own their own home, business, and farm and attend whatever church they choose, and major in whatever subject they choose in the college of their choice. Unfortunately, we have a small group of elite insiders who are secretly conspiring to rob us all of these privileges. They are doing it by recruiting hordes of illiterate masses to influence and change election results. And, in many, if not most cases, they are facilitating voter fraud.

Our Fifth District congressman, Tim Tam, is a good guy. But, in spite of his words, he has voiced opposition to the "E" Amendment in that he thinks there are some good aspects about it, but some other aspects that need to be revisited.

Gosh, folks. If that isn't a politician's answer, what is? The fact is, Tim Tam is heavily influenced by his party constituents. He loves Indiana and his district. But, he loves his power and influence more, and his wealth. Have you checked to see who is contributing to his election campaigns? It might surprise you. And don't forget, these people will expect something in return from Tim.

Let's talk about his children. Do they attend public schools here in our neck of the woods? Of course not. For them, it is elite private schools in Washington. Tim likes Washington a lot. So much that he seems to actually live there more than in his district. I guess he's gotten comfortable with fellow power brokers. You know those Washington types who think they know what's best for us. Sure, he may say that he agrees in principal with the "E" Amendment. But, just you wait. When his bosses in the party tell him no he'll be as compliant as a good hunting dog.

No folks, Tim Tam isn't going to rock the boat with his buddies in Washington. He needs to go. That's why we need to elect Wayne Plaine to replace Tim Tam in Congress. Wayne understands our values. He knows what America is all about. He knows that the "E" Amendment is the vehicle we need to protect and preserve the America we know. He scorns any politician who will compromise his people in favor of his own personal wealth and power. He knows the meaning of accountability and conscience.

Most importantly, he understands where the buck stops. Right here in Lafayette – not in Washington. Tim Tam says he understands your needs and is working for you. But, in reality, his buck stops with the masses of undocumented workers voting illegally in this country. Many of these people are functionally illiterate in English.

Let's say no to Tim Tam and his kind. Vote for Wayne Plaine for Congress. Republican, Democrat, Independent or another party it doesn't matter. This isn't about party. It is about patriotism. If you believe that English should become the official language of the United States, vote for Wayne. If you are satisfied with this tiny ruling class who are stealing your country, you should vote for Tim Tam. If you do not have a problem with support groups helping people vote multiple times to sway elections, vote for Tim Tam. If illiteracy in America doesn't bother you, you should vote for Tim Tam.

After all, this is about America. If you love America and want to do anything and everything to protect her from crimes such as identity theft, vote for Wayne. If not, Tim Tam is your man. And remember, since Tim doesn't favor the "E" Amendment in its present state, he is "un-American, un-patriotic and unfit for leadership in America!"

This is a message that could be conveyed on YouTube. It won't be text. It will be in living color. Eagle Rick Stick, will be entering a passionate plea for people to vote against the incumbent, Tim Tam. He will be essentially litmus testing Tam, claiming that because he doesn't favor the "E" Amendment in its purest form, he is against it.

The greatest difference between this approach and a traditional approach is that Stick will be using the classic sight, sound, motion, color and emotion that made television the most powerful of media. Today's opinion leaders don't necessarily get all of their information from newspapers, as they did fifty years ago. Ten years ago, it was television. Now, it is the internet.

Whether it is YouTube, Twitter, Facebook, MySpace or another vehicle, it is possible for everyone to produce their own web message. It is a much more personal message than text or even traditional television. When bloggers go online and tell their story, share their opinions, and encourage response, the receiver comes away with the feeling that the message was created specifically with them in mind. Never, have there been transmission options like this.

Without question, Tam or any smart politician, especially one in Lafayette, Indiana, will not oppose making English the official language. The challenge for Rick Stick and any other Eagles who call him out will be to convince cyberspace that he is a snake in the woodpile. In effect, Tam might agree to make the language official, but do nothing more, which is useless to our cause.

Okay, so Rick Stick in Lafayette, Indiana might be able to convince his district that Tim Tam is unfit because he doesn't embrace the "E" Amendment in its purest form. So what?

What about Juan Plantain, our Eagle in Hialeah?

Most narrow-minded bigots would presume that anyone of Hispanic origin would be against the "E" Amendment, but they are wrong. In fact, Juan may prove to be one of the highest flying Eagles. His message will tell the story.

For years, Latin surnamed Americans have been lumped into one category – those who wanted to resist the unifying effect of English as our American language. That is wrong, as we all know. Speaking multiple languages makes us smarter and better. But, when it comes down to how we communicate in our society, we can only have one language. That language is English.

I am supporting my friend, mi amigo, Pablo de la Playa. Because, unlike his opponent, Oscar Oceano, Pablo supports the "E" Amendment intact. No changes. Nada. Pablo de la Playa wants a better educated, more unified America. His opponent wants neither.

I am proud of my heritage. I love Spanish. My parents and grandparents speak it in their homes. BUT, this is America. We cannot have separate societies. We must be one. And the English language makes us one people.

Oscar Oceano isn't a bad person. But, he is influenced by his party constituents. They say that we may lose votes if the ballots are only in English. But, we must have literacy in this country for everyone. English literacy.

If we don't, we will have linguistic ghettos.

If we don't, we will have second class citizens.

We are all equal. We must have one thread that binds us all as Americans. That thread is the English language.

Pablo de la Playa has a background similar to mine. His parents and grandparents still speak Spanish in their homes. But, unlike Oscar Oceano, Pablo knows that for us to be one nation and achieve total equality, we must have one language. Not two, three, or more, but one. And that language is English.

Why is it necessary to require a high school proficiency test for a job in government? Or for a professional license? Or, to receive a building permit for a multiple housing development? Porque, desgrasciamente, people are lazy. They won't learn English unless they are forced to. Period. I know this.

Yes, it is difficult to tell people they must learn to read English to hold these jobs. But, I know in my heart that it is the only way to bring about equality for our people while contributing to a stronger and greater America.

My opponent is telling people what they want to hear. His friends in government are from the tiny ruling class of career politicians. They want to keep our people ignorant and want to stimulate bigotry, for their own personal gain. They will tell you, as Oscar Oceano will tell you, that we should be allowed to vote and work even if we never learn English. After all, it makes our people easier for them to control. But, we are not looking for the easy route. We are looking for the best route.

Vote for Pablo de la Playa and cast a vote for an America that is unified. A vote for his opponent is a vote for the old way that is gradually destroying the America we dream of. As for Oscar Oceano, he says that he doesn't favor the "E" Amendment in its purest form. Therefore, he is un-American, un-patriotic and unfit for a leadership role in this country.

Does this feeling really exist in Miami-Dade County, Florida? Visit it. You will see it more than manifested. There is tremendous patriotism there and with it, a love for this country as strong as anywhere in America. Hispanic surnamed Americans are proud of their ancestry in the same sense as German, Irish, Italian and Japanese Americans are proud of where they came from. Like everyone, they see themselves as Americans first. Contrary to popular opinion, the majority of Latinos will favor English only written driver's license testing. They will also advocate a citizenship requirement that mandates passage of a high school English proficiency test for children born to illegal aliens.

Will people in Hialeah, Florida vote out a congressman who is opposed to eliminating Spanish voting ballots in the county municipalities? Keep in mind, they were placed there at request of local officials. Now, Pablo de la Playa is saying they are instrumental in continued discrimination against Latinos.

Are we on the same planet? YES! YES! YES!

I never felt the pride in being American as great as during the September, 2008 naturalization ceremony I attended in Miami. These new Americans, many still learning English wanted more than ever to belong, to be a part of our country. Would they like to be part of this anticipatory reference group referred to as Eagles for America?

I believe that they will be some of our very strongest voices.

So what about Oscar Oceano? Is Oscar merely an anachronism? Or is he another opportunistic minority politician who sees the disappearance of Spanish translating to the end of his position as a fighter for minority interests? Likely the latter. With the gradual decline of Spanish use in America, there will be less differentiation among all peoples.

Rather than Latinos, Asians, Africans and Anglos, we will be Americans. Is that too idealistic? Maybe a little. But, in the case of Latin surnamed Americans, their historic discrimination has been language based more than any other minority group. As they make English their primary language, the perceived differences leading to discrimination quickly dissipate. A politician like Pablo de la Playa can convey this better than anyone. For those who want to see our country actualize as Lincoln visualized, they will quickly realize that the path of Pablo de la Playa is the correct one. The path of least resistance as advocated by Oscar Oceano is synonymous with ignorance, poverty and continued discrimination.

Eagles like Juan Plantain see this. They can get out the word to all who want to experience the American Dream to its fullest extent. Juan will employ the necessary passion via the internet that only television could bring. Internet users will see him moving, talking and expressing his position. In the end, he will be convincing.

If you love America, you must do your part to protect her. The "E" Amendment is the single greatest thing we can do to make her stronger and eliminate a lot of needless, foolish prejudice along the way.

Now let's visit another nest of high flying Eagles, 644 miles to the north. This is a place that has seen prosperity, war, and renewed prosperity. Much can be explained by its strategic geographical location. But the real soul of the city is exhibited by its faith, courage, resilience and a belief in a better tomorrow. I am talking about Atlanta, Georgia.

Certainly, one might think that Marietta, Roswell, Duluth, Norcross and Stone Mountain would be fertile ground for Eagles for America. But downtown Atlanta? As in the inner city? Isn't this the place where Martin Luther King gave his famous *I have a dream* speech? Are we actually saying that we could find Eagles to convince the people here that the *Voting Rights Act* should be repealed?

Are we kidding? NO! NO! NO!

For those who have lived in downtown Atlanta, as I have, a strange and wonderful thing has occurred. You see people through their eyes, not their skin colors. And, it explains a lot of things. We are all in this together and we are one, if we can get past physical exteriors. The problem has been history and the lack of communication and empathy. When we take the time to do both, things begin falling in place. The internet makes this possible.

We must remember that this country belongs to all of us. Requiring a fourth grade equivalent English proficiency test as a prerequisite for voting is not aimed at disfranchising Americans. It is, in part, a method of monitoring the progress of our public schools. It is disgraceful to learn of students who graduate from high school unable to read or write. It is a reflection, not on the student, but on the schools and the system.

There are many politicians who give this problem lip service. Privately, however, they concur that there will always be people out there who can't read and write.

There are minority politicians who have used the race card over the years to make a point. In their heyday, they brought much needed awareness to a severely overlooked ugliness in America. In the end, they were successful. Then came the aftermath. They never moved to the next level. It was as if they had pulled an upset in a football game that electrified the country, then, instead of looking ahead to the next opponent, they continued to talk about the victory and why the other team lost.

To be sure, there are a lot of Oscar Oceanos in the African American community. They have used the race card because it is easy and historically fashionable. However, it is the path of least resistance. It is synonymous with ignorance, poverty, and continued discrimination. It is also an anachronism and is doing nothing short of dividing America.

This must end and the "E" Amendment is the perfect tool to do it. Young Eagles can become a part of this new colorblind anticipatory reference group and literally transcend old stigmas that need to be laid to rest. Many Americans can look back to a sordid family history. But, we must look to the future. We must get past grievances and ancient hurts, even if they are justified. And, to be sure, they are. For the sake of our nation, we must lay them to rest. We must come together. It is absolutely imperative. It is the only way we can preserve the freedoms we enjoy and in many cases, take for granted.

Are not our leaders in favor of all of these things? Truthfully? No. Again, we are talking about a tiny ruling class of career politicians, trust fund babies, second-, third-, and fourth-generation political aristocrats, and newly knighted outsiders who were invited to the party only because this tiny group needed front men.

Can anyone out there identify any front men?

In reality, this tiny, select group representing America's ruling class doesn't care if things ever change. In fact, they like things the way that they are. Like Hispanics without English, these potential voters are easier to control and manipulate. The more they are able to comprehend for themselves, the more likely they are to think for themselves. Then, as they began to think more independently, their vote won't be automatic. Politicians will find they will need to work to retain votes.

Finding Eagles in the inner cities is not as difficult as one might think. Atlanta Eagle Freddie Freeway debuts on YouTube.

Ladies and Gentlemen, I am here because I hear the sound of change in America. And, sad to say, it may not be the change we were all looking for. What I am hearing is the sound of America's ruling class, attempting to re-introduce slavery in our country. (Boos in the background.)

You know, there have been a lot of *Toms* in the past. They would go out there and say they were with us and they were for us, but who they were really for was *the man*. One of those Toms is Cyril Skyscraper, our Eleventh District Congressman. You know, ol' Cyril is pretty real; about keeping everything the way it is. Throw a few bones our way, kiss some babies and some places where the sun don't shine. But, in the end, we are still seeing a lot of our kids on the street that can't read and write. Why is that?

Because ol' Cyril is in bed with his good friends at the NEA! No, my friends, that doesn't stand for Negros Envisioning Africa! It is the National Education Association. And let me tell you about the National Education Association! They are against merit pay for teachers.

My friend Eddie Embassy thinks ol' Cyril has had his time to shine. That's why Eddie is running for Congress. Eddie wants to see education become a real priority in this country. And it begins by making English the official language. We need to do it in the form of the Twenty-eighth Amendment to the Constitution of the United States of America!

And we've got to make it so that no sleazy lawyer's going to be able to take it away from us once we have it! Like they're taking Congressional representation from Georgia and giving it to California. Bet you didn't know about that, but it's true! They are counting bodies and not citizens when it comes census time. Ooomph! Sounds reminiscent of the three-fifths compromise! As in, slaves count as three-fifths of a person. (more boos!) Told you these folks wanted to reintroduce slavery! And with ol' Cyril in their pocket, they can get away with it!

Now, I know that ol' Cyril will tell you that to pass the "E" Amendment, we must repeal the *Voting Rights Act*. Can we do that? Think about it, for a minute. The *Voting Rights Act* was originally adopted in 1965. Dr. King helped bring it about. But, that was half a century ago. Things have changed. Some will say they haven't, but we know they have.

We passed the *Civil Rights Act of 1968*, which made discrimination based on race, color, sex, religion and national origin against the law. And, don't forget about the Fourteenth Amendment or the *Civil Rights Act of 1866*. All of that is the law! *Jim Crow* is dead. In 2008 we elected an African American president if you haven't forgotten! And guess what, ladies and gentlemen, most of the people who elected Barack Obama were white!

Now think about that and tell me we haven't done some changing since 1965! We have! But there is more to be done. Much more! In short, we have got to get everyone on the same page. We all must be speaking the same language. And everyone, EVERYONE must be able to read and write it. No exceptions. If we can't do that, then all that we have worked for, the victory that we still relish is hollow.

There are politicians out there who want to keep Americans ignorant. The way they do it is to keep them illiterate. If we do not make reading at a fourth grade level a requirement for voting, there will never be any improvements in the public schools. Just float, float and float some more! Who cares? Because remember, it is a lot easier to control someone who doesn't have the ability to read at the fourth grade level than to control someone who does! We must be smart and realize that the *Voting Rights Act* was aimed at destroying those old ambiguous *Jim Crow* literacy tests that were administered subjectively by racists and bigots.

Do not kid yourselves! These politicians who are telling you that the "E" Amendment's passage is not in your best interest are lying to you! We must have one language. For the sake of a strong America! And it is our America! We must love her more than life itself.

We cannot have a small group of elitists, with money and power, controlling all of us like we are a bunch of sheep! The quickest way to make sure this doesn't happen is to pass the "E" Amendment. Anyone opposed, including Cyril Skyscraper is un-American, un-patriotic and unfit for leadership in the United States of America.

A vote for Eddie Embassy is a vote for America. It is a vote for unity. It is a vote for equality. It is a vote against discrimination. It is a vote against America's ruling class. We are Americans. We love this country because there is no other land like ours! We will never allow a few self-indulgent, self-interested traitors to destroy her.

Eddie has seen the visions of both Dr. King and Abraham Lincoln. He knows that passage of the "E" Amendment to the Constitution of the United State of America will make the dreams of both great American patriots a reality.

Can Freddie Freeway's impassioned plea reach some potential constituents and truly make a difference? Absolutely! The power of the visual message makes it possible for the viewer to see Freddie's sincerity. His emotional appeal will not be lost on people who see progress in conjunction with continued concerns. True, African Americans in the inner cities might be skeptical of the thought of repealing the *Voting Rights Act*. After all, it was adopted only after nearly a century of setbacks and near misses. However, this is a new age.

We have accomplished a lot since 1965. But, there are still the same prevailing problems that stem from a lack of accountability in many public schools today. One organization Freddie is singling out is the National Education Association. NEA has nothing to do with the "E" Amendment. But, it is probable that its leadership will not support it.

He makes reference to sleazy lawyers. This, of course, is in regard to the "E" Amendment's immunity to legal challenge requirement that many in the legal profession will find objectionable. It is easy to create mistrust, if not hostility toward lawyers. Freddie is inserting that line in a manner that suggests lawyers will ultimately attempt to steal the victory from "E" supporters.

He also suggests that Georgia is losing congressional representation due to the current census laws. There is no way to confirm this. But it is true that most, if not all, of his constituency are legal citizens of the United States. A change in the census law to base numbers on citizenship could ultimately be beneficial to Georgia or any state with a lower percentage of non-citizens. He goes so far as to draw an analogy to the three-fifths compromise. This colonial (1787) concession allowed slaveholders to increase their congressional representation through slave ownership.

More significantly than anything, he is making literacy the key issue. He is saying in blunt fashion that the traditional leadership has given the public schools and their supporters a free pass where the students are concerned. To keep them illiterate and ignorant is the key to controlling them. This is the theme and when fully comprehended the result is anger. Anger can then be transformed into passion. Passion becomes energy. The end result is activism.

The fact that Freddie Freeway will be telling this story on YouTube will have an impact, especially on younger voters. Many young Americans are asking questions. Such as, will there be a social security system when I retire? What about the mounting national debt? Are you expecting me to pay the healthcare costs of people with pre-existing conditions? And you're going to send me to jail if I don't? Nobody said anything about this during the last election.

These young people are already suspicious of the status quo. Even with the election of an African American president, there are still question marks. They will see and hear Freddie and ask the inevitable question: Are these people in Washington shooting straight or are they simply pulling my chain?

Historically, they have experienced more letdowns than triumphs. A clear message with an appeal that reaches to the very heart of the question will have an immediate impact on some. Actually suggesting that the *Voting Rights Act* is unnecessary goes against past attitudes and opinions. Talk about politically incorrect. It is that made manifest.

Imagine building a house and running out of money halfway through construction. The original plan called for an elaborate sunroom in the back – climate controlled, with fountains and a built in hot tub. Rather than having nothing, the decision is to build a screened in back porch. The porch works great. It is used for forty years, in fact.

Now, the children of the people who built the house occupy

it and decide they want to complete the house as it was originally designed. They locate the plans. They have cost estimates done and realize that they have the money to do it. The architect tells them that in order to build it, they must first remove the old porch. When they ask why, he tells them that the floor is made of wood and to build it as it was originally designed, they need a new foundation. To do that, the wooden floor must be removed. The frame is likewise made of wood and the original plan called for steel and concrete. It has to go as well. The original plan called for fountains and a built-in hot tub. This requires additional plumbing. In short, keeping the existing porch and trying to go around it or incorporate it into the new sunroom will cost more than simply removing it.

This is pretty much the argument for the repeal of the *Voting Rights Act*. It served its purpose. Today, however, we don't have those same problems of subjective disfranchisement. What we do have is a literacy problem that must be faced. To suggest that any organization will favor creating a system that is irresponsible to this extent will be politically incorrect, at best. At worst, it will be greeted with howls and protests. How dare anyone suggest that some children are intentionally ignored because they are more valuable to certain political factions illiterate than literate?

That's why inner cities such as Atlanta will ultimately be true hatcheries for Eagles for America. We are in a different era than in the sixties. We have access to information like never before. As people begin piecing together what has happened historically, their trust in the political order further diminishes.

The internet and the use of YouTube and other alternatives make communication, especially expressing a single point, more possible than ever. People want to belong. They want to be a part of something. More and more we are asking the same questions. Why are we having such a difficult time making things work and who can ultimately get things done?

The "E" Amendment represents a rallying point. It is something that people can truly latch onto and believe in. It constitutes everything that is good in America. It excludes nobody. It is about everybody. Especially the country itself!

When we begin looking at the "E" Amendment from a universal perspective, we begin to see that it is about who loves America the most.

Why must we have one official language?

One official language will bind us as one people, making us stronger and more unified.

Why a literacy test needed for citizenship, voting and to hold certain licenses and work in certain capacities?

To insure that we are sufficiently intelligent to remain leaders of the free world.

Why ID cards with photographs, thumbprint and retinal scan?

To totally eliminate voter fraud and to deter as much identity theft as possible.

Why does this amendment need immunity from legal challenge?

Because we don't have the money or the time to waste in court arguing at America's expense.

The internet makes for an equalizer like nothing else ever conceived. It doesn't matter if you live in a penthouse apartment in the heart of Manhattan or a singlewide trailer in Smithville, Oklahoma. Online we are equals.

Friendships are developed. Even marital unions are formed online. In today's hurley burley society, people are finding it harder than ever to build relationships. We get into routines, get busy and before we know it, the day is over. The next day duplicates the previous day's drudgery. However, when we go online, another world awaits.

This cyber world in many ways is a world without scope. You can literally go where you want, when you want, ask what you want and usually get answers. The world online creates avenues to meet people from all walks of life, from every corner of the world. We learn about distant places and become acquainted with new and diverse people. Because we are all the same online, there are fewer inhibitions. We are less reserved, more assertive, often more vocal than in a normal physical setting.

Cyberspace is the perfect setting for "E" dialogue. Blogging to advance the cause of the "E" Amendment amounts to creating open participation. Every participant is relevant. Their standing equates to how much they love our country and how much time they have to contribute to the cause.

The beauty of an anticipatory reference group is its open membership. Anyone can be an Eagle. You merely need to love the United States of America and be committed to fighting anyone who doesn't. Online, Eagles will communicate with other Eagles throughout America. Friendships will be forged. Relationships centered on passing the the "E" Amendment, and stopping all those opposed to it, will be built. There is no better method of bonding that to pursue a common enemy.

How high an Eagle flies will be determined largely by how much time per day they are able to contribute to the cause. There will be some Eagles who will do nothing more than check their e-mail. Others will blog for hours, communicating every conceivable message available, to politicians, constituents and other Eagles throughout the country. The more committed the Eagle, the more time they will spend blogging.

Communication within Eagle ranks is equally important. The more united the group, the better. When Eagles regularly exchange e-mail correspondence with other Eagles, the sense of unity and belonging are fortified and intensified. Members will feed off the others' energy. They will co-blog transmissions promoting solidarity.

Strength does come in numbers. As the legions of Eagles grow, so will the idea. Soon, it will be the talk of every blog, bus stop and every dinner table – virtually unstoppable.

Thus begins the first leg of our message to America. Let's push these opportunistic self-servers out of the way and get on with the task of creating a smarter, more unified America.

Cyberspace is the first stop.

9 Where Do We Go From Here?

When people fear government, you have tyranny. When government fears the people, you have liberty.

— Thomas Jefferson

We have reached the point of putting it all together.

A constitutional amendment making English the official language of the United States is now on the table. The amendment includes methodology that will virtually end voter fraud and seriously impair identity theft while presenting a fair, compassionate plan to control immigration. We have surmised that an overwhelming majority of the country will be in support of it. We also acknowledge that a strong, vocal and influential minority will be opposed to it.

There may be constitutional concerns. There are certainly questions regarding its current legality when reviewing the Lyndon Johnson inspired, *Voting Rights Act!* The "E" Amendment is in direct conflict with the Act and will supersede it. Is the *Voting Rights Act* truly good for America at this point in time?

At best, the *Voting Rights Act* is an anachronism. We are no longer discriminating on the basis of race. There are those who would argue to their graves that there will always be racial discrimination. Without such an issue, their political action committees will be inconsequential. They will likely lose funding. In some cases, they may cease to exist. However, evidence that we have transcended racial discrimination rests with the 2008 presidential election result.

There are no *Jim Crow* laws in practice, anywhere in America. There are questions regarding other provisions of the Act. Such as, allowing alternative languages to be used on ballots at the request of municipalities. This generates the next question.

Is such a practice in the best interest of America?

I think not.

Loving America includes the desire to make her strong. To make her strong, we must be a unified people. We must transcend all barriers and have one common thread that binds us. That thread is English. We cannot allow other languages to officially co-cxist; even on a temporary basis. Section Five of the *Voting Rights Act* actually encourages Americans not to learn English. As a result, we now have places in America that English isn't even used. There are people in this country who would be perfectly content to never learn it. Why? Because it takes time and effort. Under the present laws, they need not bother.

That is why we either need to repeal it, or produce an amendment that will supersede it.

The "E" Amendment will do that.

We have discussed some of the probable opponents of our proposed amendment. We know about the trial lawyers. We know about the National Education Association. We know about the politicians dependent on the illiterate masses for their elections and re-elections. We have mentioned potential problems that may arise from loose constructionist judges. We are sympathetic to the aims of the Libertarians and their longing for smaller, less active government. The group who may be the single biggest opponent is the media.

We when talk about the media, we are referring to the federally licensed broadcast media. Print and cable are not included in this discussion. They will always be writing and broadcasting without any restraints and should be; biased or not. However, when discussing over-the-air broadcasting, there is an added responsibility. Basically, they must be above partisanship. Why is there a difference? Because there are a limited number of licenses available.

What defines over-the-air broadcasting? Over the air broadcasting is free. In other words its transmission is totally paid for by commercial sponsors. In the case of cable, the viewer is paying a fee for access. Certainly there are commercials on most cable stations, but to gain access, a viewer must contract with the cable company or one of the alternatives such as DIRECTV or DISH Network for their service. Over-the-air or free TV is available if you have a television set and affiliate stations in your area. There are a limited number of networks and affiliates. Each affiliate must comply with requirements set by the Federal Communications Commission.

To gain license renewal, each affiliate must show evidence that they are serving the public. It is required that examples be cited. Qualification can be rigorous.

Networks, such as NBC, CBS and ABC provide programming to their affiliates. In most cases, they payfees to the local affiliates based on market rank to provide clearance for programming including advertisements sold nationally through the network. In addition to clearance fees, the local affiliates are given local "avails" with which they are able to sell local spot advertising.

Much of the alleged bias is coming through the networks. Because of the limited number of media vehicles, it can have a decisive impact on public opinion.

But isn't that why it is important to reinstate the *Fairness Doctrine?* On that subject, it might be noted that, the *Fairness Doctrine* is poorly named. The title *Fairness Doctrine* is as appropriate as historians referring to the **Rome-Berlin Axis** as the "Coalition for World Peace." In a nutshell, one side had sponsors and audience. The other side didn't. The side that didn't have sponsors and audience decided they did not want the other side to exist. It sounds like what they really wanted was censorship.

More specifically, *Air America*, hosted by Minnesota Senator Al Franken bombed. It was a loser on every front. With limited audience, it was unable to generate the necessary advertising revenue to keep it afloat. Why? Because there simply wasn't a large enough audience holding similar political opinions to justify its existence. No listeners, no advertising. No advertising, no program. It's simple economics.

But what about programming that represented the opposing point of view? Is it fair to deny them the same access, if they are able to generate the necessary advertising revenue that results from a large audience?

Facts are facts. Some people may not like Rush Limbaugh, while others do. If a broadcasting vehicle determines there is an audience wanting a program, they should have the right to carry it. The obvious determiner is advertising revenue. The same would hold true if Rush Limbaugh, Al Franken or another talent paid a station for a block of time and sold the advertising internally. It simply comes down to what television viewers and radio listeners want to view or listen to.

Talk radio is a special part of a free society. It must always be a part of America. When government, directly or indirectly, attempts to impede it, they are overstepping. Without question there will be those who concede that the only way to advance an agenda is to silence any and all critics. When that happens, we face perhaps the greatest threat in this nation's relatively young life.

Network news is another thing altogether. An advertiser sponsored program coming from talk radio is comparable to a feature story in a newspaper. Hard news is hard news and there is no place for partisanship. None whatsoever! But we have it, as sure as Russia has it. Our media is quick to point fingers at Putin and Russia, but people who live in glass houses should not throw rocks.

Are we as flagrant as Russia? No. But, we are nowhere close to the oath every journalist took in their Sigma Delta Chi pledge. The 2008 election exemplified this assertion more than any other time in history. The broadcast networks presented one side to the exclusion of the other. Their flagrant bias was sufficient to make any true Sigma Delta Chi advocate cringe. Never, in history was media bias more evident than with General Electric and NBC. This kind of media partisanship is a dangerous threat to our constitutional rights.

It is perfectly reasonable for cable, magazines and newspapers to endorse candidates and side with individual political parties. Television and radio stations should be able to sell sponsorships to groups reflecting different political positions. If there is more interest in one position over another, resulting in more coverage, so be it. However, when we are talking about over the air network news, it must remain non-partisan. The influence wielded by these networks is vast. They must remain neutral. If they cannot, we are no better than Putin's Russia.

Journalists must be above politics. It is imperative that they remain objective. After all the media is another entity. It must hold to a standard that is higher than any partisan position. Utilizing federally licensed broadcast network news to influence and shape public opinion is manipulative at best. There can be no compromise. If there is, as Former House Speaker Newt Gingrich concluded, "we have *Pravda*."

Even though it may go against some First Amendment purists, there is an increasing need for a monitoring system that will insure that federally licensed broadcast network news is unbiased. It is apparent that a non-partisan commission overseeing all federally licensed broadcast properties may be necessary. This commission will grade them on bias. If they are perceived as anything less than objective, they will receive a warning. There will be no warning for a second offense. If and when the offense is repeated, the company loses its license. No third chance. No questions, no explanation. The license will be forfeit. End of story. This would apply to both networks and network owned affiliates.

Many will say that a commission with this kind of leverage will compromise the First Amendment. This is a valid argument; or is it? We are not talking about all media. This oversight will only apply to federally licensed radio and television networks, and affiliates that are owned by the networks. Keep in mind that when the amendment was written, there were no federally licensed radio or television stations. We must also remember that the *Radio Act of 1927*, which preceded the *Communications Act of 1934*, stipulated that not everyone could broadcast.

Those receiving licenses were entrusted with something very dear; a vehicle of free transmission. To have this trust abused, by exhibiting bias, makes them unworthy. In essence, if they violate that trust, they should lose this privilege.

How this concept would be introduced, delivered and executed is another topic for a different writing. It must be done. What happened in Russia could happen here, if we do not get a handle on unconscionable abuses and practices taking place every day in the broadcast media.

Who would constitute this non-partisan commission? A team of ex-journalists committed to both the First Amendment and the principles of Sigma Delta Chi, the Society of Professional Journalists. Those principles include but are not limited to, "the media is above all partisanship." Because of their grave responsibility, the television and radio stations cannot settle for a lesser standard. Licensees are entrusted to work for the interest of their public. There is no room for bias.

Okay. So we force broadcast networks such as CBS, NBC and ABC to adopt a standard of non-partisanship. What if we can't? Does that spell the end of the "E" Amendment?

No. The growing skepticism and negativity toward the media might work to "E" supporters' advantage, especially if networks or affiliates voiced opposition to it. Much of the reporting seen today is a combination of headlines and sound bytes. On a topic this comprehensive, shallow, skim over stories will be met with little real attention and even less credibility.

Certainly, the media will be intrigued with such a proposal. After all, it makes for an excellent news story. There will be media representatives who will embrace it, but they will be in the minority. The upper echelons of today's broadcast hierarchy will be pre-conditioned to report the concept as interesting, but impossible to implement. Their expert opinions supporting this conclusion will be, you guessed it, from representatives of that same circle of elite insiders who we have referenced throughout the writing.

Without a doubt, many questions will be raised. A literacy test? A photo identification card? Fingerprints? Retinal scans?

Improving American literacy while eliminating voter fraud and curbing identity theft en route to a real immigration policy are noble aspirations. But there is one very valid concern. How are we going to pay for this? It obviously won't be cheap.

The question of cost was discussed in an earlier chapter. Where will the money come from? Surprisingly, the answer eliminates still another serious deficiency in this country.

Of all the American government-run operations, the one institution most reminiscent of the former Soviet institutions is the United States Postal Service.

Have you been to the post office recently? Did you notice how casual and unhurried all of the workers were? You could see twenty people in line. There might be four postal workers. Normally it takes a postal worker three minutes per customer. Assuming there is nothing complicated. Nobody is ever in a big rush to finish. Why? Because speed and efficiency are not top priorities.

Did anyone ever mention how difficult it is to get fired from the Postal Service? If you show up for work, you generally can work there indefinitely, or at least until retirement age. When it comes time for retirement, the postal workers have better retirements than most private sector workers. In short, you have happy, complacent workers, who never have to worry about getting fired and have great pension plans. Life is good.

In addition to seeing methodical, unhurried postal workers, what most of us see are the ever rising prices for mail service. Now, there is even talk about discontinuing Saturday service. Enough is enough.

What if we sold the United States Postal Service to private enterprise? Specifically, if we sold it to five different companies in an effort to create some good healthy competition. The sales will be inclusive of any and all real estate. The postal workers' pensions will be totally at the discretion of the buyers. In other words, if UPS decided to replace the over-funded pensions with a minimal annuity, it would have that option.

Draconian? Perhaps. These companies will be paying prices set by the federal government. They must be allowed to make a profit. Money generated by the sale of the Postal Service will be astronomical. How much would be difficult to ascertain at this stage because of market considerations. But it will be eye popping.

In the end, the American consumer will have much improved mail service. We will be replacing the most Soviet-like institution in the country with the very companies who are on the cutting edge of the highest levels of modern technology.

There is an even larger revenue source that could result from the sale of the Postal Service. A residential access tax on commercially oriented direct mail will generate sufficient revenue to more than cover the cost of voter identification cards, fingerprints, and retinal scans.

Here is how it will work. For every direct mail piece, whether it be Home Depot, Kroger, Macys or any other organization that communicates a marketing message, five cents will be levied against the sender. This will also apply to political correspondence, including incumbent politicians' franking privileges. The Internal Revenue Service will administer the tax.

In essence, junk mail will fund the voter identification cards. Could it be that simple? Maybe. Think about it. A lot of what the mail carrier delivers to mailbox after mailbox is junk mail. It would not be surprising to learn that at least 75% is commercially oriented mail. To top it off, most of the senders have bulk mailing permits. This is outrageous. How can this be?

There is no easy answer. It has been going on for some time. But one thing is certain, we have constitutional protection for our homes. Why should not companies, organizations or government be required to pay for access to them?

A residential access tax on commercially oriented direct mail might be considered detrimental to the industry, right? Think again. Direct mail cost is higher than any other form of mass communication on a cost-per-thousand basis. If cost was a concern, the industry would have died decades ago. In taxing it, we are tapping into an annoying part of Americans' lives.

Needless to say, this newly found revenue source will more than cover the cost of paying for the photo ID cards and the administering of the examinations. Can anyone possibly think of a better tradeoff? What a deal.

What to do with the proceeds of the overall sale of the Postal Service is a wonderful problem to consider. The real estate alone would be worth billions of dollars. It's true that print media is giving way to the internet. Fewer and fewer people are mailing letters today. Most letter writing is done in the way of email. Time will tell.

In theory, "E" Amendment proponents will take charge of the question of funding at the same time the bill is introduced. How to pay for foolproof identification cards is already being discussed. There are a number of ideas already on the table. This plan is unquestionably more ambitious than most, but the revenue potential is there.

Could our Eagles be counted upon to help make this measure a reality? Definitely.

The problem that we have addressed is multi-dimensional. We have thousands, perhaps millions of functionately illiterate people in this country. We have others who resist learning English. Fixing that problem is part of the equation. The long-term solution is to revamp our immigration priority system.

Okay. I can hear it now. If you make fluency in English the top criteria, won't you be showing favoritism to English speaking countries such as England, India and Canada?

Yes. But, there would be other requirements as well.

Today, we have an immigration priority system that gives first preference to parents and children. Immigration through sponsorship by a sibling can take as long as twelve years. Distant relatives are close to impossible. As a result, applicants wanting to stay in the United States are seeking other methods that can get them into the country. Then, they focus on staying. In some instances, their stay isn't authorized.

Few politicians will tell you that the immigration system is perfect, or even in good shape. It is not. That's why it would be easy to amend. Adopting a points system with fluency in English as one of the factors, makes perfect sense.

Let's look at a mythical points system more closely and examine the advantages and flaws.

Educational level would begin with one point for a high school graduate, two points for an undergraduate degree and three points for an advanced degree. Immigrants with proof of a trade would be given an additional half point as would those with engineering and nursing degrees. Medical degrees would be worth three additional points.

Age could be another factor. We want and need young people

who will come into the country and contribute to the Social Security system. Therefore, if the applicant is thirty or younger, they would receive an additional point.

As for English proficiency, a half point would be given for the applicant's ability to pass a fourth grade exam, a full point for those who passed the high school test.

So, in theory, twenty-eight-year-old, Johann Bezdek of Prague with a degree in engineering and capable of passing a high school English proficiency test will have four and one-half points. Two points because he had an undergraduate degree, one point because he has high school English proficiency, one point because he is under thirty and an additional half-point because his degree is in engineering.

To be sure, there will still be consideration given for family already in the United States. Perhaps one point for siblings and parents and two points for children would be appropriate. Family connections may be skewing immigration unfairly in favor of a limited number of countries. In the spirit of American fairness, we must strive to be as diverse as possible.

This plan will not apply to political exiles or children of political exiles. America has always been and should remain the safe harbor for refugees of tyranny and oppression.

There is a strong argument to give immigrants from NATO countries a point. There is nothing discriminatory about favoring allies when it comes to determining who is allowed into this country on a permanent basis. If this is implemented, Johann Bezdek will then have five and one-half points.

The idea behind all of this is strengthening America. Those deeming any of these points as politically incorrect, may have lost sight of the main idea. We want a stronger, smarter nation.

Targeting young, well-educated immigration candidates, fluent in English is simply smart. Why shouldn't we cherry pick our new Americans? If half of the planet wants to live here, why not capitalize on it? Giving uneducated, non-English speakers a prefer-ence solely because of family connections may not be in America's best interest.

Certainly, there are those who will say that not uniting families in favor of some mythical points system is cold, insensitive and un-compassionate. Maybe it is. The question is, "What is best for the country as a whole?" Most Americans know the answer. The needs of the many outweigh the needs of the few. America comes first.

The dilemma of what to do with the twelve million or so illegal aliens currently in the country is beyond the scope of this book.

On the question of children of illegal aliens born here and whether or not they should automatically be given citizenship, the "E" Amendment offers a compromise that is fair and practical.

The key is determining, once and for all, if the Fourteenth Amendment should include children of illegal aliens. Opponents point out correctly that the amendment made reference to those freed from slavery, not children of illegal aliens. Many favor strip-ping these children of illegal aliens of citizenship on these grounds. Their contention is, the constitutional interpretation of giving automatic citizenship for children born in the U.S. is motivation for breaking the law.

Proponents are equally quick to say that the Constitution guarantees them citizenship irregardless of whether their parents broke the law.

The "E" Amendment provides a bridge for the moderates. Children of illegal aliens able to pass the high school proficiency test will be given a special classification, that might require some sort of limited service to be determined at an appropriate time. If the children are unable to pass the proficiency test, they will depart with their parents and begin the process through normal channels. Is this not what the framers of the amendment would have suggested?

Let us take a moment to visit that Reconstruction Congress who conceived the Fourteenth Amendment. At that time, it was considered radical by strict constructionist lawmakers. Its purpose was to make all of the freed slaves citizens. The ultimate goal was to win them suffrage in the hope that they would be future Republican voters. There was never any discussion regarding children of Americans who had entered the country illegally. Creators of this amendment would never have dreamed that 150 years later its application would be the hallmark for citizenship for children of parents who entered the country illegally. Such a development would have been incomprehensible – primarily, because entry into the United States was as difficult as purchasing a boat ticket.

Today, the result is anchor babies. These children born in the United States are automatically granted citizenship by the Fourteenth Amendment, often making it possible for their entire extended families to immigrate. This question can be better defined if passage of a high school English proficiency test is part of the equation. If the baby can pass the proficiency test, then the family should be treated accordingly. If not, they can resort to the normal channels required for everyone. We simply cannot live under a presumed policy that it is easier to be forgiven than to gain permission.

There will be a constitutional argument if the aforementioned plan is implemented. Opponents will cling to the Fourteenth Amendment, voicing the belief that it is intended for anyone born in the U.S. regardless of the circumstances. Amending the Fourteenth Amendment is one method of preventing a logjam in the courtroom. Including wording in the "E" Amendment requiring passage of the proficiency test, regardless of birthplace will be even stronger.

The "E" Amendment is not about immigration reform. But it naturally creates reform. Its primary objective is to make certain that all applicants for naturalization can pass an English proficiency test.

People in the country illegally won't be applying for naturalization under the present laws.

There is a strong belief that many support organizations who assist voter registration may be registering illegal aliens. A voter registration card will eliminate this problem. No illegal alien will voluntarily allow themself to be fingerprinted and photographed. There will be opponents who will claim that the very thought of thumbprints and retinal scans will frighten away legitimate voters. But this will come down to education. If these support groups can instigate illegal voting practices, they can use those same resources to educate legitimate voters of the importance and urgency of exercising their right to vote.

Of course, there will be protests from certain activist groups. The "E" Amendment will be positioned as anti-immigrant and especially anti-Latino. This is untrue. Ironically, Hispanics will benefit more from the amendment than any other group. Provided they entered the country legally. Many Hispanics have suffered greatly from the common practice of being stereotyped.

Many, if not most, Americans are totally ignorant on the subject of Latin American cultures. It's probably fair to say that 90% of Americans have never had the opportunity to live in a cosmopolitan Latino mecca such as Miami, where they can experience the differences and diversity of Latin America – its history, variety and cultures. As a people, we fail to see past the Spanish language when attempting to identify perpetrators. Naively we have a tendency to throw all Hispanics into one hopper with no regard other than the language tie. That is part of the problem.

Associating Hispanics with illegal immigration is racial and ethnic bias in its ugliest form. This is about the law, who is abiding by it and who is breaking it. Those who entered the country without permission will see it as another barrier, as they should. We want to make living in American illegally unattractive, not inviting. That is why *Phyler v. Doe* must be overturned. That is why we must have written driver's license testing only in English.

One of the sad realities of our illegal alien problem is that Americans have facilitated it. In a booming economy, it was difficult to find workers to perform some of the worst jobs for minimum wage. When the question of paying people a livable wage came up, some entrepreneurs were quick to point out that if they paid workers more, they couldn't make an acceptable profit. The argument generally ended with the conclusion that people these days just don't want to work.

I recall the proprietor of a tire dealership in Springdale, Arkansas bragging that he had a family of Mexicans managing four chicken houses he owned. On a heavily wooded tract, between Springdale and Siloam Springs, Arkansas, accessible only by a dirt road, the man had built four modern chicken houses.

Beside the chicken houses was a dilapidated doublewide trailer. Seven people were living in it. These seven people constituted his crew: Jose, his wife, two teen-age children and a seven-year-old, plus his mother and sister. They effectively managed the houses. Only Jose spoke some English.

Jose was driving a broken down pickup truck, courtesy of his "Jefe", which he typically drove to Siloam Springs or Springdale. He was paid a total of $100 per week. Cash of course. Plus, he received on a weekly basis, two pounds of coffee, ten pounds of pinto beans, five pounds of corn meal, five pounds of rice, a pound of sugar, two cases of beer, two cartons of cigarettes, a fifth of tequila and as much kerosene as he needed.

Jose's family had a small garden and, as their Jefe reminded them, they could have their fill of all of the excess of the houses. In other words, chickens who died were theirs, so they had plenty to eat.

The doublewide had no running water and no electricity. Hence, there was no paper trail from utility companies to trace their existence. There was a pond, well-stocked with catfish, and a well nearby. There were even groves of hickory and black walnut trees at the edge of the clearing that provided Jose's family with as many deliciously edible nuts as they cared to shell.

The doublewide was lighted and heated with kerosene lanterns and heaters. There was one generator per chicken house to run the fans in the hottest of weather.

To Jose and his family, this was "una vida magnifico con mucho comida y dinero sufficiente." (A magnificent life with plenty of food and decent money.) They were all in the country illegally and were actually able to save sufficient money to send a portion back to Mexico. To their "Jefe", it was a gold mine.

Chickens are dirty but very profitable. With minimum wage help it was possible to clear $20,000 per chicken house. Paying a total of six workers only $100 in addition to another $100 per week in food, alcohol and cigarettes upped his profits to nearly $30,000 per house, per year.

Had this proprietor of the tire store been apprehended by the authorities, it would have meant jail time. But who was going to blow the whistle? Not Jose and his family!

Arrangements similar to Jose's are commonplace in the United States. That is why there will never be a foolproof method of stopping illegal immigration. Fingers are often pointed at Mexicans. But they are by no means the only offenders. As long as there are jobs nobody wants, we will have illegal workers. Unless, we tap an untouched market.

The recent additions to NATO include countries with very low average household incomes. The people are generally well-educated. Because English has long been the second language in Europe, they have been exposed to it from childhood. In some cases they studied it and became fluent in English. With this in mind, we should consider giving preference to all NATO countries. A point system which automatically gave a point for NATO membership countries makes sense.

It amounts to abolishing our present country by country quota system. In its place will be a points system that favors age, education, English proficiency and their native country's relationship with the United States.

This will accomplish three objectives.

By openly rewarding our NATO allies, we will be letting the world know that we remember our friends. This will generate good will in Europe. That can't hurt. Our relations with them are frayed at best. Their experimentations with socialism have left them frustrated and also educated regarding its dangers. Secondly, we will gain better educated immigrants, many already fluent in English. Finally, we will be filling jobs that no other Americans, here legally in the country, want.

These new NATO countries may be poor, but they are typically well-educated. It is common to find Poles, Czechs and Romanians who are fluent in English with college degrees. Will they be interested in a job working in a chicken house in Siloam Springs, Arkansas? What about a job picking tomatoes in Homestead, Florida? In July? You can bet your life they will be.

The difference is that they will be here legally. They will take these jobs because they will know that in America, their opportunities for bettering their lives at a later time will be greatly enhanced.

This used to be the way our system worked. Immigrants would start at the bottom and work up. By 1960, immigration had slowed dramatically, almost to a standstill. There was a deep recession in 1963. The civil rights movement underscored the need to bring African Americans into the fold, enjoying all rights and privileges guaranteed by the Constitution. Immigrants were seen to be prime competitors with African Americans for the same jobs. Many African Americans were able to trace their roots back more than 100 years. They were justified in pointing out that due to their sordid history and tradition of racial discrimination, preference over newly arrived immigrants was justified.

As time passed, African Americans advanced. Perhaps not as quickly as should have been the case, but progress was made. By 2000, jobs that would have been readily filled by African Americans in 1960 were often going unfilled. These often difficult and rigorous jobs were filled by another minority group, Mexicans.

Mexican Americans have proven to be some of the hardest workers ever to set foot in this country. They have taken jobs that literally nobody else wanted. Most Mexicans are in the country legally. However, there are instances where Mexicans cross the border and work for a time in the states, then return to their homes in Mexico. All too often, authorities have looked the other way.

With the rising crime wave equated with drug trafficking, there is increasing concern about the security of our country. A method certain to curtail this practice is to eliminate the need for it.

The "E" Amendment, coupled with the four point immigration checklist will result in immigrants capable of assimilating into our society much more quickly. And, by emphasizing age, education, proficiency in English and their native country's relationship with the U.S., we will gain greater numbers of well-educated, English speaking immigrants.

The end result: a smarter, stronger, more secure America.

There will be immediate workers available to take the low paying jobs. Our workforce will be smarter because we will be making education a priority point of our immigration process. There will be many well-educated applicants already fluent in the language. It will have an immediate impact on our overall productivity as a nation.

Sounds great. The only problem is, the entire proposal is politically incorrect. For starters, you have the issue of taking better educated, English savvy immigrants over relatives of families already residing in the country. The opposition will call this cold, insensitive and calloused.

Then, you have the issue of race. Look at the countries making up the North Atlantic Treaty Organization. Forget about loyalty to our allies. Forget about education. Forget about fluency in English. Forget about age. Opponents of the point system and a preferential point for NATO countries will argue that advocates were attempting to alter the racial percentages in America.

Rewarding applicants from NATO countries makes sense. It will be equally smart to restrict applicants from terrorist countries. America should take the best possible candidates. Basing approval on points may be the fairest plan overall. We need to look at constructive, proactive alternatives to our broken immigration system. The "E" Amendment creates a foundation for the entire question of immigration.

We must get a handle on making everyone in the country better in the use of English. This cannot be like *No Child Left Behind* where someone had a great idea, but never determined how it would be adequately administered and funded. It all begins with the public schools and the teachers.

English taught in the classroom is not easy. In fact, it is one of the toughest courses to teach. We need the best and brightest teachers to consider teaching English. A proven method designed to move in that direction is to pay them a premium. If the choice is to be paid $42,000 per year to teach English or $35,000 to teach any other subject, more teachers will opt to teach English.

There needs to be more emphasis on grammar and usage. Anyone who has really dealt with the subject of grammar and usage will concur that this is a challenging discipline. All too often, the current English curriculum spends more time on literature than grammar and usage.

Literature is generally more interesting both to the student and the teacher. But, learning correct grammar and usage will aid students more in the long run. It is amazing how many students graduate from high school without the ability to write a business letter. This must change and will change, if we make it a priority.

English grammar needs to account for at least as much time as literature. More time needs to be spent on English composition. Every high school graduate should be able to write a business letter.

Striving for fluency in a foreign language is a very aggressive objective. Many contemporary educators will scoff at the idea. At first glance, it would seem improbable. Six years of one foreign language? Where will we get the money? Where will we find the teachers? Assuming that we did both, could all our public school students actually benefit from learning a second language? Not to mention, be able to handle a second language academically?

Let us answer the third question first. Yes, most students could. Not all, but most will finish their six years with at least some limited understanding of that language. Remember, the purpose of learning this second language is to improve their use of their primary language, English.

Where will we get the teachers? There are surprisingly a lot of people qualified to teach a foreign language who are not working in such a capacity. Why? Because they don't have educational teaching certificates. Remove this requirement and you will have a lot of qualified, energetic, enthusiastic applicants, teaching courses such as Mandarin, Arabic, Farsi, Swahili and Polish in our classrooms. In some of the smaller schools, there might be more limited options. But, there will always be at least one foreign language available and enough educated instructors to facilitate learning.

How will we pay for this? Because we have a secondary motive for our children learning a second language, we can be satisfied to use teaching methods that emphasize reading, writing and oral exercises. Thus, we are not talking about the highest forms of technology. Instead, we are taking a slow path toward gradual comprehension and practical use of a language. Exposure to a language translates to introduction to a culture. Different regions might opt for closer examinations of certain cultures over others. But the overall end result will be deeper, more diverse students, who will likewise be stronger in their use of English, which was the original goal.

Clearing this hurdle may be impossible under the present system. The NEA will be certain to resist waiving the teaching certificate for foreign language teachers. They will be vehemently opposed to the thought of paying English teachers 20% more than teachers of other disciplines.

A rival union, stressing the importance of not only paying a premium to English teachers, but instituting merit pay in general will make waves, to be sure. Many of today's schoolteachers will admit to the need of an alternative to NEA. The "E" Amendment gives them a platform.

Will there be educators who might come on board as Eagles?

You can count on it. Schoolteachers are often the first to identify wrongs and problems in a system or with an idea. Merit pay is discussed every day. Paying English teachers a premium may be novel, but it isn't radical or unethical. In actuality, it makes a lot of sense. Those in the profession know that English isn't the easiest discipline to master. Logic dictates that with a higher pay scale, there will be more applicants. The more applicants, the greater chance we will get better teachers.

Teachers are often some of the most computer literate Americans. Joining the host of Eagles and becoming engaged in e-mail communication and blogging to politicians and other Eagles will be a natural progression. Teachers are generally excellent communicators. They are often the first to grasp the significance of any movement or idea.

The "E" Amendment isn't about rich or poor. It is not about big or small. It is simply a strategy designed to create a smarter America – short-term and long-term. There is no partisanship. This is above that. Our number one priority is America, protecting her from self-interested opportunists and making her stronger.

History has proven that we are capable of reversing ourselves when it is the will of the people. Prohibition is a prime example. We repealed the Eighteenth Amendment with the Twenty-first Amendment because it was the will of the people. The proposed Twenty-eighth Amendment, the "E" Amendment, will supersede the *Voting Rights Act* because the people will determine that (a) race is no longer an issue and (b) it is not in the country's interest to allow languages other than English to hold any official existence.

Can 60,000 or so bloggers bring about the change?

Let's return to consideration of the Bolshevik Revolution for a moment. Roughly the same numbers were engaged and they brought about a monumental change. For starters, they toppled a thousand-year-old monarchy. In the process, they were breaking the law, committing high treason and, among other things, risking their lives for their cause.

The Bolsheviks had limited telephone communication. Airline travel was in its infancy. They had no television. They had no radio. They had no fax machines. The internet was decades into the future. Printing presses were extremely hard to come by.

How were they able to accomplish such an impossible mission? And why could Eagles for America be successful with a blogging campaign as earlier outlined?

The Bolsheviks succeeded because they were passionate, disciplined and purposeful. Eagles for America can duplicate the unity that was the key to their success. And it might be easier than originally predicted. Their lives won't be at risk. Their computers are in their homes. The only expense they will incur will be their time.

The country is restive. America has been apathetic in recent years. Now, almost too late, we are realizing that a small group of well connected insiders have manipulated the entire country. They have used uneducated Americans to their advantage, keeping them ignorant in an effort to control them. They have created a culture of political correctness that has undermined individualism, free thinking and expression. With power structures, such as broadcast media and the National Education Association, they have formed alliances that have facilitated their monopoly.

Eagles for America can use one of the few remaining resources of free expression, the internet, to bring nationwide awareness to what is happening. Thanks to the internet, Americans in all corners of the country are able to get in the loop regarding who is running the country and where they are attempting to take it.

There is nothing more contagious than an idea. When Americans make up their minds that they want the proposed Twenty-eighth Amendment, it will be merely a matter of time until it is adopted. What is most critical is belief in our ability to make it reality.

When compared to what the Bolsheviks pulled off, this is a piece of cake. We are obviously not attempting to overthrow the government. We are simply trying to give the average American a voice in it.

We have freedom of speech, at least for now. We have a unifying cause that includes everyone. Our cause is built on the idea that, as a nation of laws, we must live under the law, bringing about change within the law. No one is above the law or dares impede it.

Can 60,000 committed bloggers bring about the "E" Amendment? In actuality, it is probable that less than that number would be able to do it. But, expect a lot more than 60,000 Eagles for America to take flight in a unified holy war to retake America. In identifying the opposition, it is becoming clear that this tiny fragment of self-serving elitists has allowed America to slip toward mediocrity. Now, we need new voices asking new questions. To the chagrin of the ruling class, these questions will not be politically correct.

America is unique. We came from different lands seeking the same thing. Through it all, what has held us together has been the language. This cannot be compromised. If it is, we are lost.

Americans must be the masters of the English language. We must be better than every other nation in the world, even England.

We must be smarter. We must have greater accountability. And we must ask the toughest of questions. We cannot allow old forces to manipulate us, creating hatred and ill feelings between racial and ethnic groups. This has long been a tool of America's ruling class. Divide, create dissention and control. No more!

We can never be satisfied until we know that we are the best educated, most literate people on the planet. All that is needed is a catalyst.

The "E" Amendment will be that catalyst.

10 The "E" Amendment and Obama

"Obama is running for Jimmy Carter's second term."
Republican candidate John McCain
during the 2008 presidential election

In our journey down the thorny path of adding an amendment to the U.S. Constitution, we have learned that the president cannot veto a constitutional amendment. Nor, is it necessary to place a proposed amendment before the president for signing.

The little known, vaguely referenced case of *Hollingsworth v. Virginia* (1798) insured that no chief executive could deter the legislative process. This insures proper checks and balances in government. How this law materialized and what spurred its adoption is another subject for a different writing. For our purposes, however, it eases an almost impossible task of adding our proposed Twenty-eighth Amendment, which is the subject of *"E" is for English.*

That being said, the question arises, would President Barack Obama support the "E" Amendment?

When Barack Obama ran for the presidency, it was assumed that he aspired to take the country in a different direction. But what was that direction? His Republican opponent, John McCain asserted that he was "running for Jimmy Carter's second term." Obama advocates suggested and expected more.

On top of the list was accountability from the public schools, with a strong emphasis toward charter schools. Proponents for merit pay for teachers were energized when he questioned the National Education Association's position on tenure as the primary measure for teacher compensation. This set him apart from Hillary Clinton and won him critical support from independents. Without question, he is committed to improving the public schools. Recently he has teamed with like-minded activists, such as Bill Gates, to promote improved educational standards.

Obama has been a vocal supporter of Americans learning a second language. He went so far as to make this point in Europe during the presidential campaign.

I think he will favor at least the concept of an alternative teachers union that promotes merit pay and mandatory study of a foreign language.

Will he agree with the idea of paying English teachers a premium in the public schools? Maybe. It will be an interesting question to put in front of him. He seems to be committed to the idea of improved literacy in America. But, of course, what politician is going to oppose improved literacy?

Beyond that, questions emerge. Will Barack Obama favor legislation that supersedes the *Voting Rights Act?* My sincere belief is that in the depths of his soul, he will conclude this might be the only way to achieve the optimum literacy standard in America. Recognizing the lofty idealism inherent in such an objective, he will acknowledge that the "E" Amendment is right for America, in a perfect world. Unfortunately this is not a perfect world. There are other considerations.

In 1965, we had a completely different America. The country, as a whole, decided to outlaw some of the prejudicial practices that had been inherent since Reconstruction. It was not that African Americans alone brought about the change, their suffrage and enhanced opportunities were the by-products. It was White America that elected to undergo a paradigm shift.

Obama's 2008 election was the end result. Therefore, logically, the president should be at the forefront in explaining to the country that, while the *Voting Rights Act* served its purpose, it has become a hindrance to future progress. Now it is facilitating illiteracy while dividing the country.

Could the president not take this position? And, if not, why? Politics.

To be sure, Obama's core supporters include some of the best and brightest minds in America. These are the same people who supported the presidential campaigns of Edward Kennedy, Mario Cuomo, Michael Dukakis and Bill Bradley. The Right commonly refers to them as the Left Wing of the Democratic Party. They are vocal but represent nothing close to the majority in America. They are flanked by some of the wealthiest people on the globe, people like George Soros and Warren Buffet. They draw overwhelming support from throngs of Hollywood entertainers turned activists who are equally vocal, yet also small in number.

To win elections, this core needs help and a lot of it. This help comes from the masses of illiterate, would-be voters who, if located, organized and properly indoctrinated, will vote as they are told. In some cases, they will be promised something. It could be as small as a pack of cigarettes or as large as a job.

For Obama to win re-election, he will need them to vote en masse, as a block.

A fourth grade proficiency test in conjunction with voter identification cards, English only driver's license testing, and a new interpretation of the Fourteenth Amendment will completely unglue much of his organization.

Here's why. The "E" Amendment's implementation will effectively reduce the voting landscape by as much as five percent. Will these be Republican, Democrat or independent voters? There is truly no way of knowing the exact ratio, but it could have a profound impact on the electoral map. To many moderates, Republican and Democrat, it might actually give them more voice in the process.

An insightful Marlton, New Jersey restaurateur suggested, "The "E" Amendment will go in the back door and eliminate four or five percent of the voting electorate. Of that four or five percent, probably 95% will be people who would have likely voted for Obama."

As a Democrat, he professed that this development will not be all bad for the mainstream of his party. "They (the national party) have gotten away from small business, middle class and working Americans in favor of people who represent the very bottom of society. This isn't the same Democratic Party that nominated John F. Kennedy, I assure you.

"What Obama is promising is a free ride for these people on the backs of workers. Not to mention higher taxes for everyday Joe Americans like me.

"If people had to prove they were literate in order to vote, a lot wouldn't vote. The politicians would know this and refocus on Middle America, where they should have been focused all along," he added. He went on to strongly profess a belief that Obama might be linked to some of the illegal activities now being uncovered at ACORN.

Obama's career beginnings are tied to the Association of Community Organizations for Reform Now, ACORN. As the days skip by, a scandal for the ages is unfolding in Minnesota. The contested race between Norm Coleman and Al Franken was never settled, in a satisfactory manner.

As one convenience store operator in Baudette, Minnesota, a tiny fishing village on the Canadian border put it, "No way Franken wins without help from outside. I speak of illegal help such as what he received from ACORN."

There is justifiable concern over voter irregularities and election fraud. With it is a growing realization that a system better at preventing fraud should be implemented. Arguably no people in America are as cognizant of voter fraud as Minnesotans.

Following the Coleman-Franken Senatorial election of 2008, Governor Tim Pawlenty had initially issued plans to examine all 43,000 ballots done on the auspices of ACORN. Franken had been declared the winner by 312 votes. After six months, faced with a partisan state supreme court, Coleman conceded. But it was a messy affair! Republicans predicted that well more than the decisive 312 ACORN voters were (a) dead, (b) fictitious, (c) non-residents or (d) people who had voted multiple times in different precincts.

Obama will likely distance himself from ACORN. He is certainly nobody's fool. Ties to a rogue organization hurt credibility. But, the question remains: What kind of an impact would voter ID cards have had on the outcome, if they had been utilized in the 2008 election? Would the result have been the same, had the "E" Amendment been the law of the land?

Let us return to the earlier comments made by the New Jersey restaurateur. You cannot vote unless you have an identification card. To get an ID card, you must pass a fourth grade English proficiency test. How many voters will be eliminated from the electorate? Four to five percent? We are not merely talking about illegal votes. We are talking about voters who can't pass the test or are too private to participate in the qualification. Some will predict that these lost voters will represent a significant portion of Obama's constituency.

There is no scientific way to predict how these lost voters would cast their vote. It is certain that many who don't vote will be those who choose not participate in the process. Many people are private and will be uncomfortable with the thought of a thumb print and a retinal scan. These are not necessarily people who would cast their vote for Obama. If anything, they will be Libertarians or Republicans with Libertarian leanings.

Immigration control is a benefit of the "E" Amendment. With a new definition of the Fourteenth Amendment's guarantee of citizenship, coupled with English only driver's license testing and a new interpretation of *Phyler v. Doe*, illegal immigration can be reduced to a trickle. Sounds good, but does the Obama Administration truly want this?

Conservative spokespersons suggest that Obama wants to grant all illegal aliens amnesty, in anticipation of gaining new Democrat voters. There may be some validity to this argument. It is probable that most, not all, but most of the new voters will vote Democrat. Republicans fear that it will be enough to sway elections. They are quick to use California as an example.

The question on everyone's lips is "why would Obama, or anyone, want to encourage voter fraud?" And, for that matter, "Why would Obama, or anyone, want to facilitate and encourage illiteracy and illegal immigration?"

From a cynical point of view it is very simple. These disadvantaged souls are the most easily controlled. Specifically, we are talking about uneducated people who cannot read what is on a ballot. If a support group tells them how to vote, they will never question it. Especially if something tangible is offered in return. This support group could be a church, a union or an organization such as ACORN.

Still, voting is the right of every adult in this country. Shouldn't it remain so?

That is the argument. With a world that grows more complex by the minute, we must find a way to raise the bar regarding literacy. By forcing the electorate to achieve a fourth grade reading proficiency as a pre-requisite for suffrage, we will take a giant step toward achieving that goal. True, it could play havoc with the constituencies of certain politicians. But, this is about America and what will make us a smarter, stronger and more secure nation. No politician is bigger than America.

To control America, the tiny circle of political insiders we have referred to as America's ruling class must have these blocks of ignorant, illiterate voters. Requiring their participation in a voter qualification process such as the one outlined in this writing will have a profound impact.

For mainstream, middle class America, it will result in the return of their country. To self-serving elites and well-connected front men, it will be the beginning of their demise.

Literate people are more difficult to control and manipulate than illiterate people.

The same will hold true for people who continue to use a language other than English as their primary method of communication. Their peers don't necessarily want them to learn English. They can be better controlled if they are limited to their original tongue. Failure to learn English will help contribute to their remaining near the poverty level. The inability to read English will make them less prone to questioning the status quo. The lure of an all inclusive welfare state will be enticing. Encouraging class warfare through jealousy and resentment is a cowardly ploy that ultimately hurts America.

Barack Obama does not have an exclusive on this reasoning. This is the most consistent ideology harbored by the far left. It stems from perhaps the deepest, dirtiest reality of *New Deal* ideology: *"A way out for the wealthy and socialism for everyone else."*

Is Barack Obama a socialist?

Many conservatives assert that he most definitely is. Liberals describe him as "an enlightened progressive, clearly focused on today's needs and problems." Others will conclude that he is nothing more than "an opportunist and a trimmer." There are still others who believe that, while Obama is an ideologue, he is essentially "over his head and clueless" about how to handle the situation at hand.

The question remains, will there be any way for this president to support the "E" Amendment?

A September, 2009, conversation with an African American probate lawyer at a deli in Park Ridge, Illinois yielded startling insights. Describing himself as a lifelong Democrat, he admitted to having met Obama only once in passing.

"No way of truly knowing, if he (Obama) would support the 'E' Amendment," he predicted. He described the president's inner circle as complicated.

"Rahm Emanuel (then Chief of Staff) is a tough son-of-a-bitch." He described Emanuel as the person controlling things. He reminded me that David Plouffe, Obama's campaign manager, and Emanuel aren't the best of friends.

He scorned the media for making a big deal out of William Ayers and Reverend Jeremiah Wright. "Ayers is an old hippie, he's harmless. Wright hates white people."

The lawyer recounted spending nine months in Birmingham, Alabama on assignment. "Some of the nicest people I have met," he remembered. "Not especially racist. I mean, we're all racist to a certain extent. But when I think of racism, as in white people hating black people, I think of South Boston. That's racism. These Alabama people were mainly interested in sports and church. And food," he laughed, graphically describing regular southern cuisine that consisted of turnip greens, black-eyed peas, okra, sweet potatoes and fried chicken. "I gained ten pounds while I was there," he patted his stomach with a smile.

Returning to the original subject, he cited a connection between the former governor (Rod Blagojevich), Emanuel and Obama. "There's something there and it's hidden in the mists," he mused. "You must understand something. Both the president and the governor were fair-haired face men a few years ago. They were actually rivals. But their money bags were the same people. Whatever Obama did, it would need to be done with their blessing.

"However, if you are asking what he would do if the decision was his alone, I think that he would support this 'E' Amendment," the lawyer calculated. "Things aren't the same as they were when Dr. King was alive. America has gotten lazy and complacent while China is quietly taking over the world. They will take it over if we don't improve our educational standards. Kids in our inner cities are getting the biggest shaft of all."

He went on to profess his genuine belief that Barack Obama sincerely cares about educational standards and deficiencies in the country. He reminded me of the disagreement between Obama and Hillary Clinton, whose hometown we were gracing during the conversation, on merit pay for teachers.

He described the Reverends Jesse Jackson and Al Sharpton as has beens. "They're the past. This is about the future. Everyone's future," he concluded.

It begins with the conclusion that the country has progressed significantly since 1965. If we believe it has, then we can begin the removal of artificial mechanisms designed to create a level playing field for the disadvantaged. We will do this because the country, as a whole, concludes that building a stronger, smarter, more secure America is a higher priority. In our effort to help, we are hurting these disadvantaged souls by facilitating them with a crutch. The crutch is our refusal to force them to learn English.

At first glance, Barack Obama doesn't appear strong or decisive enough to bring about this kind of change. He might secretly harbor sympathy for it. But it is doubtful that he will forsake his power brokers in favor of the middle class. After all, it is not mainstream America that makes the big campaign contributions.

There is likewise a strong possibility that he truly believes in universal suffrage, regardless of one's ability to read a ballot. Certainly it is the politically correct response. In baseball terms, the "E" Amendment is a knuckle-curve-ball, thrown at an inopportune time. It can have devastating consequences for those attempting to control the country via this illiterate voting block.

This reasoning lends insight into the desire to include all persons in the census, irregardless of whether they are in the country legally. More people equates to more representation in Congress. If the census becomes legal citizen based, there might be as much as a sixteen seat swing in the House. California, New York and Illinois were all carried by Obama. Nearly all of the states that will benefit from the swing are traditionally carried by Republicans.

To prevent this minor catastrophe, there are those who advocate universal amnesty for all illegal aliens. True, they list learning English as one of the conditions of citizenship. But will they be willing to require that these new Americans pass a high school equivalent English proficiency test as a condition of citizenship? Liberals will be indignant, but moderates will see it as an enlightened compromise.

Most Americans clearly oppose universal amnesty, as Ted Kennedy and John McCain quickly learned. Barack Obama likewise supported the failed legislation and is now vocal in his support of similar immigration reform. Not surprisingly, his administration had suggested that they wanted it on the table for 2010. Could they have been thinking ahead to the 2012 election?

Without question, when non-English speakers learn English they become better integrated into society. With that, however, comes the problem for the ruling elites. When people conquer illiteracy, they start asking questions. Unfortunately, many will be uncomfortable questions. So begins the journey of self-actualization and individualism!

Are we suggesting that Barack Obama is opposed to the conquest of illiteracy? No. Or, at least, not in principle. I think he genuinely wants everyone to experience self-actualization and individualism. The rub comes with the simple fact that his support may be at odds with his aspirations to stay in office.

With the acquisition of literacy comes freedom. But this freedom for some, translates to the loss of leverage for others. Losing this leverage results in a loss of power for these rulers and this is Barack Obama's quandary. He likely believes everyone should have the opportunity to experience the American Dream. He will voice his belief that no person should be deprived of something as basic as the ability to speak or read the language. Doing something decisive to insure it happens will be another thing.

While literacy will be a thorny problem for Obama, immigration control could be an absolute nightmare.

The Fourteenth Amendment's equal protection clause is the loophole used to allow children of illegal aliens, born in the country, to stay permanently. With the requirement of passing a high school equivalent English proficiency test as outlined for the anchor babies, the president will be caught between a rock and a hard place.

His African American base will likely favor such an interpretation. Mexican voters might not be so supportive. The far left and far right will be against this measure. Obama might not be concerned with the latter. The former will vote for him regardless because they have no better option. This will leave the moderates and especially independent voters who will likely see it as a compromise. Refusing to see the "E" alternative as a bridge for the moderates could ultimately alienate swing voters.

English only written driver's license tests will be another sticking point. There are many local and regional politicians who will oppose this measure. Their arguments, and organizations, will be strong. Can Obama find a way to sell this to his base?

What about repealing *Phyler v. Doe?* While his African American base might enthusiastically support this, it is likely his overall constituency might oppose it on ideological grounds.

In reality, both measures are designed to discourage illegal aliens from wanting to stay in the country. Without the ability to drive a motor vehicle and no available entitlements, living in the U.S. will become much more difficult.

Obama might have a chance to pull it off. His African American base will support it. Moderates, independents and especially Reagan Democrats will applaud the initiative. His far left constituency will object, but there will be few alternatives for them. It is doubtful that Republicans will take an opposing view. Even Dewey-Rockefeller Republicans from states bordering Mexico will find it tough going if they oppose it.

Perhaps most difficult will be the provision making the "E" Amendment immune from legal challenge. Could a civil rights lawyer ever agree to such a stipulation? I would think, probably not. But there is always hope. Without this provision, the courts will be slammed. And that translates to good business for those in the legal profession. The best way to insure that this isn't the final verdict is to prohibit legal challenge altogether.

Obama has ties to the trial lawyers' PAC and they will never forgive him if he does anything less than denounce this provision of the "E" Amendment.

Which brings us to the original question: Will Barack Obama support the "E" Amendment?

He might favor certain parts of it.

It is likely that, had "E" been the law of the land in 2008, he probably would not have won the election. His base will be quick to point out this fact.

There were simply too many close states that would have been impacted had "E" been in place – beginning with all of the red states that George W. Bush won in 2000 and 2004. Florida, Ohio, North Carolina, Indiana and Virginia were very close. Smaller states such as Nevada, New Mexico and Iowa would have broken for McCain. Even larger states, that have historically gone blue, such as Pennsylvania, Michigan and New Jersey, would have been too close to call and may have gone red. We will never know.

What we can surmise is that the Reagan Democrats will be much more focused than they are now. These are families sharing conservative values with moderate incomes. Many feel they have been pushed to the rear by the block of disadvantaged voters courted by the far left. Republicans failed to find an answer in 2008 and a lot of these Reagan Democrats broke for Obama. Colin Powell's endorsement helped Obama immensely. The 2012 election may find these voters skeptical and more inclined to cross party lines.

The "E" Amendment is proposed legislation aimed directly at Reagan Democrats. In the eyes of most Republicans and most, if not all, conservatives, Obama is simply too liberal to entertain such legislation. He will see merit in pieces of the amendment. It might prove politically difficult for him to support a literacy test; even though he will know, logically, it is the right thing to do.

There is, however, one wildcard yet to be played.

In 2008, perhaps the single most brilliant piece of the Obama campaign was his use of the internet. The web was saturated with Obama messages. Conversely, John McCain professed to have never used the internet. Not a smart idea.

The block of voters most influenced by internet messages was roughly between eighteen and thirty-four. I refer to them as the "Yuppietechs." They receive virtually all of their news online. There is constant communication. New vehicles, such as YouTube, Facebook and Twitter, emerge every day. The Obama campaign effectively reached out to these potential voters.

Initially, Republicans were quick to reason that the level of participation in elections from this block had been minimal in years past. A few remembered Bill Clinton's effective use of MTV in the 1992 election, but overall, they were slow out of the chute. This allowed Obama to build a new, energetic constituency through this modern means of communication.

Obama was elected. As 2008 became 2009 and then 2010, many of the members of this new constituency found themselves battling for the first time, the same problems that thirty-, forty-and fifty-something Americans were facing – a brutal, worsening recession. Confidence in the president waned.

Traditionally, Americans have blamed the President for economic woes and other problems relating to a loss of income or a decrease in their standard of living. These twenty-somethings are no different. They enthusiastically elected Obama, anticipating better things ahead. A year after the election, they look at a world from the confines of their parent's home, with no job and only tens of thousands of dollars of student loans to show for the education just completed.

In some instances, there is a mild feeling of betrayal for Obama. True, he looked good and gave eloquent speeches. Now his focus and interest seem to be targeted more at the lower ends of society, not the upwardly mobile members of a new generation of voters. This might have sounded good in principal, but in tough economic times, human nature generally looks inward.

Not much has changed since the late seventies.

Jimmy Carter came into office with high ideals and the promise of a more honest, more transparent government. But as time unfolded, the Georgia peanut farmer's plain spoken candor translated into a president who was weak, indecisive and unable to handle a multitude of issues simultaneously. Worldwide, American prestige declined. The economy soured. Interest rates climbed to 20%. Inflation shot to 18%. Instead of offering hope and solutions, Carter actually went on national television and scolded America. America was in no mood for his "crisis of confidence" speech, in 1979.

The 1980 election was a rout. Ronald Reagan flew into office on a mantle of hope, lower taxes, less government and more respect abroad. It worked.

There are still those who can't accept the fact that Reagan accomplished more than any other president in the twentieth century. True, there were bumps in the road, but overall, from building a strong economy to ending the cold war, no president did more. The group of voters who made the difference was later referred to as the Reagan Democrats.

Young people who had heartily voted for Carter in 1976 also voted for Reagan in 1980. Many became life long Republicans from that day forward. In some cases, their votes were cast in anger. But, as the country gradually found its footing, even voters who professed to have previously voted only for Democrats, sang the former actor's accolades.

Obama and the Democrats greatest fear may come from the belief that both Reagan Democrats and Yuppietechs ultimately find their champion in Marco Rubio. Rubio's message of "smaller government, lower taxes and pursuits of the American dream" are from the Reagan playbook. Columnist Ariana Huffington called Rubio the "Obama of the right."

Compounding the problem for Democrats is that Marco Rubio is Hispanic. Democrat pollsters are quick to point out that Obama will need to carry Latinos decisively in 2012. An American of Cuban descent delivering a message of hope, belief in American small business and individual accomplishment would be at odds with the Democrats' promise of wealth redistribution and enhanced entitlement programs.

Would Rubio support the "E" Amendment?

Nobody knows. One thing is for certain. He could sell it! In effect, Marco Rubio represents the end result of the "E" Amendment. The "E" Amendment is all about achieving total literacy by way of accelerated assimilation. It likewise promotes the bi-lingual American. Through these objectives, we attain a "stronger, smarter, more secure" America. In essence, through accelerated assimilation, we improve all Americans' chances of enjoying the American Dream, eliminating bigotry and prejudice along the way. As a bonus, we solve the immigration riddle in a fair, practical and constructive manner that benefits the entire country.

Of course, there are those who would consider Rubio, too much of a *supply sider* to ever be considered for the White House. These same people never acknowledged Reagan's achievements. They were largely members of two catagories – the far left and old time New Dealers who saw Reaganomics as a methodical disassembling of Franklin D. Roosevelt's progressive economic creation of the thirties.

There were likewise many courthouse Democrats such as Tennessee's James Sassor who initially opposed what was referred to as supply side economics. Later, the senator reversed his position, based on the conclusion that it worked. There were many Southern Democrats who were facing similar quandaries. The national party nominated Northern Liberals in both the 1984 and 1988 elections. They were facing new, conservative opposition at home. Many ultimately switched parties.

Some interesting parallels confront Barack Obama. These same twenty-something new voters are not the most loyal. Many voted in 2008 for the first time. In the past, these younger voters have proven to be the most volatile. A continued bad economy and the frustration of fruitless job searches are prime ingredients for complete voting reversals. This, coupled with the government forcing them under the threat of fines or imprisonment, to purchase health insurance, further disillusions them. To many of these young voters, this constitutes more than deception. It amounts to outright betrayal. It is from these factions that many of our Eagles for America will be hatched.

In chapter seven nothing short of a cyber war was laid out. Because Obama is not making the upwardly mobile, college educated professional or technician his first priority, retribution at the ballot box should be in order. It could even go beyond that. Anger, passion and frustration combine in a volatile mix.

In the eyes of these Americans, Barack Obama won their vote under false pretences. They expected to be at the center of the "change you can believe in". As it turned out, they proved to be allies in a return to the Great Society days of the sixties. Initially positioning himself as a centrist, Obama has proven to be a textbook, big government liberal with a radical agenda. This is not the change they wanted or voted for.

It is the change that many Obama supporters, such as the late Ted Kennedy, John Kerry and Nancy Pelosi sought. It goes back to the original premise behind the New Deal – a way out for the wealthy and socialism for everyone else.

One of the quickest ways to raise the effective tax rate is to inflate the money, forcing taxpayers into higher brackets. This was the standard in the late seventies. When indexing was introduced, the New Dealers howled. It is likely they will attempt to raise the tax brackets once again, while repealing indexing.

This too will not bode well for middle class America. Their money buys less. Their tax bracket increases. As the deficit continues to mount, there looks to be no end in sight. Many independents are fiscal conservatives. They compare America to a drunk at a bar who continues to run a tab, even though he is out of money. When does the bartender say no?

Still, Americans are the most industrious people in the world. We have problems, but they are fixable. The key will be to allow the people a chance to build a society on the premise of insuring future world leadership by making our people more literate. This is the challenge that Eagles for America will issue to Barack Obama.

Based on earlier assumptions, it was concluded that, behind the pretty face and flowery words, Barack Obama is nothing more than a politician. In the eyes of journalist Dick Morris he is a very liberal politician. Is there anything else there? Is there more to Obama than the run-of-the-mill, Tom Harkin, welfare state liberal?

Eagles for America can quickly bring it out, if it exists.

The "E" Amendment is on the table. Barack Obama will support it. Or he will not. If he does not, he becomes a proponent of continued illiteracy in America, continued voter fraud in America, immigration without laws and borders, with entitlements for all who are lucky enough to evade border patrols, and continued identity theft.

In short, he is un-American, unpatriotic and unfit for leadership in America.

This could potentially be a very dangerous scenario for Obama. He is already perceived as soft on immigration control. Without question, he has ties to ACORN, an organization that has become synonymous with voter fraud. Identity theft is the fastest growing crime in America.

In fairness, the president has made some courageous overtures in education. He should be commended for this. But, a decisive plan to knock out illiteracy might be considered too aggressive – at least for his constituents. Many, if not most, will see his support of the "E" Amendment as disloyal. They will consider the president a turncoat. He will be despised in many of the circles that have been his greatest admirers.

In Thomas Friedman's book *The World is Flat*, the definition of *flat* translated to "creating a level playing field" for the world so that countries abroad could share and compete with America. As University of Kentucky English Professor, Dr. Kay Combs, explained, "The "E" Amendment would not only change America, it would change the world." Such would be the result if jobs utlitizing the social security numbers of Americans were not allowed to be outsourced.

These mostly low paid service positions would literally be in a foreign city one day and gone a few months later. Meanwhile, educated immigration applicants already fluent in English would increase dramatically. Often they would be the grateful recipients of these jobs that found their way home! Chronically unemployed Americans could likewise benefit .

Will Obama favor this development?

It is difficult to say. Many companies would be impacted. There would be recourse from countries that lost these jobs. On paper, the concept would be popular domestically and most Americans would favor it, even at the threat of inflation. Outsourcing is a growing issue in the country. Democrats have demonized their Republican opponents in recent times over outsourcing. This would be another aspect of the "E" Amendment that would further push Barack

Obama into a box with no backdoor. Supporting it would anger key constutuents. Failure to support it would firmly align him with the same old, Ivy League status quo that has brought America to the point of economic ruin and class warfare. Many of these supporters already considered his departure from the teachers' union line as a warning sign.

All these factors notwithstanding, let us back up and imagine an Obama as courageous as his hero, Abraham Lincoln. Historians will note, Lincoln's first priority was not to please his constituents. In fact, he made some of the most questionable decisions and appointments of any president.

They started with Secretary of State William Seward. Seward had served as the governor of New York and had been a key rival in the presidential race. When Lincoln appointed him Secretary of State, his followers were appalled. They asked, "Why Seward, Mr. President, in light of what he says of you?"

The question was fair. Seward had previously referred to Lincoln as a "home spun, corn pone, rail splitter."

Undeterred, Lincoln replied, "Because he is the best and most qualified person in the country for the Secretary of State post."

Lincoln further angered members of his party when he appointed William Stanton of Ohio as Secretary of Defense. Stanton, a Democrat, was a strange individual, who kept the tiny coffin of his dead child on his fireplace mantle. Lincoln defended his choice by reminding Republicans that he was a plurality president. He had failed to garner 50% of the votes and wanted a War Democrat, such as Stanton, in his cabinet.

At the firing on Fort Sumter, Lincoln knew the proper procedure would have been to close the Southern ports. He also knew the order would have been largely ignored by the Southern states, not to mention their European and Caribbean trading partners. Therefore, he blockaded the ports. While this action technically recognized the Confederacy as a hostile nation, it was necessary. Without a blockade, the Southern states would have had carte blanche in trading their cotton for largely European consumer goods and war materials.

Members of Lincoln's cabinet and inner circle discouraged a blockade, including General Winfield Scott. Lincoln recognized the War Between the States as a "different type of war." In retrospect, Lincoln may have been the only president in history ultimately able to hold the country together.

Let us not forget about the *Emancipation Proclamation*. This was considered the riskiest of decisions in 1863. Many of his closest supporters advised against it. But, it turned the war once and for all.

Obviously, Obama's hero and role model was more than a run-of-the-mill politician.

Which brings us finally to the million-dollar-question.

Will Obama forsake the privileged few making up America's ruling class, as well as his far left constituents, for the sake of a principle?

We will begin with the second group. The far left might compose 15% of the country, maybe as many as 20%. They support national health care, carbon and emission controls, higher taxes, less money spent on defense, and a large, centrally controlled federal government. Education improvement is not an adversarial issue, neither is identity theft. But the thought of a literacy test and ID cards will result in absolute pandemonium. They will likely be outraged by the concept of a new interpretation of the Fourteenth Amendment. They will be opposed to English only written tests for driver's licenses. They will consider striking *Phyler v. Doe* as draconian.

The good news is these people have no place to go.

It will be difficult to nominate a rival candidate when the party had a seated president – difficult, but not impossible. Party insiders will confirm that another Hillary Clinton run at the White House,

President Barack Obama

while doubtful, could still materialize. It is a foregone conclusion that no Republican candidate will make an attractive alternative for these voters.

The tiny group of elites composing America's ruling class will be another matter. Power is power. Nobody wants to lose something that they currently enjoy. The number of people potentially effected by the "E" Amendment might be as small as 5,000,000 or as large as 7,500,000 nationally. That may not sound like a lot, in a nation of 300,000,000, but in some of these close elections they could be the difference. Taking these people out of the mix, due to their inability to pass a fourth grade English proficiency test or their refusal to participate in the application process, could seriously alter the electoral map.

These are questions all of us need to ask ourselves. Should anyone incapable of reading a ballot be voting? Assuming they are, on what grounds are their decisions being made? Is voter privacy more important than stamping out voter fraud?

For Barack Obama to abandon the people who catapulted him to office will be a tall order. Still, he would not be the first. If he chooses to embark on the mission of truly bringing change to America, real change, he will have his vehicle.

In the end, our president will have a choice. He can be a politician, concerned primarily with his own lot in life, or he can be a statesman, with only America's needs and best interests at heart.

It could ultimately result in a decision not to seek re-election.

In spite of all of the negative publicity heaped on Obama from the Right, there is always the hope that they are wrong. There is always the promise that Barack Hussein Obama might actually understand the need for taking America to this next level. The positive signs are that he is genuinely concerned with excellence in education. He has proven that he is willing to cross swords with the education establishment. He understands that America cannot stand in the shadows and be content with mediocre report cards from our teachers and students. He is painfully aware of the fact that world competition will not wait.

Passage of the "E" Amendment will raise the bar. There will be better reading comprehension, better writing abilities and better understanding of the language itself. There will also be less division and, yes, less discrimination. We will benefit by being smarter as a nation.

Better than any other measure introduced, the "E" Amendment will promote unity. It will give the entire nation a point of commonality. There is nothing exclusionary about English as the one and only official language. It literally transcends skin color, ethnic origin, socio-economic standing, and religious preference. It is the glue that brings us together as a nation, binding us as one people.

Hopefully, Barack Obama can come to this realization. Without question, he will anger and alienate old friends and patrons. But, America is more important than anything or anybody. Becoming the champion advocate for the "E" Amendment will elevate Obama to Lincolnesque stature.

Championing the "E" Amendment will take him to a revered standing in the same manner that Lincoln attained such a designation because he will have chosen America first. Not 15 or 20% of it. Not a handful of affluent power brokers who in reality are similar to the oligarchs in Russia. But the true majority of Americans. The mainstream, middle class backbone of the country. In the end, when given the choice he will have chosen the many over the few.

Is this not the true essence of democracy?

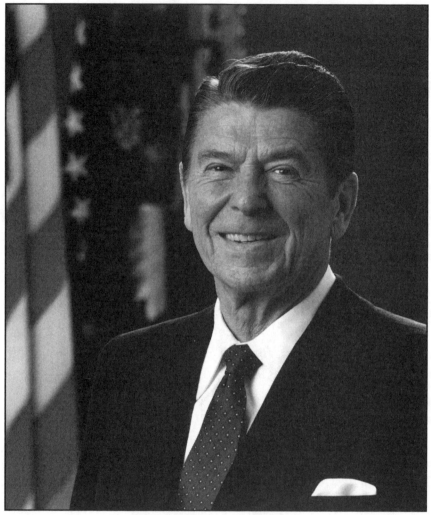

President Ronald Reagan

11 Who Am I?

In many circles, I would be an insignificant nobody.

At the same time, I am a true snapshot of Middle America. You might say Joe the Plumber, south.

I was born and raised in El Dorado, Arkansas, a little town of about 25,000 people, two hours south of Little Rock, thirteen miles north of the Louisiana state line.

My parents were both reasonably well-educated, holding college degrees. My father needed only to complete his dissertation and he would have earned a PhD in agronomy.

He was an LSU man. He and my mother met on registration day at the Baton Rouge campus. Ultimately my brother, sister, and I graduated from LSU.

My mother fondly tells stories of how my father, five years her elder and fresh from a War War II tour of duty that included nearly all of the hottest battles of Europe, overwhelmed her with his manliness and maturity. She was majoring in music and was quick to observe that the number of men in that college was minimal.

My father seldom talked about the war. But, in reviewing his discharge papers, it confirmed that he had seen such places as Omaha Beach and the Ardennes. He did share some painful reflections with his kid brother, Jim. As Jim related to me in 1976, the first six months or so after he got back from the war, "All the nights were the same. Clint would drink himself into a stupor. Then he would rattle off one experience after another, sometimes laughing, sometimes literally crying." There were obviously many recollections.

One was a friendship with a man who grew up only thirty miles from his birthplace of Bossier City, Louisiana. Jim didn't remember his name. From boot camp in Yuma, Arizona, training for the North Africa campaign, they were constantly together. While they were never sent to North Africa, they did spend seven months in England, just prior to Normandy.

Miraculously, they survived the Normandy invasion, both landing in the second boatload at Omaha Beach, dodging fire as the Allies stubbornly secured a foothold. We even found a *Life* magazine photo of my father in action there.

Having secured the beach, the Allies moved east. Both my father and his buddy were in artillery. As Dad recounted to Jim, "I was sighting a target, with my hand on his shoulder when there was a huge burst of shrapnel. I wasn't touched. They couldn't even find all of the pieces of him." My mother said the event scarred my father for the remainder of his life.

"One minute he was there. The next minute he was gone. Why it wasn't me, I'll never know," he would murmur wistfully.

While in England, my father struck up a relationship with a French woman who had escaped the continent during the Dunkirk evacuation. As Jim remembered, "The woman had a little girl about three or four. She and her husband had lived in New Orleans for several years and she spoke perfect English." Her husband was missing in action and presumed killed. Jim was likewise unable to remember her name.

Like so many French evacuees, this woman was living in a refugee camp a few miles outside London. The camp was relatively close to where the America troops were headquartered. She later moved into a nearby boarding house. During that half year, they kindled a romance so engulfing that it may have gotten my father through the worst parts of the struggle. After the surrender, he obtained a fifteen day pass and searched in vain for the woman. "Your father was absolutely heartsick over that woman. He said he looked everywhere. He said that the Limeys didn't help and didn't care. They just wanted the Americans to get out of their country."

One woman from the boarding house remembered the woman. She gave Clint an unopened letter he had mailed months before. She recalled the woman and the child leaving abruptly in the middle of the night, sometime early in 1945. She did not know where they had gone. That was it. Clint never learned any more than that. "He would go on and on over her. She must have been something," Jim added.

Returning to America, my father quickly found that, in spite of his service, there was still not much for him, as far as work. Having entered the war with an undergraduate degree, he took advantage of the GI bill and began working on his masters. In Baton Rouge, he met my mother and within a year, they were married. He worked at the agriculture experimental station, just off campus, as he completed his graduate degree.

My father was a farmer at heart. He longed to return to northwestern Louisiana. When he inquired about the prospect of taking over the family farm, 320 acres in Webster Parish, he learned that his parents didn't actually own the land. It was owned by my father's bachelor uncle, Shirley, who eventually willed it to my grandparents upon his death seven years later.

Having learned the cold truth about the farm ownership, my father turned to another option, the Red River bottomland outside Shreveport. The land would grow anything and banks were lending money at low interest rates, but the price was high, $100 per acre. My grandfather told my father, "Son, there's never been any land worth a hundred dollars an acre. And never will be." His enthusiasm doused and his dream shattered, my father returned to Baton Rouge.

While working on his doctorate, he learned from my mother's brother-in-law of the big money to be made working as a pipe fitter in Pine Bluff, Arkansas. He promptly left the graduate program and moved to Pine Bluff, first attending trade school, then working as a journeyman pipe fitter.

The money was good. In fact, in 1947 Arkansas, it was exceptional. However, to my mother's dismay, it united my father with less educated, less affluent people. She let him know about it, too. At her constant prodding and his mother's insistence, my father returned to Louisiana and completed sufficient hours to gain a teaching certificate.

Meantime, my mother completed her degree in music. She specialized in voice. As one would expect, there wasn't much in the way of employment for a music major specializing in voice. She sang in the choir and gave piano lessons to elementary school children. For real money, she returned to what she had learned in high school while employed by her father, bookkeeping and accounting.

Unlike my father's parents who both held undergraduate degrees, my mother's parents never graduated from high school. My maternal grandfather was a Registered Public Accountant who came out of the Depression in better shape than he had entered it.

Jeff Babb was forced to drop out of El Dorado High School to take care of his ailing parents. Initially, he worked for the railroad. Then, he bought into a grocery business and gradually accumulated enough money to buy rental property adjacent to his parents' homestead. J.J., as he was called, began working evenings for a courtly old gentleman accountant who blamed years of doing five dollar tax returns for his failing eyesight. Gradually, he delegated the work to my grandfather.

When he died, he left all his clients to J.J., who took the business and ran with it. Immediately, he put both my mother and aunt on the payroll. By the early '50s he was clearing better than $25,000 per year from his accounting practice, a princely sum in south Arkansas at that time.

While keeping his rental houses, he sold his share in the grocery business, putting most of the proceeds safely away, cash in a lock box and EEE bonds. He did conservatively invest in two or three oil drillings. El Dorado was, and still is, the oil capital of Arkansas. He never made or lost enough to note. There was an oil hex in the family as he ruefully pointed out.

His mother's family, the Murphys were of Irish descent and had the ill luck of selling the same exact tract of land near Norphlet, Arkansas, five miles north of El Dorado, that later was the site of the world famous "Busey Number One" that ushered in the oil boom of 1921. The sale was consummated just prior to the turn of the century. There was always that *what might have been* syndrome with regard to that ill-fated sale.

The Murphy clan in south Arkansas was large, rough, Protestant and children of the potato blight victims in Ireland in the mid-nineteenth century. Grandma Babb was sharp, acid-tongued, and mildly obnoxious. She enjoyed a dip of snuff and a wee dram of whiskey from time to time. She proudly lamented that she was not part of those, "bog trottin', flannel mouthed, shanty Irish." She let it be known that there are no Catholics in my family.

The Babbs were of English descent. They were bourgeois London bankers, of Puritan and Quaker stock. It was one of these Puritan differences that prompted the first Babb to exit England in favor of the new world.

Phillip Babb was the third son and generally the least accomplished, least respected of the children. When his father caught fourteen-year-old Phillip in bed with the chamber maid, he was brusquely ordered to get out and don't come back.

Making his way west to Bristol, Phillip signed on as a cabin boy with a ship bound for the Americas. It was 1652 when he first set foot in Kittery, Maine. Later, he was the captain of his own ship. He ultimately built a large waterfront home in Kittery. There was a monument erected in the mid-eighteenth century to him. He had arrived as an undocumented alien. Today writings describe Phillip Babb as a genuine, certified ghost.

The Willises were planters in the Lands End Region of Cornwall. The name is of Welsh origin, but my father's ancestors were all English speaking. The first Willis entered America in the 1640s, marrying the daughter of Thomas Todd and Lucy Higgenbotham. Todd was one of the earliest Jamestown settlers, landing in 1620. There are some famous Americans spawned from these original colonists. Among them were Thomas Stone of Maryland, a signer of the Constitution and Merryweather Lewis who would lead the Lewis and Clark expedition.

My paternal grandmother's people came over later, in the early eighteenth century. They were also Irish, descendents of English nobility who had been granted large estates in Ireland following English conquest. O'Brian was shortened to Brian when they entered America. Like the Willises they entered through Virginia and over the decades migrated, first to Georgia and ultimately to north Louisiana, where they carved a large cotton plantation out of the pine forests. It was there that they met the Smith family, who later married more Irish newcomers, the Levinses.

My maternal grandmother descended from French Huguenots. She was born on a small farm in Spencer County, Indiana, just outside of Booneville. Her mother and brother died during the flu epidemic of 1918. Her father worked in the lumber business. After the family's initial move to Todd County, Kentucky, they migrated further southwest to Clarenden, Arkansas where she met J.J. in 1915.

Over the years, the descendents of Phillip Babb spread throughout the country. My strain landed in Monroe County, Alabama, thirty miles northwest of Mobile, just prior to statehood in 1817. Thirty years later, they came to Union County, Arkansas, known then as Champanole Landing.

Several families routinely traveled together on these cross country marches. Making the more than 250 mile trek from south Alabama to south Arkansas with the Babbs were the Pinsons. As would be expected, they often intermarried. J.J. Babb's grandfather,

Robert Newton Babb did just that. On the day of Lee's surrender to Grant at Appomattox, he was a widower with five children in the newly formed village of El Dorado. His oldest son, Thomas Jefferson, known to his friends as T.J. and by his children and grandchildren as Big Daddy, fathered eight sons and one daughter. J.J. was the fifth and the only child who would die in El Dorado.

Unlike his fifth son, T.J. Babb held a college degree. He taught school and even did a stint in the Arkansas House of Representatives. A burly, barrel-chested man, he bore a slight resemblance to Theodore Roosevelt. He was an industrious man, learning carpentry to supplement his meager income as a schoolmaster. His ability to search deeds and records at the Union County courthouse ultimately yielded an unlikely property that could be taken for merely paying past due taxes – a schoolhouse originally intended for the large number of African American children in El Dorado.

There is a story that hinted of El Dorado's dark past that few wanted to talk about at the turn of the century. In 1881, a young man, recently graduated from Tuskegee Institute came to Union County. Very little was said about this young man, who allegedly was tutored by Booker T. Washington himself. What was remembered was his quick entry and disappearance. One report, that quickly was forgotten, was that of a body found deep in the woods, disfigured to the extent that positive identification was impossible. There was also a legend that every morning on the porch of this schoolhouse that T.J. Babb bought, an old-fashioned school bell could be faintly heard.

In this house, the family grew. T.J. expanded the original building to include a kitchen, dining room, and two bedrooms. When the children moved to different cities and states, J.J. and his Huguenot wife, Lucy, stayed, grew and prospered. My mother was born and raised in this house. My parents, brother and sister lived in it during the two years that our new house on the west side of El Dorado was being built.

The contrast between my two grandfathers was striking. J.J. never graduated from high school but owned a prosperous accounting firm. The law had always interested him deeply. He read law and, at the age of fifty-seven, took and passed the Arkansas bar exam. His final ten years of life, he died of a heart attack at age sixty-eight in 1961, were largely spent practicing title law. He left the accounting business to my mother who doubled it before selling it in 1984.

Henry Clinton Willis graduated from Louisiana Normal in 1914. As did J.J., he served in the war. His wife was a descendent of the Brians. Her mother was a Smith. Her father's name was Levins. Henry had several successful brothers. One brother, James Clinton Willis, was a surgeon and founder of the Willis Knighton Medical Center in Shreveport. Another brother, Shirley, was the brunt of a lot of jokes, the least of which were about his name.

Unlike most of the somber, taciturn Willises, Shirley Willis talked constantly. He worked in a feed store in Doyline, Louisiana, twenty miles east of Shreveport. There he would drink in stories from the farmers and ranchers who frequented the place. People liked him well enough, but by today's standards, he would likely be considered nerdy. His mind, however, was extremely agile and he inherited a special talent from his famous uncle, James William Nicholson, an uncanny ability with figures.

James William Nicholson was appointed president of LSU in 1883. The main thoroughfare that runs through the campus bears his name. He is credited with naming the mascot. Today, when people think of the LSU Fighting Tigers, they think of the Bayou Bengals. Colonel Nicholson actually named them for the Louisiana Tigers, a crack regiment in Robert E. Lee's Army of Northern Virginia that was composed primarily of Irish cutthroats, taken from the jails of New Orleans. Colonel Nicholson wrote several mathematics textbooks. He had a particular love for trigonometry. He was also a master of business math, which Shirley Willis found second nature.

Shirley would talk to everyone about literally everything. But he was likewise a great listener. He had the innate ability to bait people into volunteering sometimes very confidential information about property that might be distressed and owners who might be on the ropes. He would then take this information to others who might have the means and ultimately instigate a transaction, always carving for himself a little piece of that transaction with no out-of-pocket investment.

By the time Shirley Willis was sixty years of age, he had no wife and no children. He owned more than 2000 acres in northwest Louisiana outright, more than three hundred head of cattle and several commercial buildings, included the building housing his feed store.

His brother, Henry, always needed a push. As my mother put it, "Mr. Willis pretty much sat for his entire life." Including, sitting at Shirley's feed store as an hourly employee. One of my earliest memories entailed his scolding me for licking the salt blocks that were in the back of the store. He pretty much allowed his Irish wife, Annie Dean, to run the household. He will be always credited with a classic line, "All a man gets out of life is a little something to eat and his kids." When he died in April of 1963, it almost went by unnoticed.

My paternal great-grandfather, Gladden Willis, had Shirley's spunk, but directed in a different way. A wiry man with a sunny demeanor, Gladden always liked the ladies. He was admittedly vulnerable to suggestion, such as a friend with a car suggesting he accompany him on a little ride. This often translated to taking unplanned, last minute trips to Baton Rouge where he was always checking on papers at the capital for Shirley. It was evident that he was checking on more than paperwork while in the capital city.

My car broke down one foggy, humid, late August night. It was 1:30 A.M. on Sunday morning and I had finished my on-air shift at WAFB radio. After walking roughly a mile, I found an open Shell station. There sitting on a mechanic's stool talking to the attendant, was an older gentleman who looked to be in his early seventies. When I asked the attendant if he knew of anyone who could tow and fix my car, the older gentlemen looked at me warily and said,

"Yeah, but it's gonna cost you a little something." It was déjà vu. In effect I was looking at my grandfather, or the perfect likeness of my father's dead father. It was perfect with one exception, this older gentleman who was offering to help me was African American.

Uncle Jim could not help but laugh when he recounted some of Grandpa's escapades. He said it was a miracle Gladden lived to be ninety-six years old considering the company he often kept and the rough places he frequented.

"He always loved Grandma," Jim remembered, "but he just seemed to attract women, all kinds of women without trying. Some of them had husbands. He was a cat." Jim said he often couldn't believe that his arid father was the son of the Glad man, as his grandfather was called. He admitted that his mother, Gladden Willis' daughter-in-law, would have taken a brush to my father had he been anything like his father.

Annie Dean was something different, altogether. She was a child of Reconstruction. Her family had lost several thousand acres of land due to their inability to pay the taxes. They also owned more than 100 slaves who, having been officially emancipated, never left the estate. Instead, they looked to their former master, the same as they always had. With money that was worthless, the Levinses attempted to feed their former feudal estate with what means that they had. My father often credits the sweet potato for saving families such as his grandparents and their former slaves during the days following the war.

My great-grandfather, her father, was twelve in 1865. Alonzo Franklin Levins went from great wealth to poverty overnight. Furthermore, he and his wife lost their first three children. Two were boys. My great-grandmother watched in anguish as her husband would mount a large white stallion, gallop off and be gone for months. My grandmother's earliest memories included her mother saying, "Your Pa's off gallivanting again." He would usually end up on the river where card games could be found on the steamboats. It would often be months before his return. My grandmother told stories of her mother and sisters harvesting the crops in his absence.

Frank Levins, as he was commonly referred to, was a tall, strapping, impressive man with a powerful presence. While he looked imposing, he could be warm and genial. There was a quiet sadness that seemed to envelope him, as if his life was nothing short of a pained existence.

In his later years, he told stores of his childhood and a happy life on a cotton plantation, in a world that forever held promise. At age twelve, he tried to enlist with General Richard Taylor only to learn upon arrival in Shreveport that Lee had surrendered to Grant a month earlier. The promise of the future was to quickly become the curse of the present. Through his teenage years, he watched his family gradually lose the plantation. The taxes were high and their entire fortune had been tied up in cotton, land and slaves. Soon they were down to their homestead and the ten acres that surrounded it.

Frank Levins never recovered. He could not bring himself to talk about the three lost children. The lost land and wealth he did talk about, until his death in 1948. He was ninety-five.

After the Levins' first three children died, seven more followed. All were girls. Amazingly every one of them earned college degrees and all became school teachers. My grandmother was thrifty. She was almost as good at saving money as my mother and J.J. But, she was a casualty of the bank run in 1933. Having scrimped and saved with great care for fifteen years, she saw their life savings of $5700 disappear overnight. For the rest of her days, she never trusted banks. Her money was kept in Granny's tea kettle, which occupied a space on the hearth. In 1983, she suffered a stroke and

City Hall in El Dorado, Arkansas

was permanently hospitalized. It was then that we learned there was slightly more than $107,000 in hundred dollar bills neatly curled inside Granny's tea kettle.

I never knew my grandfathers well. I was five when J.J. passed, but I remembered him as a warm passionate person who would carry me around and give me dollar bills. He was a deeply spiritual man, took honey in his coffee, ate healthy and was very much in tune with the politics of the day. He ghost wrote a column in the *El Dorado Times*, using the pen name Tecumseh McGoogin. He predicted integrated schools in El Dorado twenty-five years in advance. From what Lucy told me, he was extremely active sexually to the day he died. They insisted on being called J.J. and Lucy, rather than Grandma and Grandpa.

My mother was very close to her father. When he died, she lost her best friend. She talks to this day of how he had almost a mystical ability to see into the future. His prediction of Roosevelt's New Deal was totally accurate. In his very words, he summed it up, "It's socialism. Everything the government gives will have strings attached."

In 1968, when they actually integrated the public schools in El Dorado, it wasn't really that big of a deal. There were a couple of riots, but they involved only a dozen or so kids. The reports of racial tensions were exaggerated. The students who were involved were generally students who were always in trouble with one thing or another. Overall in El Dorado, life went on. About 40% of the 25,000 residents were black. They were typically less affluent than the white residents. The black kids were often behind in class. It seemed like they had traded equality for their school, pride and traditions.

My brother, sister and I graduated from El Dorado High School. Was it a great place to go to school? Not particularly. There wasn't much going on there. I wouldn't want any of my children to be forced to go there, but, it was okay. It was what there was in El Dorado. Why did we stay in El Dorado? Because, my mother had a successful accounting business established there. My father did what he had done for the previous twenty years, taught school.

I would like to say that my father put helping underprivileged young boys on a higher plane than making money. He touched the lives of a lot of blue collar boys in El Dorado. Teaching industrial arts, he taught them a trade and many took advantage of it in later years. He was very well respected by all of his peers, but he earned maybe half as much income as my mother. I think she slightly resented this fact. He was a man of the people. He seemingly was more comfortable with blue collar, less educated types.

To supplement his income, he worked as the coordinator for the local 706. This was the union for plumbers and steamfitters in El Dorado. The best thing that came from this part time job was the multitude of expense paid trips for himself and his family. The annual convention at Purdue University in West Lafayette, Indiana was always the starting point for some sort of cross country jaunt. More than once we ended up in Clearwater, Florida, visiting my mother's sister. We also made a meaningful trip to Hollywood, Florida in 1971.

I was a better than average student. Not an A student, but a solid B student. My brother was an exceptional football player and my father's foremost dream was to see him attend LSU on a football scholarship. For me, he hinted that I might consider learning to be a printer.

In the end, my father would never see any of his children grow to adulthood. He died of cancer in 1973, at the age of fifty-two.

My last two years in high school were spent working as a sportswriter for the local newspaper. I received class credits through the Industrial Cooperative Training Program. I bought my first car, a brand new 1973 Mustang. The payment was $96.48 per month.

This, plus the insurance, I paid from my earnings at the newspaper. At peak, I was making about $300 per month.

I attended Arkansas State University in the fall of 1974 as a freshman, transferring to LSU in summer of '76 and graduating in May of '79 with a BA in journalism. My grades in college were actually better than in high school.

LSU is a large public school. There was a huge international student enrollment at that time, second in the nation, to my knowledge. The Liberal Arts curriculum was excellent. I had pledged Kappa Alpha Order at Arkansas State, at LSU, I affiliated and later went alumni. The diversity of my college experience left a lasting mark on me. I saw people from all walks of life, all types of backgrounds, both cultural and economic.

While in school, I hustled to make ends meet. I had a private student loan from a bank in El Dorado. I had a small Basic Educational Opportunity Grant. I worked. I spent a year-and-a-half working for two different radio stations. I worked for an advertising agency and for a printer. I worked as a stringer for two different newspapers. When that wasn't enough, I ran football cards and scalped football tickets. I managed and survived.

Would I have traded it all for a cushy ride at an Ivy League school? Who knows? Maybe. If I had, I would have met a lot of people I didn't meet at LSU – and vice versa.

One individual that I know I wouldn't have met was a dear friend from the United Arab Emirates, Abdullah Hareb. Abdullah, Abdool as my brother called him, was okay. In fact, we later learned that he was brilliant, a civil engineering major. What we also fathomed was because he had studied English from the age of six, we could communicate.

When we took him back home to El Dorado for Thanksgiving in November 1978, I watched with pleasure as my mother actually warmed up to the conversation. She was always open-minded. Abdullah was secular. He had a brother attending LSU who was a devout Sunni fundamentalist. They argued. Primarily over his association with westerners and his disdain for anything traditional. He would always end every shouting bout with his brother with the same statement, "Many of his friends are stupids and I am not a religious person."

Religious or irreligious, because we could communicate, we had made a good friend. In doing so, my brother and I realized that people are essentially the same everywhere. We may have slightly different values, but we are more alike than different.

The key was the language and the fact that due totally to his fifteen years or so of studying English, we did not have a language barrier.

We had effectively entered a crack in the curse of Babel.

Epilogue

In May, 1973, a seventeen-year-old teen was issued a proposition, "If you can recruit a baseball team, we have a sponsor."

The young man had lost his father the previous month to cancer. He welcomed the diversion. The challenge of the proposition was unimportant. He was being asked to recruit fifteen teen-aged boys for his baseball team. No more than five could be fifteen years old. At least three needed to be thirteen. The season started in two weeks. It was the Union County Babe Ruth Baseball League.

The young man went to work. Within six days he had his team. Five of his players were fifteen, three were thirteen, and the remainder were fourteen years of age. He knew and had previously coached 80% of the boys in basketball at the El Dorado (Arkansas) Boys Club. It seemed like he knew the right places to look for players. There was one distinction, the El Dorado Boys Club was fully integrated. The Union County Babe Ruth League was white only. The team the young man put on the field for the first game had seven African American players.

The Union County Babe Ruth League played its games at the El Dorado Municipal Airport, eight miles west of the city. Getting there meant procuring transportation. This may have been by design. It was often difficult for kids to find rides to the airport. The young coach was not deterred. He devised a pick-up point at a supermarket known as Razorback Food Shoppes. He arrived there before each and every game in a 1967 Ford Country Squire station wagon, offering and providing rides for every player in need.

The season began. Ham Davies Chevrolet, the sponsor, quickly drew applause from the African American community based on his insightful integration of an all white league.

Car sales reportedly soared.

South Arkansas NAACP President Bobby Joe Ross called the young coach offering assistance with anything from rides to money to anything else that was needed. He received gracious thanks but nothing more.

By season's end, Ham Davies Chevrolet was the Union County Babe Ruth Champion. They were also described as the most together team in the league. Many of the parents were surprised at how good of friends the players actually were. But the young coach wasn't.

His name was Jeff Willis. Ross, a history teacher at El Dorado High knew him from the previous summer when he had him in an American history class. He described him as a decent guy, but expressed surprise that he had the courage to do what he did.

Willis is from the same congressional district as Bill Clinton and Mike Huckabee.

Childhood friend Morgan Huffman remembered, "Nobody really thought much about it until several years had passed. Then it began to sink in on everyone what Jeff and those guys on that baseball team had actually done."

Author's Bio

What differentiates Jeff Willis from some other voices on the subject of English in relation to education and geo-politics is the direction from which he approaches it. He is not a teacher, yet he hails from a family of schoolteachers, college professors and educators. Much of their disillusionment is reflected in *"E" is for English*. Many of the ideas and proposed solutions can be attributed to them.

Willis worked for network television affiliates throughout the south for nearly twenty years, including time in Asheville, North Carolina, Nashville, Tennessee, Atlanta, Georgia, Baton Rouge, Louisiana, Fayetteville, Arkansas and Lexington, Kentucky. During this time he witnessed the gradual destruction of the New Deal that began during the Reagan years and the beginning of the age of Political Correctness, that emerged during Clinton's stay in the White House. He saw, from the eyes of local news media, the impact of national policies and changes that came with each administration.

Going back further, Willis witnessed firsthand, the public schools during desegregation. Not as an observer, but as a student participant. He has not only read about busing. He himself was bussed. He has seen school riots, firsthand. From the actual building where they took place, while they were taking place!

Willis has spent time in every American state, save four. While he still anticipates his first trips to the Orient, Africa and Australia, he has experienced Latin America and Europe. Including, the former Soviet Union.

Willis has seen Russia. Not from the eyes of a tour group. But from his eyes, speaking the language himself in the homes of countless Russian families! Not only in Moscow! But in a number of Siberian cities, four time zones east of the capital. With this experience has come an understanding of the Russian people.

Jeff Willis

Willis has experienced Miami, the new Miami that is more Hispanic than Anglo. Working in both the real estate and finance industries, he has seen the great progress made by these newcomers, determined to carve out a place for themselves in America. He has also observed the trap carefully laid by powers that strive to prevent full assimilation by Latino immigrants.

In short, Jeff B. Willis is a snapshot of mainstream, middle America. A graduate of Louisiana State University with a BA in journalism, he also has degree equivalent hours in history with minors in both English and Spanish. He is not from a privileged immediate family, but can claim a patrician past. He has been fully exposed to the front lines. Willis has experienced firsthand what some authorities on this subject have only read about.

"E" represents a collection of voices, not only academicians, but actual teachers in the trenches. This writing has been derived from their perspectives.

Notes

Chapter 1 – Politically Incorrect

1. Robert Caro, *The Years of Lyndon Johnson Master of the Senate*, "Introduction: The Presence of Fire," 2002
2. Wikipedia Encyclopedia
3. John Fund, *Stealing Elections.* 2005
4. "Phyler vs. Doe 1982 Supreme Court Ruling," Wikipedia Encyclopedia 2007
5. Nicholas Wreden, *The Unmaking of a Russian*, 1935
6. Dick Morris & Eileen McGann, *Fleeced*, "How the Teachers' Union Rips Off Its Members," pages 211-225
7. Anna Benn, *Insights into Russia*, "The Perils of Perestroika," 1995
8. "Hollingsworth vs. Virginia 1798," Wikipedia Encyclopedia 2007
9. Dana Rohrabacher, quotation, Wikipedia Encyclopedia 2007
10. Bill Lind, "The Origins of Political Correctness," *Accuracy in Academia*, February 8, 2000

Chapter 2 – Welcome to Miami

1. Ann Louise Bardach, *Cuba Confidential*, "Calle Ocho Politics," pages 101-125, 2002
2. Patrick Symmes, *The Boys From Delores*, "The Company," pages 36-89, 2007
3. Clifford L. Staten, *The History of Cuba*, "The Wars for Independence and U.S. Occupation 1868 to 1902," pages 32-44, 2003
4. Clifford L. Staten, *The History of Cuba*, "U.S. Dominance, the Failure of Reform and the Rise of Batista 1902-1952," pages 45-70, 2003
5. Clifford L. Staten, *The History of Cuba*, "The Fall of Batista," pages 71-89, 2003
6. Patrick Symmes, *The Boys From Delores*, "Miami Springs," pages 3-35, 2007

7. Ann Louise Bardach, *Cuba Confidential,* "The Man Who Would Be King," pages 126-150, 2002

8. Fernando L. Rodriguez Jimenez, *Sentir Cuba,* "Paraisoencontrado(An Earthly Paradise)," pages 5-7, 1998

9. Clifford L. Staten, *The History of Cuba,* "Revolution and the Cold War 1959-70," pages 89-106, 2003

10. Jon Lee Anderson, *Che Guevara: A Revolutionary Life,* "The Story of a Failure," pages 630-669, 1997

11. E. Benjamin Andrews, *History of the United States,* vol 5, "The War With Spain," Pgs 192-193

12. E. Benjamin Andrews, *History of the United States,* vol 5, "Cuba Libre," pgs 228-229

13. *Messages and Papers of the Presidents,* vol 13, "President McKinley's Second Inaugural Address," pg 6468

14. *U.S. and Latin American Relations,* Pearson, 2008, pg 56

Chapter 3 – English and Immigration

1. United States Citizenship and Immigration Services, Case Status Services Online, 2009

2. United States Citizenship and Immigration Services, Immigration Forms, 2009

3. United States Citizenship and Immigration Services, Laws and Regulations, 2009

4. U.S. Immigration Support, R1(Religious) Visas, 2009

5. Eli Evans, *Judah P. Benjamin- The Jewish Confederate,* 1989

6. United States Army, Enlistment Benefits, 2009

7. Mississippi Marital License Requirement, 2009

8. McCain-Kennedy Reform Bill 2007

9. The Anchor Babies, www.americanresistance.com

10. Fourteenth Amendment, 14thamendment.us/birthright_citizenship/original_intent.hmtl

11. Jack Ward, "Should Anchor Babies Get Automatic Citizenship?" newswithviews.com

12. NCLR, LULAC, MALDEF, SEIU, LHNI, Universal Health Care for Illegal Aliens, 24ahead.com

13. www.thewakeupamerica.com/ILLEGAL_ALIEN_INVASION_FACT_SHEET.htm

14. UCCS/Women and Ethnic Studies www.uccs.edu/~west/joellelopez. htm
15. finance.edigg.com/.../International_Drivers_License_Scams. shtml
16. The Threat of Non-Citizen Voting, www.heritage.org

Chapter 4 – Moscow

1. Anna Benn, *Insights Into Russia,* "Communism," 1995
2. Orlando Figes, *Natasha's Dance: A Cultural History of Russia,* "Descendants of Genghiz Khan," pages 355-430, 2002
3. Anne Applebaum, *Gulag: A History,* "The Great Terror and Its Aftermath," pages 92-120, 2003
4. Orlando Figes, *Natasha's Dance: A Cultural History of Russia,* "European Russia," pages 1-68, 2002
5. Dimitri K. Simes, *After The Collapse Russia Seeks Its Place As A Great Power* "The Unmaking of the Soviet State," pages 37-55
6. Stephen Kotkin, *Armageddon Averted,* "Idealism and Treason," pages 171-196, 2001
7. Leon Aron, *Yeltsin: A Revolutionary Life,* "The Revolution," pages 439-493, 2000
8. www.themoscowtimes.com
9. Stephen Kotkin, *Armageddon Averted,* "Reviving the Dream," pages 31-57, 2001
10. *Tourism & Vacations,* (Russian language periodical) 1998
11. Nicholas Maltzoff, *Essentials of Russian Grammar,* "Verbs," pages 142-235, 1996
12. Nicholas Maltzoff, *Essentials of Russian Grammar,* "The Declension of Nouns," pages 27-79, 1996
13. Orlando Figes, *Natasha's Dance: A Cultural History of Russia,* "In Search of the Russian Soul," pages 289-353, 2002
14. Anna Benn, *Insights Into Russia,* "The Perils of Perestroika," 1995
15. Russia and America/Not a Cold War But A Cold Tiff, *The Economist* 2007
16. F. Tyutchev, *The Spirit of Russia,* "Teachers' and Students' Activities Kit," pages 159-254, 1998
17. Anatoli Rybakov, *Children of the Arbat,* 1988
18. Krasnoyarsk, *City in the Center,* (Russian periodical) 1998

19. "Krai," (Krasnoyarsk region reference guide) 1998
20. James Michener, *Alaska*, 1987
21. Leon Aron, *Yeltsin: A Revolutionary Life*, "America, America," pages 321-350, 2000
22. V. E. Suslova & A. E. Petrova, "Kusbahs Coal," 1984
23. www.slapupsidethehead.com
24. Central Intelligence Agency, The World Fact book, 2009
25. en.worldpress.com/tag/boris-nempsov.
26. russia.foreignpolicyblogs.com
27. www.russian-customs-tariff.com
28. www.huliq.com/18983/Russian-journalists-report-media-restrictions

Chapter 5 – The Education Trade-Off

1. Elizabeth Wright, *Issues and Views*, "The Damage of Brown versus the Board of Education," 1997, Reprinted in 2009
2. Ellis Washington, *Issues and Views*, "The Brown versus Board of Education Fraud: Pop Psychology Masquerading as Legal Reasoning," July 15, 2003
3. William D. D'Nofrio, "The Truth About the Courts and What Must Be Done," The National Association for Neighborhood Schools, 2009
4. Dr. Dennis Cuddy, "Court Ordered Busing Has Failed," October 2007 newswithviews.com
5. www.reference.com/browse/Busing?jss=0
6. The Boston Busing: School Integration in Massachusetts, www.workablepeace.org/pdfs/busing.pdf
7. www.hoover.org/publications/policyreview/3563642.html
8. Genevieve Mitchell, *Issues and Views*, "The Busing Nightmare Continues," 1996
9. TrueNews.org "Separation of Church and State – What Did the Constitution Really Say?
10. www.secularhumanism.org/index.php?section=main&page=what
11. Dick Morris & Eileen McGann, *Fleeced*, "How the Teachers' Union Rips Off Its Members," pages 211-223, 2008
12. "Busing: 25 Years, Good Riddance To a Bad Idea," www.adversity.net/special/busing.htm

13. "School Prayer: A Case History," free2pray.info
14. www.allabouthistory.org/school-prayer.htm
15. Slawomir Grunberg, "School Prayer: A Community at War," Log In Productions, 4 LaRue Road, Spencer, N.Y. 14883
16. www.geocities.com/jhs_2283/termpaper.html
17. www.wallbuilders.com/LIBissuesArticles.asp?id=88
18. nytimes.com/2007/06/18/education/18pay. html?ex=1339819200&...&emc=rss
19. www.publicschoolreview.com/articles/29
20. www.actfl.org/files/public/enroll2000.pdf
21. beyondevolutionistheregod.com
22. www.intelligentdesignversusevolution.com
23. www.actionbioscience.org/evolution/nhmag.html
24. www.law.umkc.edu/faculty/projects/ftrials/conlaw/evolution.htm
25. Wikipedia Encyclopedia- 2007

Chapter 6 – The Heart Of It All

1. history.ky.gov/pages/KentuckyHistory.aspx
2. www.shgresources.com/ky/timeline
3. en.wikipedia.org/wiki/Kentucky_wildcats_men's_basketball
4. www.visitlex.com
5. www.veteranspark.org
6. James Lee McDonough, *War in Kentucky*, "I'll Fight Them as Long as I Live," pages 273-296, 1994
7. "Beshear Reverses Decision on Drivers Tests," www.kentucky.com/news/state/story/810477.html?storylink-MI_emailed

Chapter 7 – Eagles to the Rescue

1. www.gotquestions.org/christian-nation.html
2. www.termlimits.com
3. www.youtube.com
4. www.proenglish.org/issues/offeng/997.html
5. www.usenglish.org/view/575
6. www.opencongress.org/bill/111-h997/show
7. www.washingtonwatch.com/bills/show/110_HR_997.html

8. www.harrisinteractive.com/harris_poll/index.asp?PID
9. www.hola.com/forums/townhall/index.ssf?artid=206737
10. "Dillon vs. Glass 1921," Wikipedia Encyclopedia, 2007
11. "Coleman vs. Mullen," Wikipedia Encyclopedia, 2007
12. lwv.org/AM/template.cfm?Section=Voting_Rights_Act&... &ContentID=4357
13. blogs.edweek.org/edweek/.../12/are_latinos_learning_english_q. html
14. "Hollingsworth vs. Virginia 1798," Wikipedia Encyclopedia, 2007
15. Dr. Richard Labunski, "State Power Over Federal Laws," Lexington *Herald Leader*, January 16, 2011
16. Dr. Richard Labunski, "James Madison and the Struggle for Bill of Rights"

Chapter 8 – The Power of the Internet

1. bloggingblog.org/networks-
2. bestblogbasket.blogspot.com/2007/005/blogging-networks-5-pros-an...
3. en.wiki.ort/wiki/blogging/networks
4. www.pearsoncustom.com/allpages/civilrightsactof1866_bot.html

Chapter 9 – Where Do We Go From Here?

1. en.wikipedia.org/wiki/voting_rights_act
2. wee.usdoj.gov/crt/voting/intro/intro_b.htm
3. www.core_online.org/history/voting_rights.htm
4. questia.com/library.../voting-rights-act-of-1965.jsp
5. www.fcc.gov
6. energycommerce.house.gov/index.php?... id=244&catid=32&Itemid=58
7. www.fcc.gov/omd/history
8. www.history.com/encyclopedia.do?vendorid=fwne.fw..fe016300.a
9. www.museum.tv/archives/etv/F/federalcommu/federalcommu. htm
10. en.wikipedia.org/wiki/Communications_Act_of_1934
11. en.wikipedia.org/wiki/Fairness_doctrine
12. "Why the Fairness Doctrine is Anything But Fair," www.heritage.

org/research/regulation/em368.cfm

13. ACLJ. The So-Called "Fairness Doctrine"- Extremely Dangerous Legislation, www.aclj.org/FairnessDoctrine/default.html
14. www.nationalexpositor.com/news/1478.html
15. www.nato.int
16. www.answers.com/topic/nato
17. dlibrary.acu.edu.au/staffhome/...Foundation/English_As-Discipline
18. amazon.com/rise-fall-english-rconstructuring-discipline/dp/0300080840

Chapter 10 – The "E" Amendment and Obama

1. http://www.whitehouse.gov/the_press_office/Background-Briefing-on-terminations-reductions-and-Savings-in-the-2010- Budget/
2. http://www.whitehouse.gov/the_press_office/Remarks-by-the-President-on-Reducing-Spending-in-the-Budget/
3. "Voting Rights Went Wrong," georgewill@washpost.com
4. "Will Your Vote Count?" www.PewTrusts.org
5. Daniel Clark, "All an Act: Dems Assault Voting Rights," posted November 5, 2002
6. "The New Socialists"- Ideas for a Radical Change- A Critique of Linda Burnham's "notes on an orientation to the Obama Presidency," by Charlie Post
7. "The American Prospect What's the Matter With Massachuchetts? The Democrats are far too Dependent on it. Go Mid-west, Young Man," Michael Lind, December 2004
8. The Liberal Democratic Party of America, http://liberal.democratz.org
9. Hans A. von Spakovsky, "Requiring Identification by Voters," testimony delivered to the Texas House of Representatives, March 10, 2009,
10. Hans A. von Spakovsky, "Defunding ACORN: Necessary and Property and Certainly Constitutional," September 25, 2009
11. "Mischief in Minnesota," WSJ, November 12, 2008
12. Re: Voter Fraud (ACORN et al) Minneapolis recount, http://www.powerlineblog.com/achives/2008/11/022145.php
13. Barack Obama on Immigration, Ontheissues.org/

International/Barack_Obama_Immigration.htm

14. *The American Ruling Class*, Bullfrog Films info@bullfrogfilms.com

15. www.youtube.com/watch?v=LWgAzgP5fko

16. www.theamericanrulingclass.org

17. Why is Obama Trying to Incite Class Warfare?
Answers.yahoo.com/question/index?qid=20090301085053AAzdKGS

18. www.newsvine.com/wealth-distribution

19. Excavating the Buried Civilization of Roosevelt's New Deal
newgeography.com/content/001170-excavating-the-buried-civi...

20. www.socialosts.com

21. aim.org/.../obamas-international-socialist-connections

22. www.fff.org/blog/jghblog2008-06-12.asp.

23. beliefnet.com/boards/message_list.asp?boardID=425&...

24. a n s w e r s . y a h o o . c o m / q u e s t i o n s /
index?qid=20070926223605AAFYwb9

25. Completing the Reagan Revolution: Where Do We Go From Here?
www.heritage.org/Researcj/Policy/Review/PRO189revolution.
cfm

26. Dick Morris & Eileen McGann, *Fleeced*, "President Obama: What
Would He Do?" pages 13-43, 2008

27. Arthur B. Laffer, *President Ronald Reagan's Initial Actions Project*,
"The 1980 Electoral Mandate: Frame for Governing," pages 21-25,
2009

28. William E. Barton, *The Life of Abraham Lincoln*, "The Cabinet,"
pages 19-39, 1925

29. William E. Barton, *The Life of Abraham Lincoln*, "On to Richmond,"
pages 65-76, 1925

30. Thomas Friedman, *The World is Flat*

Chapter 11 – Who Am I?

1. asms.k12.ar.us/armem/99-00/OguinnJ/BuseyNO.HTM

2. www.founderspatriots.org/articles/babb.htm

3. acreetree.net/yimm.html

4. acreetree.net/ympva.html

5. www.lsu.edu/visitors/history.html

6. www.mindenmemories.org/teachers 11.htm

The Call for Eagles

Facing a landscape dominated by arrogant politicians convinced that they know better, Americans make one final stand. At stake is America as we know it.

America as we know it, is a land where ideas, creativity and entrepreneurship are hallmarks. In direct opposition is the alternative: "Government is the solution to any and all of our problems and needs."

The proposed "E" Amendment is a road map toward facilitating the former. Through improved reading skills, America becomes a smarter, stronger, more secure nation. En route, all Americans gain access to the American Dream.

The argument stems from the belief that every American is significant and relevant. There can be no substitute for individual thought and expression. By becoming masters of the English language, America secures its place as the last, best hope for humanity.

Eagles for America are the self-appointed knights of our endeavor. Through intense love for the United States of America, they stand ready to thwart any attempt to take America down the other road. Through their devotion to making the "E" Amendment the Twenty-eighth Amendment to the Constitution, they devote their energy to singling out any opposition. To Eagles for America, anyone opposing the "E" Amendment is simply "unpatriotic, un-American and unfit for leadership in the United States of America."

Opposing the amendment are those unconcerned with literacy in America, immigration reform, voter fraud and identity theft. There is no middle ground, no gray area and no compromise. The future of our country is on the line. As Americans we have a choice: "Allow the country to be manipulated by a few, well-funded, well-connected elitists on a dubious trail ultimately ending in Socialism, or, return rule of our country to the middle class."

Eagles for America are the centurions for Mainstream America. Their objective is to return the country to the people who bled for her, died for her and have paid for her.

To learn more about becoming a part of this glorious cause, visit the website:

www.eaglesforamerica.com

The battle for America is on!

Index

K

Kennedy, Edward 69, 73, 112, 113, 169, 227, 234, 240, 272
Kennedy, John F. 39, 135, 165, 228
Kerry, John 240
Khrushchev, Nikita 45
King, Dr. Martin Luther, Jr. 190, 193, 194, 232
Kotkin, Stephen 273

L

Labunski, Dr. Richard 276
Laffer, Arthur B. 278
Lee, Robert E. 256, 259
Levins, Alonzo Franklin 258, 259
Lewis, Merryweather 254
Limbaugh, Rush 204
Lincoln, Abraham 136, 189, 194, 243, 244, 247, 278
Lind, Bill 17, 271
Lind, Michael 277

M

Madison, James 170, 276
Maltzoff, Nicholas 273
Martinez, Mel 47
Mauricio, Dr. Tomas F. Jr. 167
Mayeaux, Jules 42
McCain, John 69, 73, 142, 169, 225, 234, 236, 237, 272
McConnell, Mitch 168
McDonough, James Lee 275
McGann, Eileen 271, 274, 278
McKay, Nancy 6
McKay, Pat 6
McKinley, William 37, 272
Meek, Kendrick 55
Menendez, Ariel 44
Michener, James 102, 274
Mitchell, Genevieve 274
Morgan, John Hunt 132
Morris, Dick 9, 19, 21, 23, 117, 120, 124, 241, 271, 274, 278